CRAFTING CO-OPS IN DENMARK

NEW ANTHROPOLOGIES OF EUROPE: PERSPECTIVES AND PROVOCATIONS

Series Editors:
Michael Herzfeld, *Harvard University*
Melissa L. Caldwell, *UC Santa Cruz*

The anthropology of Europe has dramatically shifted ground from its emergence in descriptive ethnography to the exploration of innovative theoretical and methodological approaches today. This well-established series, relaunched by Berghahn Books with a new subtitle, invites proposals that speak to contemporary social and cultural theory through innovative ethnography and vivid description. Topics range from migration, human rights, and humanitarianism to historical, visual, and material anthropology to the neoliberal and audit-culture politics of Schengen and the European Union.

Volume 18
Crafting Co-ops in Denmark Reworking Craftmanship, Construction and Capitalism in a Cooperative Realm
Maia Ebsen

Volume 17
Europe's Disappearing Waste: Unanticipated Conflicts between Removal and Greening
Daniel Sosna

Volume 16
The Jewish Maghreb: North African Experiences in Greater Paris since 1981
Samuel Sami Everett

Volume 15
A Border Island on the Crossroads of History: Lampedusa and the Mediterranean
Dionigi Albera

Volume 14
Where Saints Show Respect: Mafia, Modernity, and Rituals of Power
Berardino Palumbo

Volume 13
Lurking Cold War: Life Through Historical Communion
Stavroula Pipyrou

Volume 12
The Spectral Within: Fascism, New Towns and their Contemporary Lives
Elena Miltiadis

Volume 11
Rethinking a Radical Reputation: An Athens Neighbourhood between Media Hype and Social Experience
Maria Kenti Kranidioti

Volume 10
Haunting Futures: Crisis, Migration and Anticipation in Iceland
Marek Pawlak

Volume 9
Ritual, Rapture and Rebellion: The Making of Market, Mercy and Meaning Amongst the Gitanos of El Rastro
Marianne Blom Brodersen

Volume 8
Tactical Citizenships: Encounters with Everyday State in the Republic of Cyprus
Theodoros Kouros

For a full volume listing, please see the series page on our website: https://www.berghahnbooks.com/series/new-anthropologies-of-europe

CRAFTING CO-OPS IN DENMARK

Reworking Craftmanship, Construction, and Capitalism in a Cooperative Realm

Maia Ebsen

berghahn
NEW YORK • OXFORD
www.berghahnbooks.com

First published in 2026 by
Berghahn Books
www.berghahnbooks.com

Library of Congress Cataloging-in-Publication Data
A C.I.P. cataloging record is available from the Library of Congress
Library of Congress Cataloging in Publication Control Number: 2026021459

British Library Cataloguing in Publication Data

A catalogue record for this book is available from the British Library

EU GPSR Authorized Representative
LOGOS EUROPE, 9 rue Nicolas Poussin, 17000, LA ROCHELLE, France
Email: Contact@logoseurope.eu

ISBN 978-1-83695-620-4 hardback
ISBN 978-1-83695-621-1 epub
ISBN 978-1-83695-625-9 web pdf

https://doi.org/10.3167/9781836956204

CONTENTS

ILLUSTRATIONS AND BOXES

Illustrations

Boxes

ACKNOWLEDGMENTS

My first and foremost thanks go to the people who appear as builders in this book. In keeping with my promise of confidentiality, I have used pseudonyms for all individuals and enterprises represented here, which means that I cannot name those to whom I owe the greatest debt for making this book possible. I remain deeply grateful to each of you for welcoming me into your worlds, for your patience with my ignorance, and for your openness and curiosity, which kept me thinking, questioning, and learning throughout. You may remain anonymous, but your contributions will not be forgotten.

Many others can fortunately be named. At the Department of Anthropology at the University of Copenhagen, where this work first took shape, I benefited from an inspiring and generous academic environment. I am particularly grateful to Morten Axel Pedersen for his incisive questions, encouragement, and guidance, which helped shape the research that eventually developed into this book. I also wish to thank Pernille Hohnen and the Organization and Economy research group for their intellectual generosity and for fostering a strong sense of academic community during these years. I am equally indebted to Steffen Jöhncke and Bettina Skårup for securing the funding that made this project possible. I am grateful as well to colleagues who offered crucial support and encouragement along the way, including Inger Sjørslev, Stine Krøijer, Astrid Oberborbeck Andersen, and Cecilie Rubow, whose collegiality and mentorship mattered greatly, and to Tine Gammeltoft and Bjarke Oxlund for providing an institutional framework within which this work could flourish. Over the years, Asmus Randløv Rungby, Matti Weisdorf, Stine Illum, Ida Marie Lind Glavind, Ayo Marie Degett, Tilde Siglev, Ester Fritsch, Sofie Isager Ahl, Frida Sofie Gregersen, Anette Høite Hansen, Loa Kristine Teglgaard Christensen, and Samantha Breslin have been steadfast companions through the joys and frustrations of academic life. Your companionship has meant more than you know.

Michael Herzfeld and Heather Paxson played important roles in the later development of this manuscript. I am deeply thankful for their insight, generosity, and sustained engagement. I am especially grateful to Heather Paxson for welcoming me to MIT, where conversations with colleagues such as Graham M. Jones and Stefan Helmreich further strengthened this work. Michael Herzfeld additionally played a key role in guiding the manuscript toward publication, for which I am particularly appreciative.

During the final stages of preparing this manuscript, I moved to Aarhus University to take up a position as Assistant Professor in Education Studies. I was warmly welcomed by colleagues who, despite being unfamiliar with my specific research field, offered encouragement, curiosity, and support at a crucial moment. I am deeply grateful for this collective collegiality.

My close friends—Mira Williams, Cecilie Jessen Hansen, and Sophie Burisch—have read, listened, and thought alongside me for years. Your steady presence and thoughtful engagement at critical moments have been invaluable. Other friends—Anne Kongsbak, Johan Lund Pedersen, and Cecilie Askov—played key roles in shaping the visual outline of this book. I also thank my wider circle of friends and my family for providing perspective and joy, and for bearing with my periodic absences throughout the long process of this research.

Above all, I thank Mads, whose unwavering support carried me through every stage of this work. To Siv and Frej, who arrived along the way, and to their four grandparents, whose help with childcare at decisive moments made this book possible: thank you.

Finally, I gratefully acknowledge the financial support of Laurits Andersen's Fund. I also thank Brian Berg for allowing me to use his photographs in the book and for permitting one of them to appear on the cover. My thanks go to Tom Bonnington and his team at Berghahn for guiding this book through the complexities of the publishing process, and to the two anonymous reviewers for their careful readings and invaluable critiques.

INTRODUCTION

On a gray winter afternoon in late 2001, Erik, Frode and six other builders gathered in a basement in Copenhagen and took the final steps toward launching a *byggekooperativ* (craft co-op). All eight were either working in construction or had previously done so—some for a few years, others for more than a decade. Disappointed by earlier experiences with conventional construction work, they were ready—and eager—to launch a business that they could run on their own terms. From the outset, the eight builders agreed that the co-op's core operation should be construction work. However, they wanted to avoid the toxic chemicals they had often encountered in construction and were thus keen to identify and develop environmentally friendly building techniques and materials. Moreover, they were tired of working for others and did not want others to work for them. No boss. No stakeholders. Yet, at their core, the builders' ambitions were modest: they simply wanted the opportunity to do work that they found gratifying. As such, they had yet to fathom that, over the next twenty-five years, the enterprise they were about to launch would grow into a well-known institution within the Danish construction industry and beyond. Indeed, many have come to consider them a vanguard within a growing movement of activists, advocates, and academics seeking to resurrect cooperativism in Denmark.

The launch of the craft co-op coincided with a general election in Denmark on November 20, 2001. This election later came to be considered a "watershed in Danish electoral politics" (Skidmore-Hess 2003: 89). The Social Democrats, who had been the largest party in terms of both share of the popular vote and number of parliamentary seats in every national election between 1924 and 1998, suffered a historic defeat.[1] Instead, the largest party was the center-right Denmark's Liberal Party, forming a minority coalition government with another center-right party, the Conservative People's party. Both parties are among the traditional "old parties" within Danish politics; however, the coalition was dependent on the newly established nationalist and right-wing populist Danish People's Party. To the surprise of many, they and their anti-immigrant "Denmark for Danes" agenda gained considerable support, becoming the third largest party (behind the Liberals and Social Democrats) (Petersen, Petersen and Christiansen 2014). The two governing parties and the Danish People's Party were united by a key message: a *systemskifte* (a system change) was required in Denmark. Historians and public intellectuals have continued to debate the underlying motivations driving this push for political change in 2001.[2] Yet most agree that the election revealed that the political winds were blowing in a new direction in Denmark in the early 2000s. While right-leaning parties had held power on a number of occasions, for the first time, they were not dependent on support from centrist or left-leaning parties. The newly elected center-right government kept their majority until 2011 and returned to power in a new constellation in 2015.

Throughout the co-op's existence, its members have appeared in national media outlets, on the streets of Copenhagen and in courtrooms protesting political initiatives launched by center-right parties often related to labor market, migrant, and broader economic issues. Reporters have often depicted the builders' critical interventions in political and public debates through vivid portrayals of their committed efforts to rethink craftsmanship, reinvigorate cooperativism and develop eco-friendly building techniques in notable news stories with headlines such as "Meet this year's sustainable frontrunner" or "Running a business without bosses." The builders' ongoing presence in the media and public sphere has garnered the craft co-op a certain reputation, and interest in the organization has continued to grow, including among those applying to join the co-op. The list of craftspeople and apprentices applying for jobs and training placements at the co-op is often seemingly never-ending.

The numerous applicants have come to the skilled trades from wide-ranging backgrounds. Apart from the founding members who, for the most part, still work at the co-op, the workforce comprises a wide range of unskilled workers, individuals with a migrant background, university graduates, creatives, and people for whom vocational training was the only opportunity for post-secondary education. Despite their diverse credentials, these workers—like the co-op's founding members—are dedicated to craftwork as a livelihood. Many of them are representative of a cohort of Danish skilled workers who seek to harness craft practices to tackle challenging social, political, and environmental issues. Rather than words and intellectual refinement, the builders believe that real change only emerges through acts of doing. Erik, who has functioned as the co-op's daily manager for years, often repeats this message as he skillfully steers journalists who are keen to tell the story of these apparently remarkable builders. He encourages others, particularly the younger builders, to also speak up in public debates. When asked specifically about the success of their co-op, Erik often quips: "It's not a revolution. It's just common sense." For Henning, a shy but humorous builder who joined the co-op in its early years, one of their greatest achievements is the co-op's strong position in the public sphere. "We have managed to build up some economic heft through hard and persistent work, and that provides us with something of a power base, right?" he said with a sly smile one morning as we drank coffee in the sun outside the co-op's main office. In his own furtive way, Henning also referred to the fact that the builders had spent the co-op's occasional financial surplus on supporting a range of initiatives in the neighborhood where the organization is located and in the wider Copenhagen areas. The builders often termed this support and other related activities *aktivisme* (activism).

The builders were thus united by a strong belief in using their own hands to take action. Many of the newcomers had applied for jobs at this particular craft co-op as they wanted to learn the basics of *Godt håndværk* (good craftwork)—something the co-op had become renowned for since its inception. Apprentices were especially eager to learn how to move their bodies and hands with precision to navigate the multifaceted nature of construction sites; these dynamic and bustling areas where novel creations take form amid the organized chaos, one beam and bolt at a time.

Figure 0.1. A roof restoration in Copenhagen, Denmark. Photo by Brian Berg.

While craftwork at construction sites might seem pristine, newcomers, particularly apprentices, soon realize that this is far from the case; rather, it is messy, dirty, and entails a good deal of hardship. From the early hours of the morning to late afternoon, builders spend their time on strenuous yet stimulating work. During my fieldwork at the co-op in 2019, unsurprisingly, I soon realized that, for its current members, the notable stories about the co-op in the media were not entirely aligned with the realities of everyday work life, which was largely organized around the intricacies and practicalities of craftwork. As I observed these workers build shelters from repurposed or biodegradable materials, customize wooden kitchens, retrofit housing, and restore windows, I also realized that their attitudes toward and discussions of current politics often emerged from such practicalities. During these discussions, many builders expressed a critical stance toward local developments in Denmark—a stance they also extended to broader global issues related to environmental destruction, excessive industrial production, and growing social inequality. While they may not have proposed concrete solutions to these complex global issues, many had turned to craftwork and cooperativism in hope of bringing about some form of positive change.

Such discussions showed how the builders' engagement with craftwork and cooperativism was not simply about making a living. During one of my final conversations with Erik, he touched upon this when I asked him what was missing from the numerous accounts of the co-op and its activities by reporters. He responded that many of these accounts focused on what others considered their accomplishments; yet few had explored the day-to-day organizational life of the co-op. "To us, the important story is about freedom," he earnestly declared.

* * *

In this book, I explore how a group of builders' efforts to muddle through the daily challenges and contradictions of craftwork and cooperativism during a period of political transition in Denmark can be understood as "a story of freedom." To do so, I trace the historical emergence and current trajectory of the co-op presented above. I have named this co-op KLAR and refer to the members—that is, everyone working in the organization, including both founding members and newcomers—as *builders*.[3] By analyzing the aspirations of this socially diverse group of builders, their daily work at construction sites, discussions at internal assemblies, and efforts to rethink building practices and projects, I theorize their transformative actions and the underlying conceptions of agency and subjectivity. In doing so, I bring questions of diversity, creativity, and freedom to bear on anthropological studies of cooperativism and political action more broadly.

By homing in on the creative and (as Erik hinted) perhaps even emancipatory dimensions of cooperativism and craftwork, this book reveals something crucial about co-ops and similar associations that, I argue, is often overlooked in anthropological studies. Rather than questioning the autonomy of co-ops and similar associations, or simply denouncing them altogether as some studies do by revealing how power asymmetries and forms of exploitation are reproduced in these seemingly egalitarian organizations,[4] this book explores what novel forms of life such organizations enable. These include forms of social and material practice, as well as political action, that are not captured by notions of negation or submission to existing hegemonic orders.

As my understanding of KLAR matured during my fieldwork, I realized it would be difficult to grasp the drive and creative efforts that characterized the members' practices and projects if I focused solely on their attempts to implement and reproduce cooperativism as a distinct and ostensibly fixed organizational form. Accordingly, I began to approach the builders' practices and projects by examining their continual enactment and negotiation within specific contexts. As I searched for, mapped, and traced the agile actions that emerged from these negotiations, I was drawn to the activities and projects that the builders pursued in daily craftwork. Through this work, they aimed to reinvigorate "good craftwork,"" make construction "more sustainable" and redefine "social responsibility" in Denmark. These three aims have remained KLAR's core aspirations, and substantial parts of the ensuing chapters will be devoted to exploring what they mean in practice and how they are negotiated and contested in the co-op's everyday doings and dealings.

Thus, I came to realize that to comprehend the builders' self-defined transformative actions, I needed to ethnographically and analytically zoom in on their engagement with craftwork. To analyze the mutual constitution of the builders' transformative actions and craftwork—and thus how their daily engagement with craftwork and cooperativism informed or interfered with each other—this book brings studies of cooperativism and the broader field of research on political action in dialogue with existing anthropological scholarship on craftwork.[5] Drawing on these studies enables us to understand how craftwork becomes a source of creativity, novelty, and experimentation, and how the builders' work shaped them as subjects. Through this work, they did more than construct buildings; they also cultivated virtues of making and in doing so quite literally took politics into their own hands. In other words, the builders' transformative actions were characterized not by extraordinary events or political confrontation, but by a mundane yet meticulous attention to craft. I term this mode of action *tinkering together* to capture how it was guided by an aspiration to continually experiment with various projects and interventions, rather than to imagine radically alternative ways of working and living.

Overall, this book presents an ethnography of a community of builders who saw themselves as capable of inciting societal change through continuous processes of material, political, and social tinkering, both covert and overt. However, I believe that tracing the transformative actions that emerged from the builders' engagement with craftwork and cooperativism also reveals more general concerns about the contemporary political landscape in Denmark and beyond. More precisely, the book expands understandings of what qualifies as political action in the present day, thereby contributing to broader discussions about the nature of critical politics.[6] Based on my detailed ethnography of the builders working at KLAR, whose self-defined transformative actions departed from conventional notions of politics, I will argue for a concept of critical politics that moves beyond the usual association with public protest, campaigning and the interventionist techniques of contemporary social movements by showing how critical politics emerge from the contradictions and challenges of everyday life.[7] I propose that, by carefully documenting the emergence of such politics—including the coalition building, associations, disagreements, and differences they produce—we can demonstrate "how new world-making projects come into being, what their aims are, and what tensions and contradictions they bring with them" (Postero and Elinoff 2019: 15). By zeroing in on the emergent cultural and social forms produced through the builders' engagement with craftwork and cooperativism, this book sheds light on various life- and world-making projects in the midst or on the verge of becoming. To unfold these projects, we must begin by exploring the context in which they evolved: the contemporary Danish welfare state. Indeed, to understand how critical politics and practices of critique emerge, such as those expressed and enacted by the builders at KLAR, it is always necessary to explore their reciprocal links to specific formations of power (Li 2019).

STORIES OF FREEDOM IN A TRANSITIONAL WELFARE STATE

The notion of freedom was in vogue in Denmark around the turn of the twenty-first century. As such, the KLAR builders were not the only ones presenting narratives of freedom during this period. In his New Year's speech to the country, the newly elected prime minister Anders Fogh Rasmussen, leader of the center-right government, proclaimed that Danes "should have greater freedom to shape their own lives," adding that the new government "wants to break away from rigid systems, disempowerment, and uniformity. We believe that people are best at choosing for themselves" (Fogh Rasmussen 2002). Fogh Rasmussen later elaborated on these remarks, stressing that the twenty-first century would be the "century of freedom," with cooperation, peace and respect for the individual as guiding tenets, in contrast to the twentieth century, which, in Fogh Rasmussen's view, had been marked by class struggle, repression, world wars and totalitarian ideologies (Køber 2022). While the aspirations of the builders at KLAR might have been sparked by a similar hope for a "century of freedom," the meanings they ascribed to the notion of freedom were, as I will show in subsequent chapters, very different from the freedom pursued by Denmark's new prime minister and government.

As in the examples above, the newly elected government often used the notion of freedom to stress the need for greater focus on the rights, needs and duties of individual citizens, arguing that individual autonomy had increasingly been suppressed in Denmark by the impact of years of social democratic rule in shaping the Danish welfare state. Representatives from the government often repeated that this legacy had resulted in the gradual suppression of a "free and open public debate" by a cultural elite consisting of what some termed *smagsdommere* (arbiters of taste), or a "tyranny of experts," as the prime minister referred to them (Fogh Rasmussen 2002). A key message in political programs promoted by the center-right government was that if people were freed from this so-called cultural elite and from "systems" more generally, it would lead to greater individual freedom and possibilities. In their initial reform program from 2002 entitled *Velfærd og Valgfrighed* (Welfare and Freedom of Choice), the government underlined that they wanted to "strengthen respect for individuals," further elaborating, "With freedom of choice, individuals gain greater influence over their lives" (Køber 2022: 43). In the new government's view, the general election in 2001 thus marked the beginning of a new political era in Denmark, where individual citizens should be granted greater freedom to determine their own lives.

As such, the new government's initial rhetoric called for extensive and drastic change. In practice, however, the reforms pursued by the government largely followed a path that could be traced back to the 1980s when Denmark, like many Western European countries and North American Countries, witnessed the rise of neoliberalism (see Petersen, Petersen and Christiansen 2014; Køber 2022). Meanwhile, it was evident from the start that the development of neoliberalism followed a slightly different trajectory in Denmark than in many other countries; rather than austerity in the form of cuts to and reductions of the state apparatus, neoliberalization in Denmark has in many cases worked through the established welfare state institutions (Bruun, Krøjer and Rytter 2015; Bruun 2018).[8] In Denmark, neoliberal policies were thus focused on applying market principles to the state (Petersen et al. 2014) and on breaking down the boundaries between state and market (Køber 2022). These also became guiding tenets for the newly elected government. From 2001 onward, they introduced several market-oriented reforms of various branches of the public sector, ranging from the health care sector to housing and labor market policies (ibid.). Despite the government's promise to reform the Danish state, they did so through the continuation, albeit also slight intensification, of an existing process of neoliberalization.

The intensification of neoliberalism was partly guided by economic considerations, partly by a desire to change the general conversation about the trajectory of the Danish welfare state and a goal of redefining the core idea of *velfærd* (welfare) in Denmark. As ethnographies from Scandinavia have continuously underlined, welfare, or more specifically the welfare state, is not only a bureaucratic project but also an ideological construct.[9] As such, it is also "a building site of social relations and values," such as egalitarianism and community (Jöncke 2011: 49). It was values such as these that were the focus of discussions during the campaign leading up to the general election in 2001 and in the years that followed (ibid.). Representatives from the nationalist and right-wing populist Danish People's Party became frontrunners in this struggle over values. Launched in 1995, the Danish People's Party quickly doubled their number of seats in parliament during the first elections they took part in, becoming the third largest party at the 2001 election. Already in the late 1990s, the party's members became known for their xenophobic rhetoric, placing them at the forefront of a political struggle against immigration (Køber 2022). For many Danes, particularly academics, the emergence of an anti-immigrant discourse came as a surprise—especially because migration became a hot topic in Danish politics at a time when the economy was performing well and unemployment was low, as was the rate of immigration compared to Denmark's neighboring countries (Skidmore-Hess 2003). Nonetheless, the "Muslim question"—the question of whether or not Scandinavia, and thus also Denmark, had been too welcoming to Muslim immigrants—received increasing public attention from 2001 onward in Denmark as in many other countries (Henkel 2012). During this period, anti-immigration discourse became mainstream and routine across nearly the entire political spectrum in Denmark, turning the positive image of Denmark as a country shaped by anti-authoritarianism and inclusive social interaction into a more negative perception of a country known for rampant xenophobia and Islamophobia (Hervik 2011).[10] When freedom was evoked in these discussions, particularly by representatives from the Danish People's Party, it focused on (Danish) people's right to reject immigration policies that, in their view, had come to challenge core cultural values in Denmark (Køber 2022).

Although the center-right government was only formally in power until 2011 (before returning to government in a new formation in 2015–19), their policies have had a lasting impact on the Danish welfare state (ibid.). It was against the backdrop of this changing political landscape, initially set in motion by the election of a new government in 2001, that the builders at KLAR launched and ran their craft co-op. During this period, the craft co-op increasingly became a platform upon which the builders sought to navigate the seemingly contradictory spaces and subject positions shaped by the growing neoliberalization and intensifying anti-immigrant discourse that came to shape Danish society from 2001 onward. It was thus the changing formations of power produced by these economic and discursive changes that created "a sense of unease, or separation" (Li 2019: 37) among the builders at KLAR. I explore this sense of unease further throughout this book as I examine how the builders at KLAR used cooperative craftwork to understand, intervene in, and position themselves in relation to the shifting economic and political formations in Denmark since 2001. Cooperative craftwork in this regard became the builders' toolkit for social critique and transformative action as they sought to change societal orders and, moreover, to realize their idea of a craft co-op as a "story of freedom."

The builders' critique was not only targeted at issues related to craftwork or cooperativism, but also leveled at housing and labor market policies and the anti-immigration discourse introduced by the center-right government; nonetheless, this critique always emerged from the contradictions, ambiguities, and inequities that the builders faced as part of their daily engagement with craftwork.

CRAFTWORK AS PRACTICE AND IDEOLOGY

Every morning from Monday to Friday at around 6 a.m., lights and computers are turned on at KLAR and the large coffee pots brew their first batch. Henning and Erik are always first to arrive. Shortly after, other builders emerge from the silence of the city. Most travel by bike, a few by car. First things first: coffee. Many prefer it black, while some add a splash of dairy or oat milk. After having gulped down a cup or two, the builders pack screwdrivers, ladders, and apprentices into company cars, ready to depart for construction sites around the city of Copenhagen.

While retrofitting Copenhagen's housing stock was a primary task in the early days of KLAR, the builders' workload during 2019 comprised a wide range of projects. Many of these projects were unique, such as the construction of wooden saunas (see Figure 0.2) or the creation of acoustic panels from refurbished materials, which required a great deal of intricate woodwork.

Figure 0.2. Wooden sauna. Photo by Brian Berg.

Other projects were more standardized, including the replacement of windows in an entire residential building or loft conversions. In this book, I refer to these diverse projects as construction projects; however, I refer to the builders' work as craftwork and not construction work in acknowledgment of the great value that the builders ascribed to the unique, handcrafted projects they often worked on.[11]

The members of KLAR have a mutual commitment to the co-op's various projects and share a dedication to craftwork as a livelihood. One apprentice, Liv, was particularly outspoken on this matter. Liv had initially chosen a different educational path, but after struggling to find a job upon finishing her studies, she reconsidered her educational choices. "I was quite sure that I had to do something else. I had to figure out what it was, but it didn't take long to find out," she explained during an interview. "I knew that I had to do something with craft, something with wood, because it comes naturally to me." Liv had thus decided to embark on an apprenticeship in the skilled trades. She had soon come to value her daily engagement with craftwork immensely; in her own words, this work had given her a strong belief in herself as "a creator." She had been particularly inspired by what she described as the "curiosity of craftwork": "I think that's important, that curiosity, the willingness to try new things, and the courage to say, 'Of course we can do it.' Because that's what we need to do, and that's how I feel too." Like Liv, many of the other builders considered this ability to experiment key to craftwork.

During my fieldwork, I realized that they sought to nurture this ability through the material engagements and practical logics of craftwork as they learned the skills of carefully repairing, refining, recalibrating, remodeling, or simply renewing. In their view, society no longer valued such skills, and craftwork in general suffered from misrecognition. A common goal among the builders was to reverse this development.

A spate of recent studies has revealed that craftwork is currently undergoing a renaissance across European and North American contexts, underscoring that this revitalization has been underway since the 1990s (Marchand 2021) as craft practices have since emerged as sources of new cultural and social value (Paxson 2013). This was also the case among the builders at KLAR, who, like other modern craftspeople, had seemingly come to consider craftwork as not only a practice, but also a social ideology (Marchand 2021). Ideology in the sense that the builders' material and bodily engagement with craftwork, and the contradictions, ambiguities and inequities they faced as part of this work, provided an entry point for ordering their individual and collective conceptions of the world and the large-scale power structures that encompass these conceptions (Haugbolle 2018).

Why had the people working at KLAR decided to dedicate their professional lives to craftwork? And how did they come to associate craftwork with certain virtues and politics? These were some of the questions that emerged during my fieldwork as I tried to understand why the KLAR builders had turned specifically to craftwork and the meanings they had come to associate with this work. Throughout the book, I answer these questions as I unfold my interlocutors' dedication to craftwork and their aspirations of redefining the significance of this work in contemporary Denmark. To gain a more comprehensive understanding of these answers, I draw on existing scholarship on craftwork.[12] This work allows me to zero in on the particularities of craft practices, and more precisely, on the builders' efforts to learn how to experiment practically with different solutions, invoking "the curiosity of craftwork" that seemingly guided these efforts. In this book, I refer to this ability as *tinkering*.[13]

The notion of tinkering has a somewhat composite scholarly trajectory.[14] It has rarely been associated with craft, as it is typically understood as an unskilled attempt "to meddle" in an unhelpful manner—which is not necessarily equivalent to craftwork.[15] Meanwhile, in recent years, the notion has increasingly been used in studies from the field of Science and Technology Studies (STS), particularly in research focusing on technological advancements.[16] As tinkering has turned into a scholarly concept, its meaning has been refined. Tinkering has thus generally come to be perceived as a form of focused and purposeful "attentive experimentation" in the field of STS.[17] Overall, I draw on this understanding of tinkering to grasp the builders' engagement with a form of focused and purposeful "attentive experimentation" under contingent circumstances.[18] The notion thereby allows me to capture how the builders were guided by an aspiration of collectively and practically experimenting with various projects and interventions rather than imagining radically alternative ways of working and living.

With their strong belief in the benefits of tinkering, the builders prided themselves on being highly adept at a type of agile action that bore a striking resemblance to what has previously been referred to as the ability to "muddle through" (Scott 1998), "débrouillardise" (Reed-Danahay 1993) and, above all, the notion of "bricolage" (Lévi-Strauss 1978).[19] Like tinkering, these notions share an interest in the skill of using whatever is at hand to create something new. Yet, importantly, they also stress that such acts of "making do" can be applied as a kind of "social manipulation" and as "modes for the creation of new cultural meaning."[20] The aim of creating new cultural meaning was reflected in the builders' aspiration to tinker. They were generally guided by a strong "willingness to try new things," as Liv stated, and by a belief that experimentation always yields something new in a material, political, and social sense. When I use the term tinkering in this book, I integrate attention to craftwork's material and bodily engagements with this focus on social and political manipulation. I do so to ensure that tinkering is not reduced to a material or technical operation; rather, tinkering emerges as simultaneously a material, social, and political activity, as I also refer to with the notion of *tinkering together*. By homing in on this translatability of tinkering throughout the book, I underscore its capacity to intervene in and thus transform material, social, and political contexts.

Overall, the concepts outlined above emphasize that social manipulation or new cultural meaning might arise from agile actions such as tinkering. Meanwhile, they do not necessarily focus on how such modes of action might also comprise a form of self-transformation.[21] However, as scholars working with craft argue, people engaged with transforming the material world also transform themselves in the process, making work and subjectivity mutually constitutive (Kondo 1990; Paxson 2013). Much can be gained from studying the "self-crafting that accompanies artisanal production," as described by Michael Herzfeld (2004) in his ethnography of apprenticeship in Cretan artisans' workshops (Herzfeld 2004: 25). By attending to the politics of the body in craftwork, Herzfeld shows how bodies and selves are shaped in workshops, revealing the "encompassing hierarchies of cultural value that [apprentice and master] reproduce through the practices of apprenticeship" (ibid.: 207). In Chapter 2, I return to the question of how this "self-crafting" unfolds among the builders at KLAR as I show that, while busy tinkering with their material and political surroundings at construction sites, the builders were also engaged in more reflexive processes of tinkering with themselves.

Hence, while tinkering among the builders was an ability that inherently sprang from their material and bodily engagement with craftwork, my goal with this book is to show how the builders subsequently transposed this ability to other domains and practices as they sought to turn tinkering into a collective mode of action in their attempt to spark change within Danish society. The kinds of political agency and agentive strategies adopted by the builders were thus elaborations and translations of their shared engagement with craft practices.[22] In other words, craftwork and the associated ability of tinkering became the means through which the builders collectively attempted to carve out space to realize their occasionally divergent perceptions of freedom within the context of society's shifting economic and political formations. In this regard, the book also moves beyond a focus on how global politics shape contemporary craft practices—a concern often raised in scholarship on craft (see Herzfeld 2004; Jones 2011; Marchand 2021)—to also explore how new forms of local politics might emerge from the persistent curiosity and search for novelty that characterizes the craftwork pursued by people like the builders working at KLAR. It was also this specific form of local politics that had shaped the builders' efforts to fulfill their aspirations toward cooperative action and thus their participation in reinventing cooperativism in Denmark.

REINVENTING THE COOPERATIVE TRADITION IN A "NATION OF COOPERATORS"

Builders and apprentices applying for jobs at KLAR were typically looking for an opportunity to take part in the numerous creative projects that the co-op had taken on. Yet all newcomers were also aware that KLAR was organized as a cooperative. For some of the builders, this organizational form was just as important as the co-op's persistent focus on "good craftwork" and environmentally friendly ways of building. Several of the younger builders were outspoken about their interest in cooperativism and more broadly in finding new ways of working and living. This was particularly the case for Astrid, who had joined the co-op as an apprentice in the mid-2010s. During her twenties, she had traveled extensively to different parts of the world. During her travels, she visited co-ops and similar associations, talking to people who, for various reasons, had decided to pursue a professional life within these organizations. These conversations had stoked her interest in cooperativism.

The builders working at KLAR were not alone in their belief in and commitment to the cooperative business model. By the time I began my fieldwork in 2019, the idea of cooperativism was flourishing in Denmark.[23] That is not to say that it had ever completely vanished, but it seemed to be receiving renewed attention and significance. In conference rooms and halls across Denmark, various private and public actors congregated to share practical experiences regarding how to launch a co-op. Representatives from *Kooperationen* (The Danish Cooperative Employers' Organization) and similar organizations traveled the country holding assemblies that provided information on contemporary cooperative activities and organized courses encouraging people to launch new or reorganize existing enterprises as co-ops. A think tank called *Demokratisk Erhverv* (The Danish Research Institute for Democratic Businesses) was established by a group of professional advocates for cooperativism. National and local government advisory boards were launched. And people working in cooperatives, including Erik and the other builders at KLAR, organized events for people interested in cooperativism.

One of these events took place one afternoon in the early summer of 2019. After a long day working at various construction sites, the builders from KLAR were among those gathered in a recently retrofitted factory hall for the launch of a new Copenhagen-based network of co-ops. When I arrived at the launch, many of the builders, still dressed in workwear and thus proudly showcasing the company logo on their backs, were already enjoying a draft beer or a glass of cava provided by a Spanish co-op to quench their thirst after a long day of work. The doors of the hall were open, and attendees had gathered outside in smaller groups, basking in the sun. Inside, the walls were decorated with green posters and banners displaying the name of the new network. The aim of the network was to bring together people with an interest in cooperativism to share experiences and knowledge and thereby support the ongoing growth of co-ops in the Copenhagen area. The network's vision was expressed more clearly on green postcards that were strewn around the hall, stating that the new network was founded on "sharing practices and ideas opposed to the competitive mentality of capitalism."

Almost one hundred people had gathered in the old factory hall and the space was buzzing with conversation. However, the room fell silent when a representative from the network clinked two glass bottles together and announced that they had invited a few people to speak at the event. The first speaker was the president of *Kooperationen*. She began her speech by saluting the network's founders, underlining that this new initiative filled her with both hope and pride. "Cooperative organization is the answer to many of the challenges we have to confront nowadays," she stated, adding that "It's been a good solution for a long time, but now our time has come, especially with the climate crisis and growing inequality." Her speech was met with a wave of applause that rippled through the audience. Next up was one of the founders of a long-established co-op in Copenhagen. He humorously recounted the haphazard events and decisions that had resulted in the launch of this particular co-op. While he was supportive of the newly established network, he also warned the participants: "It's not the first time we try this out. There were numerous co-ops in the city back when I grew up. So, what went wrong?" He continued by explaining, "It's a special history and tradition that we must remember now as we seek to revive this corporate form."

As in this case, the historical trajectory of cooperativism was often emphasized during the various briefings, networking events, and workshops on cooperativism that I attended during my fieldwork. This trajectory was also frequently repeated in books and reports published during this period by public intellectuals and cooperative practitioners, who, like the president of *Kooperationen*, were busy promoting cooperativism as a solution to a wide range of societal challenges.[24] These historical accounts often emphasize the "special history and tradition" of cooperativism in Denmark, as the second speaker at the event put it, by recounting how it all started. They typically begin by describing the emergence of the first Danish co-op—a consumers' food co-op (*brugsforening*)—which was launched in 1866 in Thisted, a small town on the North Jutlandic Island. This co-op was founded by Hans Christian Sonne (1817–80), a pastor who had moved to Thisted only a few years earlier. During a visit to Copenhagen, he had heard about the British cooperative movement, which he thought could provide a potential solution to poor living conditions among the emerging Danish working class (Jensen 2016). The rise of cooperativism in Denmark is therefore often associated with the formulation of the cooperative principles developed by the Rochdale Society of Equitable Pioneers in Rochdale, close to Manchester, England in 1844.[25] Subsequently, popular historical accounts often go on to describe how cooperativism spread across Denmark in the latter part of the nineteenth century as it gained traction among farmers, who in 1882 joined forces and established the first dairy co-ops around Hjedding, a small village on the west coast of the Jutland peninsula. The peasants translated the cooperative principles into the now widely known mantra *hoveder over høveder* (heads not hooves), indicating that each cooperative member, regardless of production size (number of cattle), had one vote at general meetings. From the 1880s, dairy co-ops spread across Denmark at unprecedented speed. Thirty years later, they numbered approximately thirteen thousand. One cooperative practitioner described the development during these years as follows: "A wave has risen by the North Sea and it will not stop but flood the whole country" (Niels Petersen in Mordhorst 2005: 60).

Contemporary accounts tracing the history of cooperativism in Denmark often primarily focus on this golden age of cooperativism, as this brief overview demonstrates. In these accounts, the rise of co-ops at the end of the nineteenth century is often presented as the epitome of "a distinct Danish economic-democratic tradition" that also paved the way for the formation of modern Denmark, invoking the idea of Denmark as a "nation of cooperators" (Claus 2020). Similarly, policy reports present cooperativism as a "unique Danish innovation" or a "Danish tradition," which, if mobilized, could enable the Danish nation to surmount pressing challenges in the global economy.[26] Cooperativism, it seems, is not only portrayed as a treasured historical past, but also promoted as a stable cultural resource and tradition inherent to Danish national identity. In this sense, the builders and other contemporary cooperative practitioners in Denmark, such as those attending the event described above, seemingly position themselves as "bearers" of the Danish cooperative tradition.

The notion of tradition is debated in scholarship on both craft and cooperativism, although it has occupied a more prominent role in recent studies of craft practices.[27] As noted here, traditions are inherently deceptive (Jones 2011). Far from fixed, they are "dynamic and always situated at the confluence of continuity and change" (Marchand 2009: 25). Meanwhile, stressing the dynamic construction of traditions and the fact that they are always "invented" (Hobsbawm and Ranger 1983) also raises the question of "who does the inventing" (Ulin 1995: 520). In this regard, traditions can serve as means of exclusion in certain contexts, with those considered "bearers of tradition" sometimes associated with an incurable "backwardness" (Herzfeld 2004). In other contexts, however, those identified as "bearers of tradition" might also be the ones constructing the historical trajectory of a so-called tradition (Terrio 2000). Interestingly, the builders at KLAR seemed to adeptly navigate these two seemingly contradictory positions, occasionally taking advantage of the role and authenticity ascribed to them as "bearers of the cooperative tradition," while, in other situations, selectively reconstructing this tradition. I explore this duality in Chapter 1, where I describe how the founding members' personal and political trajectories shaped KLAR from the beginning.

Taking into account the invented and thus selective nature of traditions further begs the question of how selectivity plays out in popular accounts of cooperativism's historical trajectory in Denmark and the grand narratives of Denmark as a nation of cooperators that are recounted above. Indeed, these accounts leave out some important details regarding the history of cooperativism in Denmark. First, they do not disclose that the historical rise of cooperativism in Denmark in many ways resembles the trajectory in other European countries, such as the UK, Germany, and France, which allows them to portray Denmark as the "home country of cooperativism."[28] Second, they do not emphasize that prominent leaders in the workers' movement in Denmark were initially rather skeptical about thc idca of cooperativism.[29] Partly due to internal disagreements within the workers' movement, the mostly city-based worker co-ops started by workers and the rural producer co-ops started by peasants never really joined forces (Als, Clausen and Oksen 1979), which is a key difference when comparing the historical rise of cooperativism in Denmark to developments in the other European countries mentioned above. Third, the accounts also omit the period that followed the golden age of cooperativism in Denmark and thus the story of the decline that took place during the 1970s and 1980s, as cooperative organizations faced a number of challenges related to increasing industrialization, declining trade union support and a growing expectation that they too should find ways to thrive "on market terms" (Grelle 2012). These challenges had led to the almost complete disappearance of co-ops from the Danish socioeconomic and political landscape by the turn of the twenty-first century. Overall, the omission of these details disguises the ambiguous relations that cooperative organizations and associations have had with other significant institutions in Danish society, such as the workers' movement and the state. It also prevents us from recognizing the different configurations of and shifting meanings ascribed to cooperativism throughout history.

With this changing significance in mind, I was initially interested in exploring the meaning ascribed to cooperativism in Denmark by the people who are currently trying to reinvigorate this historical phenomenon. Surveying the contemporary landscape of co-ops in Denmark, KLAR, which was often highlighted as something of a vanguard by members of other co-ops, seemed like an apt site for an ethnographic investigation of this question and, moreover, for understanding the extent to which the resurgence of cooperativism in Denmark parallels developments in other countries, where cooperative initiatives have similarly re-emerged.

TRACING THE RESURGENCE OF COOPERATIVISM IN DENMARK AND BEYOND

It is not only among the builders at KLAR or elsewhere in Denmark one finds a growing interest in co-ops and similar associations, with various scholars having shown that this is also the case beyond the Danish context (e.g., Ferry 2002; Stephen 2005; Bryer 2010; Vargas-Cetina 2005, 2011; Rakopoulos 2015b, 2018; Narotzky and Homs 2019; Plender 2021; Snikersproge 2021). These scholars have highlighted that what is commonly defined as the "solidarity economy movement" is experiencing a resurgence as people in different national and continental contexts search for "new frontiers between the economy and politics" in times of capitalist crisis (Laville 2010). Many of the builders working at KLAR took a sympathetic view regarding a diverse range of cooperative projects and programs around the world and had come to consider their own endeavor as part of a global movement. Several had visited the well-established Mondragon co-ops in the Basque region, while others had traveled to places such as Greece and Argentina to seek out cooperative organizations and similar associations, hoping to learn from these emerging initiatives.

Despite my interlocutors' focus on the similarities between their own co-op and the cooperative endeavors of people in other contexts and countries, important differences should be noted. These differences become evident if we take a quick glance at the historical development of cooperativism in Denmark since the turn of the twenty-first century. Many of the market-oriented reforms introduced by the center-right government from 2001 onward were particularly targeted at the labor market. Overall, these reforms reinforced ideas of flexibility and individual responsibility in the Danish labor market, causing the emergence of various forms of precarity (Hirslund et al. 2020). More precisely, the reforms marked a shift from "welfare" to "workfare," which, in brief, implied a "work first" strategy, requiring individuals to participate in various job-training activities if they are to receive unemployment benefits (Rasmussen, Hansen and Juul 2020). This shift also came to shape the re-emergence of co-ops and similar associations at the turn of the century, with many of the co-ops founded during these years assuming the task of job creation in one way or another. By engaging with this task, these organizations also implicitly redefined the relationship between cooperativism and the state in Denmark, positioning themselves in closer proximity to the state than had historically been the case.[30] During my fieldwork, no one seemed to question this proximity. Indeed, many of the builders working at KLAR or other cooperative practitioners whom I met appeared to consider the Danish state an influential actor supporting their efforts to combat "contemporary forms of capitalism," as they often put it, for instance stressing the importance of introducing a legal framework for co-ops.[31]

The proximity between cooperativism and the state is an important vantage point when comparing the former's current resurgence in Denmark with the emergence of a growing number of co-ops and similar associations in other countries. In Italy, for instance, co-ops are often the result of top-down planning rather than grassroots initiatives or experiences (Rakopoulos 2018). The opposite is true elsewhere, such as the establishment of organic food co-ops in Catalonia, where participants seemingly sought independence from the market and the state (Narotzky and Homs 2019). Neither of these agendas seem to fit the Danish case. Here, the resurgence of cooperativism has been driven by a wide array of local actors, who often directly engage with both state and market. Current co-op initiatives in Denmark thus appear to distinguish themselves from similar activities in other regional contexts insofar as they were neither initiated by the state nor positioned outside or in opposition to the state or the market. Instead, as I suggest in this book, they were shaped by an ambition of finding ways to actively engage with the ongoing transformation of the Danish welfare state and a capitalist market economy. Importantly, however, this did not prevent people engaged with these initiatives, such as the builders at KLAR, from envisioning their cooperative aspirations and actions as an emancipatory endeavor.

To address the ostensibly liberating dimensions of the cooperativism pursued by my interlocutors, I move beyond analytics that question the autonomy of cooperative practices or simply denounce them. These analytics have come to dominate contemporary studies due to their restricted ethnographic focus on first the Global South and East, and subsequently on Southern Europe and South America.[32] Through ethnographic studies in these contexts, scholars have primarily sought to unravel how people have turned to cooperativism in order to adapt to the economic and political exigencies of a global political economy, such as the austerity climates that arose in these places in the aftermath of socioeconomic and political crises in the first decade of the twentieth century (e.g., Rakopoulos 2015a; Narotzky and Homs 2019; Plender 2021). Such analytics center on how people struggle to secure a livelihood in the aftermath of crisis; thus, they focus on how various forces (whether external or internal) regulate or constrain social action. Put differently, they have tended to examine actors' engagement with cooperativism or related activities through an "adaptionist model" of social action (Yanagisako 2002). However, analytics of austerity and adaptation are not necessarily the best way to understand the social lives of agentive subjects, such as Erik, Henning, Liv, Astrid, and the other builders working at KLAR, as well as other contemporary practitioners of and advocates for cooperativism in Denmark, who have come to pursue cooperativism as "a story of freedom."

To take questions of creativity and ingenuity in social action seriously, we must find ways to grasp how cooperativism is envisioned and enacted as what I term an *economy of freedom* in Chapter 1. This approach allows me to examine the multifaceted cultural, affective, ethical, and political dispositions that guide the builders at KLAR and other cooperative practitioners and advocates. Rather than try to pigeonhole cooperativism as a specific economic or organizational form, I approach these organizations as life- and world-making projects through which people seek to create a good life for themselves and others.

However, engaging collectively in such world-making projects is not an easy task, as my ongoing conversations with Astrid often reminded me.

Although Astrid had become committed to cooperativism over the years, she still harbored some misgivings. "The co-op has such great potentials, and there are so many great things about the way it is organized. But there is also something dangerous about it," she explained. "People really feel responsible. You get involved personally. You truly begin to care about people. But this also entails what I consider one of the pitfalls of the project: that you might take part in your own exploitation."

Like Astrid, most of the builders considered their working lives at KLAR to be both fulfilling and disappointing. During more intimate conversations, some would question the extent to which KLAR succeeded in fulfilling the cooperative ethos, or whether they simply "took part in their own exploitation," as Astrid put it. For builders like Astrid, the political impact of their work was a vital yet dubious issue. This was particularly the case in relation to what Astrid and other builders often described as the current development of "capitalism." In various conversations at construction sites and assemblies, a builder would evoke capitalism when debating broader global challenges related to environmental destruction, excess industrial production, and growing social inequality. Yet the builders also found it difficult to articulate exactly what they meant by "capitalism." When I asked them to explain what capitalism meant to them, many responded by asking me for a definition, underlining that, as a researcher, I should be more capable of explaining what capitalism is. In seeking to change political and economic conditions, which the builders often referred to as "capitalism," they constantly negotiated the complex question of whether and where something "outside" of these political and economic conditions might exist, in Denmark and beyond. As such, many had complicated feelings about their own endeavors and often (some more than others) expressed not only dedication but also confusion, disappointment, and indifference.

Ambiguity is not only a defining element of how the builders at KLAR engaged with cooperativism; it has haunted studies of cooperativism in the social sciences ever since the emergence of the first such organization. Karl Marx was one of the first scholars to stress this ambiguity, arguing that co-ops represent "the first sprouts of the new," yet are simultaneously bound to reproduce "the shortcomings of the prevailing system" as "workers in association become their own capitalists" (Marx, *Capital III*, in Bottomore 1991: 112). Marcel Mauss, himself an enthusiastic practitioner of cooperativism, was less skeptical than Marx. He argued that "the union and the cooperative society are the foundations of the future society generated within capitalist structure," and thus, contrary to Marx, sincerely believed in these organizations as a form of "practical socialism" (Mauss in Nash and Hopkins 1976). The divergent positions espoused by Marx and Mauss have continued to shape ethnographic studies of co-ops and similar associations.

While, initially, the majority of such studies subscribed to Mauss's optimistic belief in co-ops, subsequent studies took a more critical approach as they sought to nuance scholarly representations of co-ops by showing that even though these organizations may present themselves as egalitarian, they may in fact reproduce capitalist exploitation.[33] Contemporary ethnographies have sought to challenge both approaches by examining how social relations "outside" the cooperative framework may also threaten the ethos of cooperativism, thus showing how external social forces might also be the source of ambiguity in cooperativism.[34]

By homing in on the ambiguity of cooperativism, this book likewise moves beyond the binary approach of either celebrating or criticizing cooperative organizations (Rakopoulos 2020). However, rather than suggesting that internal divisions are defined by what happens "outside" the cooperative framework (Rakopoulos 2018), I examine how multiple social formations and bifurcations are continuously initiated and negotiated through the mundane messiness that shapes social life in a co-op, as in any other organization. To shed light on these multiple social formations and bifurcations, I trace the builders' complex affective investments in cooperativism, as exemplified by Astrid, and the dynamic and contested everyday meanings of cooperativism, craftwork, democracy, power, and value that they engender. I thus describe both the political and social affinities that bring KLAR's socially heterogeneous workforce together and the frictions that pull it apart as the co-op seeks to build new forms of solidarity. Overall, I argue, this shows that cooperativism must be approached as an elusive project that demands continuous reinvention, rather than an ostensibly fixed organizational form or an all-or-nothing proposition.[35] As I will show, tinkering—that is, a form of focused and purposeful "attentive experimentation"—is one way to overcome this elusiveness, which, to some extent, seemed only to intensify as a result of KLAR's position as a contemporary craft co-op operating in the construction industry.

COOPERATION IN CONSTRUCTION

Running a craft co-op in a volatile construction industry has not always been easy, explained Erik and Frode, another founding member; the first years were arduous. To secure a solid financial foundation for the co-op, the eight founding members worked every waking hour. Gradually, the project steadied as they cultivated a customer base and learned to navigate the delicate collaborations that characterize contemporary construction work. Meanwhile, their growing business soon faced a new challenge: recruitment. In the mid-2000s, finding craftworkers who wanted to work in a co-op based on principles such as equal pay turned out to be a challenge. Through job advertisements in various magazines, they tried to convince prospective applicants of the advantages and possibilities of working in a co-op. With time, this recruitment strategy proved successful: immediately prior to the financial crisis in 2008, the co-op's workforce had increased to more than fifty people. However, their prospects dried up overnight as the construction industry felt the first shockwaves of the crisis. To avoid downsizing, the builders collectively decided to reduce their wages; nobody should be laid off in these troubled times.

By 2019, KLAR had moved beyond these challenges. While the co-op's workforce had waxed and waned a few times during the intervening years, it had stabilized at around seventy members in 2019—sixty men and ten women aged between sixteen and sixty; a size that many members considered appropriate for an urban craft co-op. Six members worked as construction supervisors; two were in charge of accounts and human resources; and the rest (including thirteen apprentices) specialized in different trades including carpentry, woodwork, welding, electrical work, and bricklaying.

KLAR's commitment to equal salaries and the cooperative organizational form set it apart from the rest of the Danish construction industry, which, as in other countries, is generally marked by precarity and vulnerability to the global economy's cycle of boom and bust. There tends to be a high turnover rate among those working in the industry, as they move between temporary jobs and different contractors for different projects.[36] Most builders work in fixed crews or at smaller companies (less than ten employees) and receive piece-rate remuneration according to the number of units (e.g., drywall panels) they install.

Moreover, recent decades have seen a change in working conditions in the Danish construction industry due to an influx of foreign labor, primarily from Eastern European countries that have become members of the EU. Trade unions in Denmark have faced substantial problems in maintaining the principle of equal treatment for domestic and migrant workers and thus upholding labor market standards, with the treatment of some migrant workers falling far below the purported minimum standards (Arnholtz and Eldring 2015). This development is generally referred to as "social dumping" and has posed great challenges to the organization of the Danish labor market, or what is known as *Den Danske Model* (the Danish Model) or the "flexicurity model."[37] This model is based on collective agreements between employers' organizations and trade unions that cover not only minimum wage levels but also a range of other additional payments and rights and differs from labor markets in most European countries, which are heavily regulated through national legislation. As few migrant workers belong to a trade union and many do not participate in local bargaining processes, Danish trade unions have generally come to see migrant workers as a threat to the traditional active participation of workers in determining wages and working conditions (Arnholtz and Eldring 2015). Overall, the consequences of the increase in migrant workers have become a central theme in any debate concerning the construction industry in Denmark, also among researchers (Arnholtz, Krause-Jensen and Juul 2015).

At KLAR, a number of builders were employed who faced certain challenges due to a migrant or other form of marginalized background. For instance Yusuf, a young builder who had worked at KLAR for a number of years, had as a teenager come to Denmark from Iraq. When he first arrived in Denmark, Yusuf took part in a series of job-training programs for a few years but continued to struggle with the Danish language. By chance, someone noticed his craft skills and gave Erik a call. Like Yusuf, a number of the builders at KLAR had previously struggled to find permanent full-time employment and had thus experienced life at the margins of the Danish labor market. Some of them had been excluded because of illness, disability, or personal circumstances that had at times hindered their ability to maintain a full-time job. At KLAR, the builders continuously worked to secure jobs for colleagues like Yusuf by accommodating individual needs and offering special terms and flexible hours.

Issues related to migrant workers like Yusuf, as well as broader structural constraints and their impact on working conditions, have also been a key focus in ethnographic studies of the construction industry in various countries. Considering the empirical context of these studies, this might seem unsurprising: ethnographic studies of construction work have tended to focus on large firms with complex organizational structures, on informal employment and the exploitation of migrant workers, or on marginalized workers in the Global South.[38] With its strong focus on specialization and strict division of labor between architecture and construction, for instance, construction work (and workers) easily lends itself to analyses of power imbalances and class struggles. Yet, recent ethnographic work suggests we should pay critical attention to such divisions, particularly those between different professional groups (Dharia 2022).

For a sizable number of the builders at KLAR, working with craftwork in the Danish construction industry was a carefully considered decision that in a few cases had meant leaving behind a university education. These builders seemed closer to what Trevor Marchand (2021) refers to as "vocational migrants" in his study of a British Building Crafts College; that is, people who make "a deliberate decision to pursue carpentry as a practice to which they would dedicate their whole person—heart, mind, and body" (Marchand 2021: 16). Throughout my fieldwork, it became increasingly important for me to understand how and why these builders had come to associate the repetition and industriousness of construction work with certain virtues and, furthermore, how they perceived this work as a path to solving social, political, and environmental challenges.

To explore these questions, I had to consider the builders as sources of knowledge and as theorists (and not simply practitioners) in their own right by engaging with them as "coanalysts, cointerpreters, and cotheorists of economy and society, and even as cocritics of capitalism" (Miyazaki 2013: 6). Thus, this book demonstrates that builders or construction workers are also "thinking subjects"; that is, subjects "engaged in dialogue with a variety of broader intellectual debates and projects" (ibid.: 9). Reckoning with my interlocutors' ways of interpreting, knowing, theorizing, and critiquing piqued my interest in understanding how they—while simultaneously also critiquing their own transformative actions—nonetheless continued to muddle through the daily challenges and contradictions of construction work and their cooperative venture. The builders' engagement with a form of double movement—that is, their simultaneous engagement with and critique of both cooperativism and construction work—emerged as an important line of inquiry.

METHODS

Since I was interested in examining forms of contemporary cooperativism that extend beyond discursive representations, the bulk of my research focused on the daily life that unfolds in co-ops—more specifically, craft co-ops. Fortunately, Erik had similar ideas when we first met to discuss the possibility of me conducting fieldwork at KLAR over an extended period. As I walked through the co-op's front door for this first meeting, I was greeted by Erik—a compactly built man with glasses and stubble. "Grab a cup of coffee if you want one," he offered, pointing toward a large coffee pot on the table in the shared kitchen area. I joined Erik at a small wooden table in an adjacent meeting room and gave him a brief introduction to my project, underscoring that I was keen to center my research on this particular co-op. I quickly sensed that Erik was impatient. He later told me this was deliberate, a tactical move. He was a firm believer in first impressions and quick decisions. Erik thus interrupted my introduction and said that I could do fieldwork at KLAR on the condition that I participate in the co-op's daily work. The other builders, he assumed, would refuse to participate in my research if I only conducted interviews and observations. I decided to accept Erik's offer.[39]

My first official day of work at KLAR was on Monday February 4, 2019. I left home just after 6 a.m. and biked through a dark and empty urban landscape as silence blanketed the city. It was a routine I followed for eight months, accompanying the builders in their daily work at construction sites four or five days a week. On these days, I arrived at the co-op between 6:30 and 7 a.m., changed into workwear, and either drove to a construction site with a crew of builders or walked to the workshop. I followed the builders' daily schedule and joined them in the trailer during their morning break between 9 and 9:10 a.m., where we had coffee and ate bread and cheese. Lunch was 12–12:30 p.m., when everyone made their own open-faced sandwiches. After work finished at 3 p.m., I drove back to KLAR's head office with the builders and changed back into my regular clothes.

Overall, I followed the builders' work on four major construction projects and various smaller projects. To gain a deeper understanding of these projects, I also interviewed some of the people who collaborated with the builders, including architects, subcontractors, representatives from companies manufacturing building materials and research scientists at Danish technical universities. I also read architectural or technical reports, participated in events, and followed media discussions regarding these projects. As a point of comparison for my analysis, I also spent a month conducting research at a "conventional" construction company. Materials generated through all these activities have informed my understanding of the builders' specific projects and of construction work more broadly, even if they are not directly referenced in the book's ethnographic accounts.

On some projects, I spent most of my time observing the work, making coffee during breaks, or chatting with builders. On others, I was assigned regular construction tasks. In these situations, I sometimes became so absorbed in the work, I did not pay much attention to the social interactions taking place. I recognized this challenge from other ethnographies about craftwork, such as Heather Paxson's (2013) account of artisan cheesemakers in the US. Paxson noted that she was prone "to thinking of labor not only as inherently value-creating, but as a value in and of itself" (Paxson 2013: 44). Overall, my fieldwork was therefore focused on the *participatory* aspects of participant observation. My participation in the daily craftwork generated detailed insights into how the builders organized, performed, and negotiated the various practicalities and techniques.

Member assemblies, meetings, and similar gatherings play a crucial role in cooperativism. Yet scholars have often excluded such activities from their ethnographic accounts of co-ops and similar associations (an issue I return to in Chapter 4). During my fieldwork, it became clear that the builders' vivid engagement in the various intellectual discussions during joint activities were key to understanding their ongoing engagement in and negotiation of cooperativism. These activities ranged from a monthly member assembly, meetings in a "discussion group" (which at times resembled a focus group), seminars with external speakers, excursions to completed construction projects, voluntary workdays, informal social gatherings in the workshop, various parties and celebrations, and a yearly four-day company trip to a destination in Southern Europe. During these events, the builders discussed a wide range of topics: from the co-op's daily operations to matters related to construction, contemporary political issues (e.g., retirement age) and climate change. It was not unusual for someone to reference a Marxist doctrine or another seminal sociological work during such discussions. Astrid occasionally asked for my opinion about books she had come across, wanting to know, for instance, whether I had read Hardt and Negri's *Empire*. As such, the ostensible differences between myself, as an anthropologist, and the builders were continuously negotiated. This also had practical implications. For instance, a few of the builders asked if they could listen to recordings of their interviews, as if we in some sense were both researchers. In these situations, it was clear that the contrast between the "we" with which the anthropologist identifies and the "they" of the research subjects is an outcome of, rather than a starting point for, doing anthropology (Candea 2011a).

Furthermore, conducting interviews brought me closer to understanding the builders' many reflections regarding their engagement with craftwork and cooperativism as I got a chance to talk one-to-one with individual builders. A few months into my fieldwork, I began interviewing some of KLAR's founding members (Henning, Erik and Frode) before interviewing some of the builders whom I had worked with for extensive periods (Astrid and Liv among many others). I sensed that some of the builders would not feel comfortable participating in interviews, and I thus approached people in a way that allowed them to easily turn down my request, which a few did. The majority of my interviews resembled life story interviews (Atkinson 1998), with a focus on the builders' educational and professional choices. I interviewed twenty builders individually, conducting two or more interviews with key interlocutors: a total of twenty-six recorded interviews.

Most of these interviews took place at the co-op or at various locations in the city. A couple of the builders invited me home for chats, dinner, or birthday celebrations. However, these visits were rare. In Scandinavian ethnographies, scholars typically note that the home is a restricted place.[40] As such, although my study falls within the category of "anthropology at home" (Jackson 1987), domestic matters did not receive a great deal of attention during my fieldwork. At the same time, "the home" figured less prominently in many of the accounts than is generally assumed in Scandinavian ethnography. Many of my interlocutors lived in small apartments or rented rooms in Copenhagen, and many of the younger builders moved home quite frequently as they either struggled to find permanent housing or were unsure of whether they wanted to stay in the city. As such, for many of my interlocutors, KLAR was the locus of their social lives. It was somewhere their children, partners, and roommates would occasionally stop by. In other words, the builders also brought "home" to work.

Although the bulk of my fieldwork was conducted at KLAR, I never considered this site to be a *bounded entity*—neither conceptually nor methodologically. While my fieldwork centered upon this particular co-op, I also interviewed a handful of representatives from other organizations working with cooperativism in Denmark. I furthermore participated in a number of public events on topics related to cooperative practices and visited some of the other novel co-ops that continuously emerged during my study. In these situations, I often conducted informal interviews with key members or representatives. Finally, I collected documents, reports, and newspaper articles that helped shed light on the discursive formations of cooperativism in contemporary Denmark. This additional material helped to highlight how the KLAR builders' cooperative project simultaneously shaped and was shaped by discourses of cooperativism in Denmark and beyond.

My urge to understand how these discourses were produced or reinterpreted in a co-op's everyday doings and dealings brought me back to the diverse community of people connected to KLAR, who became the main interlocutors of my study. While I occasionally joined them during activities outside the co-op, I spent most of my time following life inside the organization. While doing so, I realized that the co-op consisted of a community of people characterized by a strong sense of commitment and interdependence, but also varying degrees of intimacy and professional distance. Some of the builders brought family and friends to staff parties and social gatherings, moved in together, or fell in love. Others left work promptly at 3 p.m. and only stuck around for assemblies or social activities if their colleagues invited them personally. As I began crafting my ethnography of the co-op, I continuously searched for ways to represent this heterogeneity, which I achieved through storytelling and a focus on the perspectives of individual builders.

ETHNOGRAPHY AS CRAFTWORK

Several recent scholarly contributions have reminded us that ethnography is itself a craft, stressing the importance of the craft of writing when doing ethnography, with some even offering detailed practical guides to ethnographic writing (e.g., Narayan 2012; Wulff 2016; McGranahan 2020). Writing has attracted attention from anthropologists for quite some time.

However, this attention to the tools and craft of writing seems once again to be gaining momentum within the discipline. In anthropological debates about contemporary ethnographic writing, scholars have noted a renewed focus on "storytelling"—that is, on the use of stories "to bring material, data, beliefs, and theories to life" (McGranahan 2020: 76). Yet storytelling, even ethnographic writing more generally, is never simply a descriptive exercise. Stories are analytical, due to their inherent analytical qualities.[41] They also always include attempts to transform the inchoate and the imponderable encountered during fieldwork into comprehensible prose (Herzfeld 2013).

While writing this book, I found great inspiration in these contemporary discussions of the craft and storytelling of ethnography. Like the builders at KLAR, who considered craftwork a source of creativity, novelty and experimentation, I use ethnography to craft novel depictions of the builders' various life-making and world-building projects in the midst or on the verge of becoming. The book's approach to the craft of ethnography can thus be seen as an attempt to imitate the builders' efforts to tinker. Many of the ethnographic accounts within are presented as stories of tinkering as, in various experimental ways, they each represent the builders' ongoing engagement with the elusiveness of cooperativism and with craftwork more broadly. In the following chapters, I first present the stories of and from KLAR's founding members before turning to those of and from subsequent generations of builders. I also tell the stories of the places, projects, and practical work that constitute construction. In all of these accounts, I strive to convey a sense of the experimental nature of the social life that I observed and participated in during my fieldwork at KLAR.

While such storytelling is an important aspect of ethnography, scholarly writing is also about commitment. This commitment entails "a form of accountability and an ethical practice" (McGranahan 2020: 3). In my case, commitment has also revolved around finding ways to handle my interlocutors' differing perceptions of my research. The builders at KLAR were often puzzled by the length of my fieldwork and about the results such a project should produce. "Your book is probably going to be written in a smarty-pants language so no one can read it," Henning remarked teasingly. Like Henning, several of the builders were skeptical about knowledge claims and not fond of academics. Thus, some kept their distance from me and occasionally questioned my intentions. During a drunken celebration, one builder repeatedly declared, "She's a journalist," revealing a possible mistrust of my intentions. Throughout my fieldwork and writing process, I did my best to navigate KLAR's diverse social landscape and accommodate individual builders' acceptance or refusal of my research.

OUTLINE

The remainder of the book takes readers to construction sites and to political assemblies and social activities involving the co-op's members to explore tensions between the promises and pitfalls of craftwork and cooperativism. Like other works on craft and construction, the ethnographic structure of the book largely mirrors that of a typical building process (e.g., Marchand 2009; Dharia 2022). In addition to this, the chapters trace analytically how the builders cultivate the ability to tinker through their daily engagement with craftwork and how they subsequently transpose this ability to other social domains.

At KLAR, assembling a crew was one of the first tasks undertaken when embarking on a new project.[42] Hence, the first part of the book introduces the KLAR crew, both the founding members and recent newcomers, focusing on the promises of cooperativism and craftwork that bring them together. More specifically, in Chapter 1, I outline the professional and political trajectories of the co-op's founding members, showing how ideas of freedom have always played a key role. I expand on the concept of *economies of freedom* presented in this introductory chapter to further unfold how the founding members came to envision cooperativism as an emancipatory endeavor. This lays the groundwork for one of the book's key claims: cooperativism must be approached as an elusive project, that demands continuous reinvention, rather than an ostensibly fixed organizational form or an all-or-nothing proposition.

Chapter 2 turns to the newcomers at KLAR and the daily work at construction sites, exploring in greater detail how and why, like other craft actors in contemporary Euro-American societies, the builders came to perceive craftwork as a liberating, creative form of work. One specific group of workers was particularly instrumental in understanding this question: women builders and apprentices. The chapter traces these builders' attempts to insert themselves into male-dominated trades and explores how they both conformed to and contested prevailing ideas of "good craftwork." In doing so, the chapter also shows how the builders sought to nurture the ability to tinker through their engagement with craftwork.

Chapter 3 picks up where the regular workday at construction sites ends, exploring the informal social interactions among crew members at social events taking place at KLAR during afternoons, evenings, and weekends. It homes in on the interactions between the founding members and newcomers, and thus on the role of intergenerational relations in the social organization of co-ops. I show how the entrepreneurial legacy of the co-op is renegotiated through encounters between different generations of builders.

This reveals how the builders' commitment to cooperativism simultaneously united and divided them during disagreements concerning how to practically realize the ideas and ideals behind the co-op. These divergent perspectives show that the meaning of cooperativism is not static but changes over time; moreover, they underscore that persistent tinkering is required to fulfill cooperativism's elusive promises.

In the remaining three chapters, we move from the composition of the KLAR crew and the co-op's internal workings to an examination of the challenges the builders faced as they sought to realize the promises of craft and cooperative endeavors. I begin by examining the challenges faced by the builders as they grappled with cooperativism's idea of democratic control at the co-op's numerous assemblies in Chapter 4. In the view of many of the builders, these assemblies rarely operated as democratic forums, particularly during deliberation processes, due to the complications that arose from the competing norms associated with craftwork and cooperativism. The chapter details how the builders strove to reconcile these norms in an effort to secure the democratic structure of their organization and thus ensure that their craft co-op did not end up as a conventional construction enterprise. I argue that they did so by continuously tinkering with the practical organization and operation of their assemblies.

In Chapter 5, I move back to the construction sites to show how the builders engaged with cooperative craftwork as a source of critical resistance to hegemonic social and political structures. This chapter highlights the builders' understanding of craftwork as expressed through the idea of *kloge hænder* (wise hands). By tinkering with the regulatory frameworks of construction, the builders sought to redefine the value and meaning of craftwork to challenge the misrecognition and devaluation that have come to dominate perceptions of craftwork in modern societies.

Finally, in Chapter 6, I examine the completion of construction projects. Analytically, the chapter returns to a concern outlined in this introduction and asks: Can cooperative practitioners act simultaneously within and beyond a capitalist market system? This chapter highlights the ambiguous nature of cooperativism through an exploration of the builders' evaluation of three selected building projects. I analyze the value that the builders aspired to produce through these construction projects and argue that the builders aspired to tinker with capitalism by trying to act simultaneously within and beyond a capitalist market system. I propose that exploring this double movement allows us to move beyond a binary approach that either celebrates or criticizes cooperatives by revealing cooperative practitioners' complicated relationships with capitalist practices—practices that they simultaneously refused, ridiculed, and reproduced.

The conclusion, "Taking Politics into One's Own Hands," synthesizes the book's major findings and arguments. It further discusses the historical effects of tinkering as a transformative action and suggests directions for further scholarly inquiries into craftwork, cooperativism, and critical capitalist practices in contemporary societies.

NOTES

1. As the Danish electoral system involves multi-party proportional representation, where it is the norm that no single party gains an overall majority, the largest party does not necessarily form a government.
2. See, e.g., Skidmore–Hess (2003), Lykkeberg (2008), Petersen et al. (2014) and Køber (2022).
3. A recurring question during my fieldwork was whether to protect the identities of my interlocutors. For ethnographers working with highly literate populations, confidentiality and anonymity are much easier to promise than to guarantee, as nothing can prohibit a sufficiently determined reader from trying to decode the text (Bosk and de Vries 2004). Nonetheless, I decided to pseudonymize the co-op and anyone mentioned in the book. A colleague suggested that I named the organization KLAR. I considered this a suitable suggestion, as the Danish word *klar* can be translated as both *evident* and *ready*. In my view, this choice of name reflects the builders' drive and creative efforts, which are explored in this book. I furthermore refer to everyone working at KLAR as a *builder*, including supervisors and office staff. In a few cases, I also found it necessary to alter demographic details (primarily age or gender) or deliberately leave certain ethnographic details vague in order to protect participants' identities.
4. See, e.g., Kasmir (1996), Rakopoulos (2015b, 2018) and Narotzky and Homs (2019). I return to this assertion in the section "Tracing the Resurgence of Cooperativism in Denmark and Beyond."
5. See note 12 for an overview of these studies.
6. While many references could be mentioned here, I draw specifically on Li (2019) and Postero and Elinoff (2019).
7. Here, I draw on Tania Li's conception of politics as "concrete, historically situated practices that fracture and disassemble formations of power, and subject them to an effective, critical challenge" (Li 2019: 33).
8. Many scholars have underlined the importance of looking at local manifestations of the concept of neoliberalism instead of framing it as an overarching and coherent global trend (see, e.g., Gershon 2011; Eriksen et al. 2015).
9. See, e.g., Gullestad (1992), Bruun (2011), and Bruun, Krøjer and Rytter (2015) for elaborations of this argument.
10. See also Sjørslev (2011) or Rytter (2010) for elaborations of these assertions.
11. As Marchand notes, the dynamism of craft renders it notoriously difficult to define, and as such it might best be approached as a "polythetic category" (Marchand 2021: 9). I draw on Marchand's approach, relying on an emic definition of craft in this book.

12. Presenting an adequate overview of the scholarship of craftwork would in many ways be unfeasible. Within anthropology, more specifically, the intricacies of skilled practices have received in-depth attention from a number of scholars (see, e.g., Cooper 1980; Moeran 1984; Kondo 1990; Ulin 1996; Ingold 2000, 2013; Terrio 2000; Herzfeld 2004; Marchand 2009, 2021; Venkatesan 2010; Portisch 2011; Paxson 2013; Sutton 2014). Although most of these studies refer to participants as "artisans," I use the terms "craftworker" and "builder" when referring to my interlocutors. Following Sennett (2008), I consider craftworker to be a more inclusive category than artisan.
13. While I would have preferred to use an emic term to describe this ability, as Beltrán (2023) does in his study of hackers and Reed-Danahay (1993) in her study of the Laviallois, non-verbality was a shared virtue among the builders at KLAR, as I unfold in Chapter 2, which makes it hard to identify a suitable and shared emic term for this particular ability.
14. Historically, the concept of tinkering has appeared in studies of evolution (Jacob 1977); however, it has recently appeared in studies of, for instance, urban planning (Elmqvist et al. 2018).
15. This is partly due to the etymology of the term. The word "tinkering" is typically defined with reference to "Tinkers"—denoting a group of people who travelled from place to place, selling or repairing things. Drawing on this description, tinkering is often defined as "to make small changes to something in order to repair or improve it, especially in a way that may not be helpful" (Oxford Dictionary of English, 2005).
16. The notion of tinkering has, for instance, been used in educational studies inspired by STS, particularly those concerned with STEM education (Martinez and Stager 2016); in studies of digital security (Kocksch 2024) and digitized, data-driven and personalized health care (Jansky 2024); and in STS-inspired studies of environmental adaptation (Quimby et al. 2023). The latter approach tinkering as a "sociotechnical" and "situated practice and actor agency"—an approach that evidently shares certain affinities with the concept of tinkering applied in this book.
17. This concept of tinkering was introduced by Annemarie Mol, Ingunn Moser, and Jeannette Pols (2010). Broadly speaking, they presented tinkering as a form of focused and purposeful "attentive experimentation" in their anthology on care practices (Mol et al. 2010: 13). More precisely, they stated that "seeking a compromise between different 'goods' does not necessarily depend on talk, but can also be a matter of practical tinkering, of attentive experimentation" (ibid.). This conception of tinkering bears some resemblance to earlier STS-inspired research. Karin Knorr-Cetina (1979), for instance, used tinkering to describe the work of experimenting as a creative, material and ad hoc exercise.
18. Although this conception of tinkering has also sneaked into anthropology, the notion has not spread significantly (see, e.g., Van Der Kist (2024) for an exception).
19. The notion of bricolage advanced by Claude Lévi-Strauss (2014 [1978]) is particularly relevant here, as tinkering can be translated to bricolage in French. In Lévi-Strauss's writings, the concept of bricolage refers to the process that leads to the creation of what he describes as "mythical thought"—a kind of "intellectual 'bricolage'" (Lévi-Strauss 2014 [1978]: 24). In this regard, Levi-Strauss reminded us that bricolage—or tinkering, I suggest—is not only relevant when describing a technical operation; it can also describe an intellectual movement.
20. The citations are taken from Deborah Reed-Danahay's (1993) work on *Débrouillardise*.

21. Insights from what has been dubbed the "subjective turn" in resistance studies (e.g., Krøijer 2015; Razsa 2015; Alexandrakis 2016; Laszczkowski 2019) have been particularly concerned with the relation between transformative action and self-transformation.
22. Hector Bertrán has identified a similar inclination among hacker-entrepreneurs, as hackers "use coding logic to provide a foundation for honing their ability to manage themselves and their practices in order to scrutinize their relationships with the state, private companies, and their valued hacker communities" (Beltrán 2023: 33). I draw on this argument in asserting that builders similarly use the strategies of one social practice—cooperative craftwork—as techniques to change societal orders.
23. I am here referring to the fact that a conversation about cooperativism was once again flourishing in Denmark. Due to the lack of an official definition of a cooperative organization and, moreover, the lack of a legal framework for cooperatives in Denmark, it is hard to ascertain whether or not there has been a quantitative increase in cooperative organizations.
24. See, e.g., Skytte (2016), Pedersen and Nayberg (2019), Jørgensen (2020) and Gjerding and Rask (2021) for examples of written accounts.
25. The principles were formulated as a number of ideals for the operation of co-ops and have since 1844 been key to the development of co-ops worldwide (Rakopoulos 2020). They have been revised on several occasions by the International Cooperative Alliance (1995). The most recent version is presented in The Statement on the Cooperative Identity, published in 1995, where the principles are described as 1) Open and voluntary membership, 2) Democratic member control, 3) Members' economic participation, 4) Autonomy and independence, 5) Education, training, and information, 6) Cooperation among co-ops, 7) Concern for community.
26. See, e.g., Johansen, Skovgaard and Hyllegaard (2010) for an example of a policy report on social innovation, or Mordhorst (2005) for a broader discussion of the links between innovation and cooperativism in Denmark.
27. See Terrio (2000), Herzfeld (2004), Marchand (2009), Jones (2011) and Paxson (2013) for examples from scholarship on craft. Within scholarship on cooperativism, the notion of tradition has not been debated to the same extent, yet it does for instance appear in work on the relation between anti-mafia movements and cooperatives in Sicily (Rakopoulos 2018) and on wine cooperatives in southwest France (Ulin 1995).
28. I borrow this phrase from Bertel Haarder, a prominent Danish politician (Bertel Haarder in Gjerding and Rask 2021: 208).
29. Political leaders of the labor movement were initially skeptical of the expansion of consumer co-ops in Denmark. In the early 1870s, however, this changed and discussions on cooperativism began to flourish among workers in the cities who, inspired by developments in France and Germany, gradually began to launch their own worker co-ops (*Produktionsforeninger*). Despite this enthusiasm, only eight worker co-ops managed to get off the ground before an economic depression hit Denmark in 1875. None of the worker co-ops survived the crisis (Als, Clausen and Oksen 1979). Meanwhile, cooperativism re-emerged in the workers' movement at the end of the nineteenth century, partly due to a nationwide lockout. During the following decade, numerous building co-ops were launched (a few of which are still operating today) (Grelle 2012).

30. Cooperative actors and advocates' engagement with the state in Denmark has been a point of discussion among scholars (see, e.g., Henriksen, Smith and Zimmer 2012; Sievers 2016; R. E. Jørgensen 2017). However, by approaching domains such as the state as a priori entities, none of the contributions to these discussions focus on how people involved in current forms of cooperativism also actively take part in creating the state. That is, how they construct the Danish welfare state through everyday discursive practices (Bruun et al. 2015).
31. This point resonates with arguments presented in other anthropological accounts from Scandinavia, which emphasize the nearly invisible boundary between civil society and the state (Bruun 2018). Some have even suggested that Danes see the state as "a neighbor that is ever watchful and interested without necessarily being an interfering busybody," as most are accustomed to enjoying the advantages that it offers (Jenkins 2012: 199–200).
32. Due to an upsurge of co-ops and similar associations in the mid-1970s in rural areas of Africa, Asia and Latin America, scholars tended to focus on these regions (see, e.g., Nash and Hopkins 1976; Attwood and Baviskar 1987; Attwood and Baviskar 1988). Later ethnographies also turned to European contexts, yet they centered mainly on Southern Europe (see, e.g., Holmstrom 1990; Kasmir 1996; Ulin 1996).
33. See, e.g., Nash and Hopkins (1976) for an example of an early "optimistic" ethnography of cooperativism, and Sharryn Kasmir's (1996) study of the renowned co-ops of Mondragón for a subsequent, more critical ethnography.
34. This is a main focus in Theodoros Rakopoulos's (2018) work on Sicilian agricultural cooperatives operating on vineyards and farmland seized by the Italian state from convicted mafiosi.
35. Gabriela Vargas-Cetina (2005) makes a somewhat similar argument, suggesting that we need to see co-ops and other local organizations as "ephemeral associations" that are highly context-dependent and in constant flux. Yet, whereas ephemeral in this case underscores the short-lived character of a social phenomenon, elusive indicates that a phenomenon might be difficult to find, define or achieve (Oxford Dictionary of English, 2005).
36. It is estimated that 30–40 percent of construction workers in Denmark change jobs yearly (Arnholtz, Krause-Jensen and Juul 2015), with notice of resignation or termination customarily given only a few days in advance.
37. The "flex" prefix refers to employment protection legislation that affords employers considerable leeway, while the "-curity" suffix refers to security in the form of generous income support for the unemployed.
38. See, e.g., Applebaum (1999), Paap (2006), Thiel (2007) and Pink, Tutt and Dainty (2013) for examples of ethnographic studies of construction work in large firms with complex organizational structures. Swider (2015) also provides an ethnographic study of the informal work and exploitation of migrant workers, while Hirslund (2019) and Dharia (2022) offer examples of ethnographic studies of marginalized workers in the Global South.
39. While Erik accepted my request to conduct long-term fieldwork at KLAR during our initial meeting, a legal process followed this meeting where both Erik and I signed a customized non-disclosure agreement (NDA). The purpose of the NDA was, on one hand, to provide the co-op with a mechanism to protect their business secrets, and on the other, to ensure my academic freedom. The NDA further

included a description of how I was to handle data from my fieldwork in order to comply with the General Data Protection Regulation (GDPR).

40. Marianne Gullestad (1992), for instance, argued in her seminal study of everyday life in Norway that social life is home-centered in Scandinavia, as the home is considered an intimate space. See Tjørnhøj-Thomsen (2003) or Bruun (2012) for similar assertions.
41. Kirin Narayan unfolds this assertion in a chapter in *Writing Anthropology: Essays on Craft and Commitment*. The assertion draws on a quote from Renato Rosaldo (McGranahan 2020: 74).
42. Rather than beginning with what is typically considered the first stage of a construction process, a so-called "site survey," as others have done (Dharia 2022), I follow the construction process as it unfolds from the perspectives of the builders at KLAR.

CHAPTER 1

AN ECONOMY OF FREEDOM

The Foundations of KLAR

KLAR is located in one of the most densely populated neighborhoods of Copenhagen, which is situated close to what is referred to colloquially as *søerne* (the lakes). Readers familiar with the city of Copenhagen might know that this particular neighborhood was at the center of several political struggles in the 1980s. However, few are probably aware that it was the locus of the city's industrial development before it emerged as a working-class district at the end of the nineteenth century (Federspiel 1997). This history has left traces in the architectural outline of the neighborhood, which is characterized by a blend of city blocks with nineteenth-century buildings, industrial spaces and a modular architecture style that has spread across Copenhagen because of large-scale urban renewal schemes developed in the 1980s. On one of the central streets of the neighborhood, you find a smaller building with a brightly colored facade that today houses the main office and workshop of KLAR squeezed in between housing and industrial spaces.

The geographical location of KLAR might sound like a minor, although slightly paradoxical detail, since larger construction companies are normally located at the outskirts of urban areas. Yet KLAR's location in this part of Copenhagen is not arbitrary. While the builders relocated to the building at the end of the 2010s, the main office of KLAR had been in this neighborhood since the co-op was launched. Many of the people working at KLAR lived in this neighborhood, and, over the years, the builders had developed a preference for working on construction projects in this neighborhood or at locations nearby. Cycling through the streets of this vibrant part of the city, where the bicycle is a favored mode of transportation, KLAR's logo frequently emerges on scaffolding like a beacon, proudly displaying the co-op's presence and work. Over the years, the builders have also taken part in organizing festivals and similar activities in the neighborhood, such as urban bike races. KLAR is clearly tightly connected to this neighborhood. Hence, it is difficult to chronicle the history of KLAR without also recounting the builders' current and past connection to the urban context of this neighborhood.

Co-ops are context-dependent organizations. This argument is often repeated across studies of contemporary co-ops and similar grassroots organizations. Many emphasize that these organizations are required to "reinvent themselves constantly, to keep up with global and local changes" in both the surrounding environment and institutional arrangements (Vargas-Cetina 2005: 229). Others have highlighted that an attentiveness to how co-ops are always "embedded" in local histories and social codes is key to grasping the contextual character of these organizations and further to understand "the subjective experience of participating in" cooperative activities (Rakopoulos 2018: 196). In this chapter, I push beyond such assertions by demonstrating how the craft co-op KLAR has not simply "adapted to" or become "embedded" in a local context; rather, as I shall show, it *emerged* from this context. While it may seem a minor quibble whether we employ notions of embeddedness or emergence, it has, I argue, analytical consequences. Indeed, focusing on the emergent nature and thus elusiveness of cooperativism enables us to move beyond the "embeddedness paradigm" (Ho 2015: 173), which has come to dominate contemporary studies of cooperativism. Scholars have used this paradigm in their considerations of how individuals and collectives seek to "re-localize" and "re-embed" the economy in social life in response to austerity measures emerging in many contexts in the first decade of the twenty-first century. Many have in this regard turned to Karl Polanyi (1944).[1] Taking the obvious affinities between Polanyi's discussion of the social situation engendered by economic collapse and the resurgence of co-ops and similar associations into account, this turn to Polanyi seems sound. Yet, as several scholars have stressed before me, Polanyi's depiction of economy as "embedded" risks reproducing the idea that the economic can somehow exist outside of social life.[2] As such, embeddedness verges toward economically reductive interpretations of social action, which can overlook how inventive economic actions and ideas are perhaps also key to cooperativism.

To emphasize the role of inventive and liberating economic actions and ideas in cooperativism, I attend to cooperativism as an *economy of freedom* in this chapter. In developing this notion, I take my cue from a body of newer studies within or related to economic anthropology, which explore the cultural dynamics and contingencies that underpin economic processes.[3] This body of literature insists that economic activity is also social activity and, like all culturally meaningful actions, such activity is "incited, enabled and constrained by sentiments that are themselves the products of historically contingent cultural processes" (Yanagisako 2002: 11). In drawing attention to the distinct cultural processes which motivate and shape cooperative endeavors, I show how cooperativism emerges from historically situated sentiments, desires, and commitments.

In this chapter, I unfold how and why KLAR can be perceived as an economy of freedom by exploring the ideas and plans that originally guided the establishment of the co-op. The ethnography presented in the chapter largely takes the form of autobiographical narratives, as I piece together the educational and professional trajectories of some of the founding members of KLAR. Through these trajectories, I outline the entrepreneurial ethos of the co-op by attending to the founding members' historically situated dreams, drives, and desires. Rather than situating their entrepreneurial aspirations within the monolithic concept of "neoliberalism," I pay attention to how these aspirations have emerged within a specific historical context of Danish society. In this way, we can better understand how economic goals and actions are produced in historical periods among specific cultural actors. The first step in this line of examination is to return to the story of how KLAR initially came into being.

HOW IT ALL BEGAN

Ahead of one of the co-op's latest anniversaries, an account of the beginning of KLAR circulated under the headline: "We would do it again even if we knew how much hassle and trouble we would go through." As in the Introduction to this book, this account describes one of the meetings that took place in late winter of 2001, during which eight builders met to discuss how the craft co-op, which they were planning to launch, should be organized. At the meeting, the group debated the fundamental framework of the co-op and jotted down four principles, which can be loosely translated as follows:

1) Everyone had to put extra effort into the work during the first year to ensure that the co-op got off to a positive start and they could realize their collective goal of operating an entrenched enterprise.
2) Everyone had to be sincere about their relationship to the community and their expected work contributions (i.e., they had to inform the others about any family matters or other social obligations that might restrain their work efforts).
3) Honesty was essential and they wanted to make lasting agreements during collective meetings and write these down in minutes.

4) Last, if anyone wanted to leave the co-op for a longer period, they had to resign from the collectively run council and further ensure that it did not affect the customer base.

Subsequent parts of the text describe how KLAR developed in the years since it was launched. It details how the workforce of the co-op had grown from 5 to 60 builders, and that the builders had trained more than 100 apprentices and convened more than 140 member assemblies. The account further included a few quotes from Erik, who stated that the cooperative members were happy and proud of having provided urban dwellers with more sustainable building solutions over the years, and moreover of having contributed to the development of the local neighborhood by organizing different activities and events. But, Erik stressed, they were equally proud of the daily construction work they had engaged in, ranging from the installation of kitchens, to the construction of bathrooms and renovation of facades. "We still get up at the crack of dawn and that's hard work, but the many exciting projects and our jovial customers continue to make it worthwhile," Erik added. The account underscored that running a co-op had not always been easy. Over the years, the builders had confronted several crises, such as the financial collapse in 2008. However, the community of KLAR had been the force that had enabled them to get through these challenging times. Everyone had made an additional effort whenever they had too much work, and they shared the tasks when there was too little work. The celebratory account finished with the following declaration, "The Community is our driver."

The history of KLAR is typically presented in this way in written material or in media reports. The account, therefore, represents what we might term the "official" history of the craft co-op. Yet such "official" histories of enterprises rarely represent the sole historical account of entrepreneurial endeavors. In her work on family firms in northern Italy's silk industry enterprises, Sylvia Yanagisako (2002) shows that histories of the beginning of enterprises can be told in different ways, as they include some details while omitting others. The selective nature of these historical accounts can be illuminated if we attend to them as narratives of origin not dissimilar to the stories of coming-into-being examined by anthropologists since the onset of the discipline (Yanagisako 2002). Important insights can thus be gained if we approach historical accounts of KLAR as narratives of origin. Doing so does not imply that these accounts are ungrounded in facts. Rather, these narratives are discursive practice that can provide novel perspectives on the entrepreneurial motives and actions guiding the inception as well as the development of KLAR.

The "official" history of KLAR, for instance, leaves little doubt about the importance of the notion of "community" to the development of the co-op.

Irrespective of whether the focus of the narrative is on the achievements or the daily work of the craft co-op, the account underlines that KLAR is and will always be a collective endeavor. This portrayal is further supported by the rather insignificant and anonymous depiction of the people who initially launched the craft co-op, as they are simply described as "a small group of builders." KLAR is clearly presented as the creation of a community of people.

Looking across the literature on cooperativism, the fact that the community is described as the center of a co-op is unsurprising. The notion of "community" often plays a significant role in accounts of cooperativism, although scholars typically also recognize the varied and ambiguous role of claims to community in cooperative organizations. More broadly in the economic anthropology literature, some stress the importance of a critical reading of these "community ideologies" (Narotzky 2004), while others argue that important insights can be gained from inquiring into what exactly is meant by community on the ground (Rakopoulos 2015b). While I tend to follow the latter proposal, for now, I focus on the implications of foregrounding community in "official" histories of KLAR. When merely emphasizing that KLAR is the result of collective efforts, the past and present role of the founding members of the co-op remains opaque.

In the following, I explore the role of the founding members of KLAR from a historical perspective by unfolding three alternative historical narratives of the co-op. Piecing together these alternative histories allows me to ask questions about what preceded the beginning of KLAR; a time that convincing origin stories often suppress as they, similar to the account above, tend to focus on the movement from the moment of creation to the future of an enterprise (Yanagisako 2002). Analyzing these narratives allows me to uncover the close connections between KLAR and the founding members' personal life trajectories. This shows that the co-op was not the creation of *any* community; rather, it was created by a specific group of people, whose personal stories and perceptions of freedom continue to shape the social life of KLAR. Overall, the analysis thus underscores how cooperative endeavors emerge from historically situated sentiments, desires, and commitments produced among specific cultural actors.

THREE KLAR ORIGIN STORIES

I never heard anybody from the "small group of builders" who initially launched KLAR refer to themselves as "founders" of the craft co-op. Nonetheless, the meetings convened during the late winter of 2001 were considered the founding moment of the craft co-op. During the prelude to these meetings, twenty-two builders had shown an interest in the project, Erik explained during an interview. However, several withdrew as they started working on the initial outline of the co-op. When those gathered took the final decision to launch KLAR, only "eight loyal soldiers" decided to join the adventure, according to Erik. During fieldwork, three of the "eight soldiers" were still working at KLAR. The others had quit over the years, either because the physical work had become too demanding or because they had moved on to new pastures. Several, however, continued to take part in the co-op's assemblies and social activities.

Erik's account of the 2001 meetings again highlights the importance of collective effort in the foundation of KLAR. His use of the notion of "soldiers" further indicates that loyalty and commitment were prevalent sentiments from the beginning. Launching and running a co-op was envisioned as a kind of struggle, where the "eight soldiers" had to stick together. However, as with any origin narrative, this story also contains traces of a past that begs to be brought to light. How had the people, who either initially showed interest or who eventually joined KLAR, come to know each other? This question turns our attention to what I deem the second origin story of KLAR.

Frode, who had been one of the "eight soldiers," explained during an interview that some of his fellow founding members of KLAR had met at a different craft co-op where they had worked together for some years. I will name this craft co-op MODSTRØM in the following account. According to Frode, many of them—himself included—were initially quite happy about working for this co-op. "I really learned a lot from working at that enterprise—both about the methods used to collectively run the co-op and also about the work itself. I learned something, which I needed professionally. They knew a lot about sustainability in construction work," Frode recalled. He added, "We took these values with us when we launched KLAR." MODSTRØM was located outside of Copenhagen, but on Erik's initiative, the members moved a division of the enterprise to the city, so the builders living in the city could avoid the daily transit. However, the majority of the construction projects they obtained remained located outside the city, and after a few years most of the members living in the city grew tired of driving long distances. "It didn't make sense to drive 100 km every day in a diesel car. And I had very young kids at that time so it was tough," Frode highlighted. Henning—whom most consider to be a founding member of KLAR although he was not part of the "eight soldiers"—further explained that some of the members of MODSTRØM had faced some collaboration challenges. More precisely, the principle of equal pay for all had supposedly been disregarded in MODSTRØM. "The money simply dropped into a black hole," Henning said. For Frode, Erik, and Henning, who had all worked at MODSTRØM during this period, this was only a symptom of a more substantial discord, which they attributed to their different backgrounds. According to the three of them, the founding members of MODSTRØM were "hippies" and "people from the countryside," whereas they were "people from the city." Frode explained that, for him, this difference manifested in the form of divergent work ethics. After some years, they decided to leave MODSTRØM to instead establish their own co-op, where they could, to a larger degree, stick to the principles which they considered foundational for a co-op, such as equal pay for everyone.

According to this account, some of the founding members had known each other for years before they decided to launch KLAR. The account further introduces a distinction worth noticing; that is, the difference between "people from the countryside" and "people from the city." While Frode did not detail why or how this manifested as two distinct work ethics, the distinction nonetheless underscores that the founding members of KLAR considered themselves connected to and shaped by urban living. They were, in other words, people of the city. While it remained implicit, I knew that they did not refer to any city, but rather more specifically to the city of Copenhagen. This connection to urban living and to Copenhagen more specifically turns our attention to what I deem the third origin story of KLAR.

While this third story was told in more elusive terms, Erik fleetingly recounted that he had met some of the people who joined KLAR in its nascent years in the early 1990s. He had also collaborated with a few of them on a construction project that he had obtained in 1993. In brief, the project was a renovation of a large housing construction infected with dry rot—a type of wood decay caused by fungi. Erik explained that he was hired to do the work as he had experience with retrofitting old housing constructions plagued with dry rot. He subsequently reached out to people whom he had cooperated with before to gather a crew of builders who could help him solve the task. After the work was done, several of the crew members decided to continue working together and applied for jobs at MODSTRØM. Several of the founding members had thus met each other in the early 1990s, which hints that they were somehow connected to the same social milieu in the city.

Overall, the three narratives blur the "official" historical account of KLAR. They demonstrate that even the founding members themselves trace the history of the co-op back to different events and encounters, which makes it hard to pin the beginning of KLAR to one particular moment. Rather, these stories point to the multiple events, motives, and actions of the founding members that shaped the social foundation from which the co-op initially emerged. The three stories also reveal that different identities can be ascribed to the co-op. In the first narrative, the co-op emerges as a sudden idea quickly turned into reality. By suggesting that the translation from words to action was brief, KLAR is portrayed as a place of action. The second narrative, in contrast, emphasizes practicalities—the long driving distances, having a family with kids—which portrays the founding of the co-op as a practical solution to the challenges of finding the right work-life balance. In the third narrative, the question of identity is not clear-cut, but hints that some of the founding members of KLAR had crossed each other's paths earlier on. As we shall see in the following section, this was indeed the case, as some of them had met in the same politico-social milieu emerging in Copenhagen in the 1980s and early 1990s. A milieu that had not only introduced the founding members' to the possibilities of craftwork, but also come to shape their perception of freedom significantly.

STORIES FROM THE '80S

It was primarily conversations with two of the founding members that drew my attention to the connection between certain politico-social milieus emerging in Copenhagen during the 1980s and the origins of KLAR. In examining this link, this section therefore zeros in on the personal trajectories of two individual builders, Erik and Frode. During interviews, I asked them to describe their respective lives during the 1980s. While I had one illuminating conversation with Frode about his youth in the 1980s, which I recount in the following sections, Erik conveyed his past experiences in fragments weaved into other conversations. Based on these patchy stories, I will unfold Frode and Erik's descriptions of the political environment in Copenhagen during the 1980s and examine how they relate these experiences to their current engagement with KLAR.[4]

The "No-Future" Identity

Around 1980, Erik moved to Freetown Christiania—popularly referred to simply as Christiania. Christiania is a large ex-military area with dismantled barracks located close to the city center in Copenhagen, which a group of squatters occupied in 1971. Youngsters, hippies and homeless people quickly moved in, and the place was organized as a village community. At the time, it was perceived as a "social experiment" even by policymakers and public authorities (Mikkelsen 2002). Erik had been involved in the political activities of Christiania since the early 1970s, but in 1980 he decided to finally move in. "I was part of a telephone tree already in 1976. I was only twelve back then," he said and added that, "I was raised in this activist environment, where everything was possible."

Erik worked and lived in Christiania for the next thirteen years. During these years, he was highly involved in various artistic and political activities unfolding in the community. By organizing concerts and events, he and others collected money for various construction, social, and political projects. Erik underlined that these projects taught him and his companions to build, renovate, and mobilize people to take part in the work. This practical yet prolific work also shaped his perception of political activism. "It wasn't simply an activism against something," he explained. "If you are against something, it's also great to build what you want instead." This approach had become foundational for his future engagement with political activism. "I don't have time for waiting around," he told me, "I build what I want now."

In the early 1990s, Erik decided to move for reasons he did not specify. However, he stressed that his decision to leave had been swift. "I simply handed back the keys," he said as he described how he had resigned from his position at one of the local venues at Christiania. He thus refrained from claiming his right to ownership of the organizations or the buildings he had taken part in constructing while living at Christiania. For him, this move was a question of taking their collective rejection of private ownership seriously. This rejection is generally considered a defining principle of the Freetown, and it had remained a central tenet in Erik's personal ideology even after he left.

While living at Christiania had shaped Erik in many ways, his young adulthood had also been defined by the demographic and economic processes shaping Copenhagen and Denmark more broadly at the time, like many others of his age. Erik summed up his experience of the 1980s as follows:

> First of all, we are a huge generation. We are the baby boomers of the post-war era. We grew up in a time where the two world wars had finished only twenty years back and which was the only thing the locos talked about. So, the fear of war was still around, and we grew up in the craziest cold war era, where everything was tense. In contrast to this, everything was quite easy, because it was either black or white. There wasn't anything in between. We grew up with clear distinctions between developing and industrialized countries. The world population has doubled since I was born. When I was a kid, there were places that weren't yet explored. At the same time, the 80s marked the grand victory of the social democrats in Western Europe, as they were supported by the Capital [capital interests], who had to support them, because otherwise people would move to the east. Then there was Thatcher and Reagan and the whole right-oriented yuppie-wave in Denmark, where everyone had to be the master of their own destiny, with clothes, fashion, cars, and that whole sucky way of seeing the world. Actually, it's quite interesting to look at the two legs of this development. There was the ultra-liberal development with the yuppies and the super-solidarity-oriented youth, which emerged simultaneously.

The societal picture that Erik draws in this account flags some of the reasons why the youth of the 1980s became known as a "no-future" generation.

Not only did they grow up in a society that was seemingly degrading, the "fear of war" was also, as Erik stressed, looming. However, for Erik, it was also a decade when "everything was black or white," which had, he thought, made life easier in certain ways. The tensions and uncertainties of the Cold War somehow made it impossible to plan a future, which apparently felt liberating. "There were possibilities everywhere. There were empty houses and factories. We could do what we ... it was a land of milk and honey," he tellingly described.

The 1980s had, according to Erik, been riddled with opportunities, and a certain "pioneering spirit," as he termed it, had thus characterized activist social life in the city of Copenhagen. This was also partly owing to a degree of unrest dominating the city during this decade. Erik described this in the following way: "We lived in a highly industrialized city, which was close to bankruptcy in 1986. However, they still allowed a project like Christiania to grow at the same time." "The city was extremely poor," Erik explained, "But it was great at the same time. You could always find a place to live. And you could always slip under the radar of official authorities."

Listening to Erik's descriptions sheds new light on his ceaseless entrepreneurial drive. He vividly described how he had always been capable of finding or creating a livelihood for himself. However, for him, this had been a necessity. "You need to remember that there were 360,000 young people out of work when I left school in 1980. There was nothing," he reminded me, before continuing his explanation. "There was enormous unemployment, so we simply stopped believing that you could apply for a job," he highlighted; "If I wanted a job, I had to create it myself. That was stuck in our minds. Everyone can become an entrepreneur. It's not like it's a genetic disposition. It always starts with a need of some sort." Finding ways of making a living had been important to Erik from an early age. "I have never received any support from the state," he proudly mentioned once.

Although Erik did not expect things to be easy, he rarely talked about frailty. He had become a persistent fighter—but not a lonesome one. Erik's personal story was told from a "we" perspective. As he alluded to, he had always been part of groups. "We learned to believe that—hey—if you can gather a crew, they can't break you. Always a crew, make sure you do something with a crew," he said with a gleam in his eyes.

A Squatter's Life

While living at Christiania, Erik also participated in the emerging squatter movement in Copenhagen in the early 1980s, known as the BZ movement (the Danish abbreviation for squatting), which Frode also joined. Initially,

Frode had simply participated in the street demonstrations. However, owing to his evolving interest in photography, he had begun carrying his camera to the demonstrations to take pictures of the confrontations between police and demonstrators. The police reacted strongly to this, and Frode was arrested at one of the first demonstrations. "I was beaten up quite badly, which made me connect even more with the [BZ] movement," he explained, "So, when I was released, I contacted some people whom I knew were part of the movement."

Frode joined the BZ movement only a few weeks after it was set in motion. While the origin of the movement is debated among scholars, most agree that it developed from earlier squatter movements that emerged in the city in the 1960s and 1970s; furthermore, it was set in motion by the eviction of *Byggeren*—a public leisure area in a central neighborhood in Copenhagen—in 1980.[5] Initially, the movement's central claim was a youth house in Copenhagen, but struggles quickly intensified over a lack of housing, high rates of unemployment, and large-scale slum-clearance schemes sweeping across the city. Years of street fighting with the police followed. Protests peaked with a massive struggle in 1986, when activists blocked the streets for nine days. Subsequently, the BZ movement splintered into factions, which later turned into various autonomous communities (Steiger 2018). In addition to Frode and Erik, some of the other builders who joined KLAR in its nascent years met in these communities. These included Henning and Torsten, whom I will introduce later in this chapter.

Frode did not remember exactly when he left the movement. Although he had cared deeply about the community and his co-squatters, the squatting work was exhausting. "We occupied a house and fixed it. Then we were thrown out, and it was torn down. Then we occupied a new house and fixed that," he explained. "I began to think that we were moving in circles. There were also some personal and political disagreements about the future of the movement." In his youth, Frode had sworn that he would never enroll in any sort of education. But after leaving the movement, he embarked on vocational training. "Trade school seemed like an obvious choice, because I had done so much construction work in the houses," he explained. Craft skills had, in other words, become a necessity for him as a squatter.

Erik provided similar reasoning, "The only thing we could do was to start renovating houses. And renovate some cafés and workshops and apartments. Craftwork was definitely a necessity," he recounted, and added that, "It was about finding a place to live, and things came by easily back then. I think that shaped us to a great extent." The renovation of houses was further perceived as a means to provide people with jobs. "We quickly realized that you can create jobs for forty people if you renovate instead of building something new. So, our argument was simply that we could reduce unemployment by renovating houses," Erik explained.

Creating jobs, or to be more specific, enabling people to support their own livelihood, had been important to the squatters. "We had to help each other," Frode underlined, "The strong shoulders had to carry the weak." These caring relations between members of the squatter movement were perhaps further nurtured by a strong disbelief in "the system," Frode explained, and their numerous struggles with the police during the early 1980s. "It's still imprinted in me in some sense. I don't have much belief in the established, in the system," he explained. "I don't want to spend too much time on it, because I think—I have experienced so many times how, at the end of the day, it wasn't possible to find a solution anyway, because it had to be discussed at a higher political level." In Frode's own words, he had come to consider himself "anti-authoritarian." He values his independence.

* * *

Frode and Erik considered the projects, protests, and life lived in Copenhagen during the 1980s as foundational to their subsequent life trajectories. In this sense, these narratives also resemble a form of personalized origin stories. Frode and Erik's engagement with different social movements during this decade had not only paved the way for their future professional trajectories in construction. It had also provided them with a "pioneering spirit," as Erik described, and taught them the importance of collective action. Despite the societal challenges characterizing Copenhagen during the 1980s, their lives had in their perspective been packed with emancipatory opportunities. In that sense, Frode and Erik's "stories from the '80s" also constitute what I will refer to as *tales of freedom.*

TALES OF FREEDOM

During one of our conversations, Erik briefly touched upon the sense of liberation which had seemingly defined his engagement with the different politico-social movements emerging in Copenhagen during the 1980s. He described how his participation in these movements had somehow provided his life with a certain temporality. More precisely, he said he had learned that things are only temporary. "Whenever we developed or built something ... whenever we found something that could be ours, it was only temporary," he explained. "Everything is temporary. Don't believe that you own anything. Never believe in forever," he said in passing. I must have responded with a serious look, because he corrected himself straight away and said that perhaps this came out too demotivating. He explained that these temporary engagements and experiences had rather made him believe that new opportunities always arise. "We learned to believe in our own powers," he underlined. In a sense, Erik had come to perceive temporary engagements as empowering or even liberating.

For Frode, this belief had also been supported by his and his fellow squatters' strong commitment to collective action. He stressed that his engagement in the community created by the movement had made a great difference to him as a person. "I was quite sensitive back then. I couldn't figure out how to be alone. I was very insecure," he recounted, and added that, "I found great support in the people of my age who were also part of the movement." The collective, mobilizing force of the movement had been a source of liberation for Frode. "It was very much about having the liberty to decide for ourselves," Frode stated as he described how they were struggling to secure housing back in the 1980s. Being part of a larger movement had taught Frode how individuals can—if they mobilize—induce real change.

At a time when ideas and promises of continuous socioeconomic advancement were breaking down in wider society, youngsters like Frode and Erik somehow continued to believe in the possibility of a better future. This seemingly paradoxical emergence of discourses and configurations of freedom amid various forms of precarity dominating contemporary societies has increasingly become a concern for anthropologists (e.g., Tsing 2015; Sopranzetti 2017; Rajković 2018). The forms and effects of precarity described in many of these writings could perhaps be translated into Danish society in the 1980s, a decade marked by rising youth unemployment and reductions in social benefits. However, neither Erik nor Frode's descriptions seem to convey the form of precarity portrayed in anthropological accounts, where precariousness is often described as a sense of insecurity caused by the deregulated market and flexible labor conditions (Rajković 2018). Rather, Frode and Erik continuously stressed the numerous possibilities and opportunities which, in their experience, continued to arise.

In a memoir of the 1980s generation in Denmark, a Danish philosopher, Asger Sørensen (2012), reflects upon this generation's optimistic attitude—a generation he also belonged to. According to Sørensen, his generation took on the "No-future" mantra with good reason, as the national economy of Denmark was on the edge of an economic abyss and youth unemployment was skyrocketing during the 1980s. However, Sørensen also notes that, interestingly, the youth did not worry about this. Indeed, he emphasizes, like Erik, that this situation provided them with plenty of time at their disposal, "because we didn't have to work for a future. There was no future, no reason to plan anything, so we had plenty of time to do all sorts of interesting things" (Sørensen 2012: 9). He further adds, again reiterating one of Erik's points, that "We [the youth] had freedom as a precondition and ideology, we were astounded by the inconceivable possibilities of life and our own possibilities" (ibid.: 13). According to Sørensen, part of the reason for this was that this generation grew up in times of progress, as material and economic conditions had been secured during the 1960s and 1970s; they were "kids of the welfare state" (ibid.: 9, 12). Hence, they became a generation with a strong belief in progress, who neither worried nor gave risk or insecurity a second thought. Indeed, as Sørensen points out, "freedom" became both "a precondition and ideology" for the generation of youngsters in Denmark, of which Erik, Frode, and the other founding members of KLAR were a part.

In a context where "freedom" is continuously brought up, it seems worthwhile to remember that freedom is a ubiquitous concept that carries multiple meanings (Venkatesan 2023). It is also "a concept about which anthropology has [historically] had strikingly little to say" (Laidlaw 2002: 311), although one would think that questions regarding how freedom is exercised in different social contexts and cultural traditions would be crucial to cultural anthropology.[6] Many anthropologists who have engaged with the notion have often conflated emic invocations of freedom with individual autonomy, which is putatively opposed to the kinds of things that interest anthropologists (Venkatesan 2023). Yet rather than attending to metaphysical and ahistorical ideals of freedom, anthropologists are well-positioned to turn attention to contextual understandings of freedom encountered in ethnographic engagements (Sopranzetti 2017). Doing so involves interrogating what people mean by freedom when they invoke it, and what efforts they expend to achieve such freedom.

Among the builders, freedom was indeed polysemic. Erik and others often used the term interchangeably with words such as *selvstændighed* or *uafhængighed*, which can both be translated to independence, and the expression of "*at klare sig selv*"—"to manage on one's own."[7] Indeed, Erik and Frode had a strong belief in their own abilities. As Erik said, he and his peers had "learned to believe in our own powers." Their disbelief in "the system" and external interference that Frode described appeared to have become a tenet to many of the founding members of KLAR. As such, Erik, Frode, and many of the other founding members seemingly considered themselves strong believers in negative freedom. That is, a freedom from external restrictions, forces and actions (Venkatesan 2023).[8] It was this sense of freedom that also seemingly guided the founding members' entrepreneurial aspirations and thus also the entrepreneurial ethos that came to guide the formation of KLAR in 2001.

In some regard, this sense of negative freedom seems to resemble the freedom described by the center-right government, which gained power in Denmark the same year. With their claim to pursue a *systemskifte* (a change of system) in Denmark, this government was invested keenly in finding ways to limit external interferences from both the state and the so-called cultural elite in Denmark. Yet, while their goal was to strengthen the freedom of individuals, the founding members of KLAR had a strong belief in collective action and thus in the possibility of collective freedom. Taking Frode's remark that "The strong shoulders had to carry the weak" into account further indicates that the founding members' sense of freedom, rather, seemed to represent a continuation of the redistributive intentions of the universalist welfare state logic, which the new government was trying to redefine. This intention underscores that everyone should provide for themselves most of the time and only take advantage of the collective benefits that they need (Jöncke 2011). Considering this difference, the freedom depicted by the founding members of KLAR seemed to combine a continuation of these intentions with a certain "anti-authoritarianism," as described by Frode.[9]

Although a search for negative freedom might have guided the eight people who initially decided to launch KLAR, they had to renegotiate this search as they embarked on converting their idea of freedom and the entrepreneurial ethos associated with it into a corporate structure. In Erik's words, this conversion constituted a "professionalization of activism." Already at the outset of this professionalization, the builders were confronted with requirements posed by external restrictions and forces, as exemplified by corporative state regulations.

BUILDING A CO-OP STRUCTURE

The formal registration of a corporation in Denmark comes with certain state defined requirements. To shed light on the founding members' attempts to navigate such requirements, I describe the puzzles they faced as they initially had to work out the legal framework, economic principles, and organizational structure of KLAR.

Legal Framework: Eschewing Dependence on Specific Persons

While the cooperative organizational form has existed in Denmark for more than a century, the form is not specified in any particular legal framework.[10] Rather, practitioners have to choose between different frameworks when launching a co-op.[11] Hence, one of the first hurdles, which the founding members had to overcome, was to decide on a legal framework for KLAR.

One of their primary concerns was the question of ownership. Living in Christiania had taught Erik the importance of collective ownership; a tenet he repeated when he described how they initially sought to implement this principle into KLAR's corporate form. "Personal ownership corrupts people," he said. "As soon as somebody can access money, they will take it." Accordingly, the founding members did not want a specific person(s) to be registered as the formal owner of KLAR. Rather, they thought the co-op should be considered a self-governing entity in a legal sense. Moreover, they wanted to ensure that everyone employed at the co-op had access to benefits in times of difficulty. Accordingly, all the members had to be considered wageworkers, formally speaking, which in the Danish context implies that none of them could be registered as business owners.

With the help of a lawyer, the founding members customized a legal framework that enabled them to launch the co-op as a jointly owned enterprise. The question of ownership was resolved by registering the co-op as an industrial foundation.[12] While this form enabled the members to eschew dependence on one person, it produced a different challenge, as initial capital is needed to establish an industrial foundation, thus presupposing a gift or an investment from a donor or a founder. The founding members resolved this challenge by taking on additional work—"a lot of work" emphasized Erik and Frode—through which they managed to earn enough money to reach the required amount of initial capital.

Additionally, the establishment of an industrial foundation also requires some articles of association and a description of an overall objective of the foundation, which cannot be changed subsequently. The founding members formulated the main objective of their foundation as follows:

> To operate a collectively managed and sustainable business within the construction industry, property management, or the service trades. The object of the foundation is further to support social, collectivist, socialist, or economic projects operated from a grassroots level (projects must rely chiefly on the work of those involved); and the formation of companies, which provide sound and social jobs. The foundation can support projects based in Denmark as well as abroad.

This overall objective has, together with the four principles presented earlier in the chapter, remained central to the operation of KLAR.

Thus, by formulating the ownership of the co-op in terms of an industrial foundation, the founding members succeeded in legally eschewing the question of personal ownership. According to Torsten, one of the founding members who had met Erik when he moved to Christiania in the mid-1990s, this structure had turned out to be the right choice, as it had ensured that any revenue was continuously reinvested in the co-op. "The fact that KLAR is owned by a foundation means that no one can take the lion's share," Torsten explained. "That is the most basic concept. That's definitely kept me engaged for all these years."

An industrial foundation is typically run by a board, which ensures that the financial base of the foundation is used to accomplish the overall objective. This was also the case with KLAR. In the following discussion of the organizational structure of KLAR, I will refer to this board as *the council* (a title often applied to organizational entities like this in the literature on cooperativism).

Economic Principles: Equal Pay for Equal Work

While the question of legal structure turned out to be a challenging task, the founding members had a more straightforward approach to the economic framework of KLAR. In brief, they wanted to ensure that everyone working at the co-op received the same salary. Several of them had worked at other construction companies before embarking on this project, where they had received differentiated rates of payment. However, such discrepancies simply did not make any sense to them. Therefore, they were determined to organize the economy of KLAR differently. To realize this principle, they decided that everyone working at the co-op should be paid the same hourly rate. They further agreed that everyone would be expected to work thirty-seven hours a week, which also generally constitutes a full-time work week in Denmark. Individual arrangements could be settled if somebody needed to work less because of personal needs.

The builders have persistently followed this principle for the past twenty years, thus sharing both risks and rewards. Budget surpluses have also been used on collective investments, such as a shared summerhouse and car which individual builders could lease for private purposes. When surpluses turned to deficits, the builders handled the situation collectively and equally. For the builders, these principles constitute the core of the cooperative idea. Henning, in particular, felt strongly about this matter. For him, the single most important principle of KLAR was the equal pay. "The whole project will collapse the day we compromise equal pay for everyone working here, or the day we begin distributing profit," he explained. "The whole point is that we build a community and an economic platform, which we control ourselves." Consequently, if this principle of equal salary ever became compromised, Henning was determined that he would leave the co-op. "The day it becomes an individual thing, we will be just like any other construction company that builds houses," he said. "There are plenty of them. I would not want to be part of that." In this sense, *økonomisk demokrati* (economic democracy), as the builders term it, has remained a key principle to KLAR.[13]

Organizational Structure: the Democratic Control of the Co-op

Apart from the equal pay, the cooperative principle regarding "Democratic member control" (the second principle of cooperativism in the Rochdale principles) was also key to the founding members. Initially, they decided to have a meeting every Monday morning where they would discuss the daily operation of the co-op along with overall strategic concerns. However, they soon realized this was unfeasible, as it delayed the beginning of their workday. To accommodate this challenge, they revised the organizational framework of KLAR. During my fieldwork in 2019, the organizational map of the co-op looked like this:

- *General assembly*: once a year, the entire membership of KLAR (i.e., everyone working at the co-op) convenes as a body to attend to the broad concerns of managing the co-op. They discuss the annual business plan, allocate earnings, determine the hourly pay for the following year (for apprentices and builders) and elect the daily manager of the co-op.
- *The council*: the council consists of several builders and people with connections to KLAR (the exact number of members is not predetermined), who convene once a month to discuss the daily operation of the co-op. While this body is not directly supposed to oversee the daily manager, the daily manager is required to share and discuss overall considerations with the council.
- *The daily manager*: the daily manager is appointed by the General Assembly and is accountable to that body. This person is largely responsible for the daily operation of KLAR and they also represent the co-op outwardly.
- *The monthly member assembly*: on the first Thursday of every month, the builders at KLAR convene for their monthly member assembly. This body represents the General Assembly to a certain extent. However, the monthly assemblies are primarily concerned with pressing issues in relation to the operation of KLAR.
- *The union steward*: an employee representative is elected at the yearly General Assembly as the union steward of the co-op. This person is connected to the union and is responsible for keeping builders updated on concerns related to union issues. They can, in certain cases, take up members' concerns with the daily manager.

While this outline represented the ideal structure of the internal governance of KLAR, it did not represent how decisions or authority were negotiated during everyday life at the co-op. During my fieldwork, for instance,

I never managed to participate in any of the activities or meetings of the council. With the builders' aversion to having too many meetings, I suspected that the council rarely convened. When I asked builders about the council, they often undermined their influence, stressing that they only acted as an advisory board. Moreover, no one described any formal process of election for the council. The informality, seemingly guiding the work of the council, made me presume that the council resembled an extended network of the founding members, which was brought into place when difficulties arose. I explore further how everyday workings of the co-op diverged from the ideal structure of the internal governance of KLAR in Chapter 4. As the analysis of this chapter will show, the builders were highly aware of this discrepancy. While they partly ascribed this to certain internal dynamics, they also perceived it as the result of externally imposed requirements, which they had become aware of early on in the development of KLAR. As the founding members were getting ready to complete the formal registration of KLAR, they were, to their surprise, required to list a formal director of the co-op, which obviously violated their idea of collective management. Frode outlined this concern, as he described some of his memories of their discussion:

> Just after we decided to leave the other co-op and start our own, we found out that it wasn't as simple as we imagined. To give an example, it was during this initial phase that I ended up as the director. We tried to convince them [the Danish business authority] that we were all owners of the co-op—but they didn't accept that. You need a director, they said. But if the co-op is owned by a foundation, it's owned by a foundation, we argued. They didn't accept that. We had to register somebody as the formal director. Then we somehow ended up appointing me as the director.

Hence, to comply with the regulations from the Danish business authority, the founding members randomly appointed Frode as the official director of the co-op—a role he has assumed since. When I asked Frode whether the title meant anything to him, his first response was, "No, not really." However, when elaborating, he said that ideally he thought the members should have taken turns assuming the role as director, perhaps by holding an election of some sort every fourth year. They had looked into this at one point, he explained, but it had turned out to be a complex matter of changing the names on all of the official papers. "My name is everywhere. A lot of clearing has to be done. We would need a lawyer to look into it. We could do that of course," he explained, "But we haven't made any decision on that yet. It's probably because the title doesn't really matter—you can't find an enterprise where it means less than it does here." Nevertheless, Frode's name is today an essential part of the official stamp of the co-op.

Together with the other challenges described in this and the foregoing sections, this last point demonstrates some of the difficulties experienced by the founding members as they decided to launch a craft co-op in Copenhagen in the early 2000s. Although they were keen on shaping the co-op according to their own ideas and desires, this was only possible to a certain extent. Already at KLAR's inception, the builders, therefore, became aware that they had to be agile if they were to succeed in running a co-op on their own terms. While they occasionally managed to find inventive solutions, such as when they customized the legal framework of the organization, they also sometimes had to align with conventions, such as in the case of choosing a director.

CONCLUDING REMARKS

As this chapter has demonstrated, it was not simply "*a* group of builders," but rather a very specific group of builders who launched KLAR in the early 2000s. By tracing in detail the past professional and political trajectories of these people, I have argued that KLAR not only became "embedded" in these trajectories; rather, it *emerged* from them. With this chapter, I therefore aimed to move beyond the idea that co-ops are launched and run by seemingly impersonal "communities," to instead examine how a co-op, like any other entrepreneurial endeavor, emerges from historically situated sentiments, desires, and commitments.

The professional and political trajectories of the founding members of KLAR had, according to them, been shaped by their engagement with various politico-social movements emerging in Copenhagen during the 1980s. This engagement provided the founding members with a belief in progress and a strong entrepreneurial drive, which are today some of the foundational characteristics of the entrepreneurial ethos of KLAR. To emphasize the importance of freedom to these builders and their engagement with inventive and liberating economic actions and ideas, I have attended to cooperativism as an economy of freedom in this chapter.

Today, the founding members represent a minority at KLAR. Various people have entered the craft co-op since its inception in 2001. From the outset, it had been a core goal for the founding members to establish a co-op which could easily be passed on to future generations of builders. As such, they also wanted to establish a corporate entity that, legally speaking, did not rely on the presence of certain individuals. Yet the close interconnectedness between the founding members' life trajectories and KLAR makes the objective of eschewing dependence on specific persons appear slightly paradoxical. However, by implicitly drawing on a form of "jural transcendentalism" that turns legal fictions into social guarantees (Yanagisako 2002: 84), the founding members of KLAR somehow managed to evade this paradox. By doing so, they managed to inscribe a form of legal continuity into the project, which makes KLAR appear as if it can remain the same entity over time despite changes in membership. But, as we shall see in Chapter 3, the question of continuity is not that simple.

Many of the newly arrived builders at KLAR were familiar with the founding members' past political trajectories. They knew that some of the founding members, like Frode and Erik, had been involved in political struggles for years and considered this a source of inspiration. "It definitely says something about their conscious and critical approach to the world, which matters a lot," an apprentice emphasized during an interview. Frode and Erik's personal histories, therefore, also became important markers of authority. The personal attitudes and values of those in key positions often make a mark on the ways co-ops and similar organizations are structured and function (Vargas-Cetina 2005). Today, some of the founding members, particularly Erik, occupy key structural positions within the organizational framework of KLAR. It would be easy to explain Erik's authority with reference to this position. Yet the deep entwinement between the professional and political trajectory of the founding members and KLAR complicates such analysis. It points to the fact that the founding members will always occupy privileged positions, although they occupy different structural positions within the organization.

Scholarly accounts of co-ops and similar associations have often focused on how external, impersonal forces impose themselves on these organizations, leading to the creation of internal stratification, among other things (e.g., Kasmir 1996; Narotzky 2004). The discrepancies faced by the founding members as they sought to "professionalize" some of the beliefs and experiences they had amassed during the 1980s and 1990s and launch their own craft co-op partly point toward similar arguments. The director dispute, for instance, reveals that certain structural positions were created in the co-op, as the Danish business authority requires companies to have an official director. On the other hand, the founding members' efforts to customize a legal framework that enabled them to launch the co-op as a jointly owned enterprise showed that they also sought to move beyond externally imposed requirements. The founding members' negotiation of challenges such as these provide some initial impressions of the builders' attempts to simultaneously act within and beyond societal arrangements, which this book seeks to describe and theorize ethnographically. Indeed, it is this ability that I seek to grasp with the notion of tinkering. To understand how the builders sought to acquire this ability, we must delve into the builders' engagement with craftwork. This exploration necessitates shifting our focus from the founding members' oral histories of KLAR to the construction sites and the newly arrived builders and apprentices' embodied engagement with craftwork, which I do in the following chapter.

NOTES

1. The work of Karl Polanyi is currently experiencing a revival within cooperativist studies and more broadly within economic anthropology (see, e.g., Hann 2007; Carrier 2009; Hann and Hart 2009; Dale 2010; Holmes 2012; Prudham 2013; Levien 2013; Hann 2016). Many of these studies draw more specifically on Polanyi's concept of the "double movement," which has had something of a renaissance over the past few decades (Dale 2012; Holmes 2012).
2. Scholars have stressed Polanyi's functionalist tendencies to represent "society" and "market" as active forces in their own right (see, e.g., Graeber 2001; Burawoy 2010), and further argued that locating the economic as always "embedded" within wider social, political and cultural structures reifies the "tacit assumption that a core of pure economic calculus somehow exists autonomously from whatever society surrounds it" (Højer and Pedersen 2019: 74).
3. Here, I build on the notion of "economies of sentiment" proposed by Heather Paxson (2013). I further draw on a range of studies that move beyond essentialist notions of economy by questioning the boundedness of the economic itself (e.g. Yanagisako 2002; Ho 2009; Miyazaki 2013; Bear et al. 2015; Tsing 2015; Rofel and Yanagisako 2019). Roughly speaking, these anthropologists draw on two theoretical strands. One has emerged from Michel Callon's (1998) science and technology studies inspired work on the performativity of economic theories, and the other with the idea of "economic diversity" pioneered by critical feminist scholars such as Gibson-Graham (2006). Critics of such an approach argue that it risks "subordinating all to culture," thus not recognizing that "economies may possess some relative autonomy or at least some difference from the more changeable discursive space of cultural practice" (Blim 2005: 317–18). However, the critical consequence of the perspectives outlined in this section is that the "autonomy" of any economy is heterogeneously made through processes of aligning multiple projects (Bear et al. 2015).
4. In underlining the patchiness of these narratives, I am not suggesting that they are somehow imprecise or incomplete. Rather, I highlight that there are undisputedly several parts of these stories which Erik and Frode did not share with me, and thus stress that although they appear as protagonists in the following descriptions, I have compiled these accounts from different narrations.
5. See, e.g., Mikkelsen and Karpantschof (2001), Schmidt and Mariager (2009), or Steiger (2018) for historical discussions of the BZ movement in Denmark; or Krøijer (2015) for an anthropological account of how the BZ movement came to shape subsequent social movements in Copenhagen.
6. I have added "historically" to Laidlaw's phrasing since the concept of freedom has attracted some attention from anthropologists generally associated with "the anthropology of ethics" in the subsequent years (see, e.g., Faubion 2011; Fassin 2014; Mattingly 2014).

7. These emic terms and their associated sentiments are not unique to the founding members of KLAR. Scholars have described these as key to a specific version of an "egalitarian individualism" dominating Scandinavian countries (see, e.g., Gullestad 1992; Bruun 2011).
8. Negative freedom is often juxtaposed with positive freedom, which in brief can be defined as the ability or capacity to act upon one's free will and realize one's own potential. Yet, while positive freedom is often used to emphasize self-mastery and self-realization, it also carries the risk of being used to justify control or coercion under the guise of helping individuals achieve their true potential (Venkatesan 2023).
9. As Venkatesan reminds us, a sustained attention to our interlocutors' different approaches to freedom often shows that these approaches are "multifaceted and the product of different intellectual and political traditions" (Venkatesan 2023:16).
10. In many other countries (e.g. Germany, France, Italy, Finland, Argentina and Colombia), co-ops have a specific legal framework, which makes it easy to count these organizations and thus update statistical overviews of the number of co-ops in a given country.
11. See Gjerding and Rask (2021) for practical examples of legal frameworks.
12. In Denmark, industrial foundations are officially defined as independent, self-governing entities, without private owners. See Thomsen (2017) for a historical and present account of industrial foundations in Denmark.
13. The principle of equal pay sets KLAR apart from many other contemporary co-ops in Denmark. During interviews and visits to other co-ops, members often stressed that they considered KLAR's principle of equal pay radical and difficult to implement. Several had thus decided to customize other economic principles in relation to salary. One of the other craft co-ops had, for instance, decided to distribute an equal salary among founding members, and pay a different salary to members who worked part-time or temporarily at the co-op. Another renowned co-op in Copenhagen had pursued an even more radical solution in terms of payment, as members had to subtract money they received when taking on extra work outside of the co-op (e.g. lectures or talks) from their monthly pay.

CHAPTER 2

BECOMING BUILDERS

Learning the Norms and Forms of "Good Craftwork"

Workwear is a prerequisite when working on construction sites, which entails safety shoes, heavy pants with pockets and room for extra padding on the knees, and a t-shirt, sweatshirt, or jacket with the company logo. At KLAR, all of these elements are black except for the standard safety shoes that have a yellow or blue line running between the body of the shoe and the sole. Historically, the color of a uniform indicated belonging to a certain skilled trade. Painters dressed in all white; bricklayers wore white pants and a striped shirt; plumbers and electricians dressed in blue; and woodworkers wore khaki-colored pants. An all-black uniform is new, but has become a popular choice among many young construction workers in Denmark. It is also the preferred color among the builders working at KLAR.

Like any other new apprentice, my first day of work included a visit to the storage room with Erik. I followed him as we walked through the workshop and entered one of the smaller rooms at the back of the building. Erik looked me up and down before choosing different sizes of pants, shirts, and shoes from the racks. "Try these on," he said and left the room. I slipped on the newly unwrapped pants. The zipper and button closed easily, and I stood there looking down at what seemed to be the pants' knee protection, which was located closer to my feet than my knees. I unwrapped another pair and looked at the label. One size smaller. I tried them on. The legs were still about 8 inches too long, but the knee protection was located closer to my knees. I added the sweatshirt. Standing there, I felt like a little girl dressed up in grown-up clothes. I later learned that this is the experience of many women working in construction, as most workwear is designed to fit a stereotypical male body.

Workwear plays a significant role in construction work, both practically and symbolically. Getting dressed is the first thing builders do in the morning, as they get ready to begin the work at construction sites. This uniform moves with them every day in the dirt and dust of construction sites, becoming a second skin that offers protection, pride, and empowerment. Putting on the workwear thus also marks a change in identity. As the builders stand fully dressed and ready, they transform from individuals into a unified force, with logos on their backs revealing their shared professional commitment to KLAR and trade excellence work more broadly. Workwear signals the builders' dedication to the work of crafting; a type of work which many of them have come to associate with certain virtues and politics. In this chapter, I put on my workwear to further outline how these virtues and politics emerge from the builders' everyday efforts at construction sites.

At construction sites, hands, legs, and backs of builders are in constant use, working together to accomplish the myriad tasks required in all construction projects. Bodily movements and techniques are constantly refined to attune to the requirements of a specific task. Craft skills can always be improved. Exploring how the builders engage with this refinement through constant evaluations of specific skills will not only allow us to better grasp the builders' perception of "good craftwork." It is also of immense importance for understanding how and why the builders acquired the ability to tinker through their daily engagement with craftwork.

Yet when people engage with transforming the material world, they also transform themselves in the process, making work and subjectivity mutually constitutive.[1] As the builders continuously worked on refining their technical skills and sensory engagements with materials, they might also be involved in a more fundamental process of reworking their bodies and selves. Indeed, as the builders were busy acquiring the ability to tinker on the construction sites, they were also, I shall argue, engaged in a more reflexive and embodied tinkering of their bodies and selves.

Apprentices' learning process and their commentaries on this process are illuminating when seeking to understand how builders engage with the daily craftwork and why they come to draw certain meanings from this work. Hence, this chapter particularly focuses on the apprentices working at KLAR and their engagement with more experienced builders, who take on the position as instructors in daily craftwork. How do they learn to perform and evaluate the techniques and skills of craftwork? The female apprentices working at KLAR were particularly good at explaining this. An apprentice like Liv always tried to translate into words what she was doing, in order to help me understand the ongoing adjustments she was making regarding the materials and her own body while working.

Yet as the above description of my first encounter with workwear hints at, the female builders and apprentices also faced certain challenges as they tried to fit into the role of a craftworker. They sometimes struggled with the exigencies of the bodily performance of craftwork and particularly with conforming to the masculinized forms and norms inherently shaping these performances. Indeed, to make a place for themselves in the trades, women have to struggle to reconfigure prevailing interpretations of cultural categories such as productivity, capability and competence (Weston 1998). Tracing these female builders and apprentices' attempts to insert themselves into male-dominated trades allows us to explore how they as part of learning a craft both conformed to and contested prevailing ideas of "good craftwork." In this regard, it may also suggest that the ability to tinker may not be equally attainable to everyone.

The chapter traverses numerous construction sites and surveys different projects, also introducing a broad range of people who worked at KLAR during 2019. The chapter opens with a description of the apprentices working at the co-op and the contemporary and historical development of vocational education and training in Denmark more broadly to highlight some of the structural challenges currently defining these educational programs. In the remainder of the chapter, I follow the work of the apprentices as I examine their efforts to refine their craft skills, as they simultaneously reworked their bodies and selves, and in this process, also reconfigured established societal norms and expectations.

OBTAINING A TRAINING PLACEMENT

While apprenticeship is a widespread institution, it is by no means a universal construct (Lancy 2012). In Denmark, apprenticeship is, as I shall demonstrate in more detail in this section, a formalized educational program organized by state-owned technical schools. While part of the vocational training takes place in these schools, apprentices also spend a considerable amount of time in work-based training at individual enterprises. According to apprentices, it is during these periods of training that they learn the fundamentals of *godt håndværk* (good craftwork). Obtaining the right training placement can thus be important for apprentices.

Apart from a number of temporary interns, KLAR had thirteen to fifteen apprentices during 2019. With diverse educational trajectories and work experiences, the apprentices had arrived at craftwork for various reasons and with different motivations. Astrid, for instance, had temporarily embarked on a vocational education program to learn the basic skills of woodworking while deciding which university degree to choose. Astrid had not imagined that she would complete the program, but had, to her own surprise, grown fond of craftwork. There was also Peter, in his late thirties, who had decided to embark on vocational training after having some legal problems a few years previously. Although he was only completing his second period of training at the co-op, his loud laughter and good sense of humor had already become trademarks, together with his temper and lack of precision, which sometimes got him into trouble. Then there was Karl, who was close to finishing his apprenticeship. Karl told me that he suffered from a form of ADHD (attention deficit hyperactivity disorder), and that school had never been his "thing"; hence, he had always known that his educational path would be vocational.

The diversity among the apprentices at KLAR is quite unusual for a construction enterprise in Denmark. In describing an apprentice in carpentry or woodworking, most Danes would probably depict a young man in his late teens or early twenties, who has done poorly in school. This is a stereotype, which most statistics confirm (e.g., Erhvervsuddannelser i Danmark 2019). An increasing proportion of the students on vocational education programs received low grades in primary school and they often struggled with other disadvantages; only a small proportion of the graduates continue to higher education (Jørgensen 2018). Vocational education is, therefore, considered "a dead end" by many Danes. Part of the explanation for this can be found in the historical development of vocational education in Denmark.

As in most other Northern European countries, the Danish vocational training system has its roots in the *lavsorganiseringen* (craft guilds structure). The guilds have had a strong influence and determined what *håndværk* (craftwork) entailed from their beginning in the fifteenth century, when the guild tradition arrived in Denmark from Germany, up until the mid-1850s. During these years, apprentices received exclusively work-based training, and guilds were in control of final apprenticeship examinations and certificates. With the de facto abolition of the guilds in 1856, vocational schools slowly began to take shape in order to ensure the quality of apprenticeships.[2] Mandatory periods of full-time school attendance during the day became a reality across the trades with an educational reform in the postwar period. While other Scandinavian countries restructured vocational education into full-time, school-based training, the introduction of mandatory schooling in Denmark was, in fact, aimed at preserving apprenticeships by reducing the educational responsibility of master tradespeople, thus making it more attractive for them to take in apprentices.[3]

The postwar reform was only the beginning of political intervention in vocational education in Denmark. During the 1970s, vocational education increasingly became part of the national youth and education policy, as policymakers sought to preclude a future shortage of skilled workers caused by decreasing rates of enrollment and increasing dropout rates. Increasing youth unemployment and the growing number of young people without educational training became a priority for the government during the 1980s. In the 1990s and early 2000s, several political reforms sought, on the one hand, to provide vocational students with better opportunities to achieve eligibility for higher education, and on the other, to fulfill a politically formulated target that 95 percent of a youth cohort should complete an upper secondary education.[4] These reforms thus sought ways for vocational education to ensure social inclusion, while at the same time avoiding the devaluation of these educational programs. This situation continues to define vocational education in Denmark today.

Currently, vocational training in Denmark is organized according to the “dual system” and consists of a basic course of six to twelve months, which is broad in scope, and a main course lasting three years in a work-based training placement with five alternating periods of school-based education and training at a workplace. Students apply for admission to the basic course, but cannot begin the main course without having settled an individual training agreement with a workplace, which is the responsibility of the student. Private enterprises can thus pick and choose among apprentices, and most placements tend to be allocated through informal networks. Certain groups are thus continuously excluded, particularly students from gender and ethnic minority backgrounds (Jørgensen 2018). This serves to uphold male dominance in the skilled trades particularly, and more generally reinforce the gendered divisions which shape the Danish labor market.[5]

The builders at KLAR are working to reverse the structural inequality produced in vocational educational programs through the distribution of training placements. As such, they have a preference for employing apprentices who otherwise might have a difficult time finding a training placement. Indeed, the builders prided themselves on (and to some extent are known for) being capable of creating learning facilities for different kinds of apprentices. Moreover, they always had more apprentices than they were duty-bound to admit according to formal agreements, and they also paid a higher salary to their apprentices.[6]

Likewise, KLAR has earned the reputation as an attractive training place and aspiring apprentices know that it takes additional effort to get a training placement at the co-op. On some mornings, an unfamiliar person would stand awkwardly waiting outside the main building or appear lost in the kitchen area asking for Erik. Everyone knew that this was an aspiring apprentice who had been told that showing up early is important when applying for an apprenticeship. “It shows discipline,” Astrid told me. When Astrid had first applied for an apprenticeship some years back, Erik had been hesitant;

they did not have space for another apprentice at the time, but Astrid had persisted. She showed up at parties to get to know the builders working at KLAR, underlining the sincerity of her application. "I also showed up at 7 a.m. four days during a week to show that I really wanted it," she explained. After some months, she managed to get a spot. Sune, a builder, had similarly done some "apple polishing work," as he described it, when he had applied for a training placement at KLAR some years back. "I showed up at some of the voluntary workdays, I helped clean up after the parties, and participated in a lot of the parties too," he explained. "I made sure that they noticed who I was." Sune had also been fortunate, as Bjarne, a good friend of his who had worked at KLAR for several years, had vouched for him.

While apprentices were generally expected to show initiative, exceptions were also made. On one occasion, I overheard Erik receive a phone call from a parent asking whether his son could get an apprenticeship at KLAR. Normally, Erik rejected calls like this, he said afterward, but he knew that the son in question was going through a rough time. Similarly, people from the neighborhood and representatives from youth organizations sometimes approached Erik if they knew someone in need of work. Yusuf, whom I mentioned in the Introduction, had moved through various job-training sessions for some years, but still struggled with the Danish language. By chance, someone noticed Yusuf's woodworking skills and gave Erik a call. Erik offered Yusuf a job immediately. Like Yusuf, Peter had also struggled to find an apprenticeship, as most companies were not particularly fond of hiring an apprentice with a questionable record. Some apprentices had decided to complete the first period of their work-based training at other construction enterprises, hoping that a training placement would meanwhile become available at KLAR. These apprentices told stories about rough work environments. Some described these places as *Lærlingefrabrikker* (apprentice factories), where apprentices were recruited to do the repetitive work as they were a source of cheap labor. While the severity of their experiences varied, many of the stories they told revealed that the hazing found in historical descriptions of apprenticeship was not confined to the past.[7] Yet hazing was not experienced by all apprentices to the same degree. Rather, it was often targeted at minorities, such as the female apprentices and builders.

ASSUMING THE ROLE OF THE LEARNER

Although the female apprentices and builders were reluctant to talk about hazing, they would occasionally retell stories that conveyed the gendered norms and expectations they were confronted with in work situations and in school, as they were typically the only ones with gender identities other than cis male. Astrid explained that when in school, she was constantly concerned about how to demonstrate her abilities "properly," making sure that she neither performed too well nor too poorly. Another female apprentice told me that her classmates referred to her as "mother," a nickname she had also overheard the teacher repeat. In rare incidences, workers from subcontracting companies or other enterprises would also use such nicknames on construction sites, sarcastically referring to female builders as "princesses" or "honey." Liv stressed that she had only on a few occasions heard conversations on construction sites that had made her uncomfortable. But rather than interrupting or correcting these conversations, she simply walked away. For Liv, the challenge was to avoid positioning herself as "the woman in the company." "I don't want to attract attention simply because I'm a female builder," she said with slight frustration in her voice, thereby refusing to accept the minority position that she and other female builders seemingly occupied in these male-dominated workspaces. A strategy often adopted by tradeswomen, as they have done their best to get away from discussions of gendered traits (Weston 1998).

Based on this, one might ask: Why do these women, knowing full well that they go against the grain when embarking on an apprenticeship in the skilled trades, continue to consider craftwork a gratifying and even at times liberating professional path? When I discussed this question with Liv, her answer was simple. "It's about freedom," she said, "freedom to do things myself." Craftwork had provided her with an "outlet for my desire to build," as she described it. Liv's dream was to build a house. "I can fulfill that dream now," she elucidated. "How great is that? I can actually realize my own dream if I want to." Interestingly, Liv was not the only female builder or apprentice who talked about being capable of building a house. Indeed, many of the female apprentices appeared to have deliberately picked carpentry, as they wanted to work with construction and not some kind of "fiddly-handiwork," as Liv put it. The female apprentices and builders, thus, in many ways repeated the stories of freedom that founding members narrated about craftwork and cooperativism.

Already early on their path to becoming builders, apprentices had to find ways to handle the norms and forms of "good craftwork"; yet, this was rarely communicated directly to apprentices. They had to figure out themselves that showing up early in the morning or joining parties might enable them to obtain a training placement at the co-op. They also had to find ways to handle the nicknames and gendered expectations that seemingly shaped general perceptions of who might become a good craftworker in Denmark. Despite these gendered differences, everyone apparently had, to some extent, to endorse a certain perception of craftwork that portrayed this work as a gratifying and liberating professional path in life.

Figure 2.1. A wooden roof construction of a shelter. Photo by Brian Berg.

Becoming a builder is a complex process of learning through which identities are also transformed. Learning a craft entails acquiring embodied skills, such as subjective sensory apprehension and tactile bodily knowledge, and combining this with a form of rational objectivism.[8] Yet learning a craft also involves assuming its forms of expertise and traditions (Herzfeld 2004; Jones 2011). To stress this latter argument, anthropologists studying apprenticeship in various craft practices have typically followed Jean Lave and Etienne Wenger's (2003) anthropological theory of learning and their notion of "situated peripheral learning" in examining how newcomers become part of "communities of practice" after initially arriving at the margins of a group (e.g., Lancy 1980; McNaughton 1988; Kondo 1990; Singleton 1998; Terrio 2000; Herzfeld 2004). This perspective emphasizes that just like a skill that is learned, so too are the social values and attitudes within which the skill is practiced. A common critique of this perspective is its negligence of conceptions of conflict, difference, or change, for that matter.[9] These are important questions when attending to the female apprentices and builders and their struggles to conform to the masculinized forms and norms of craftwork. Indeed, social integration in apprenticeships might not only be accomplished through processes of external social impositions—that is, through processes of inculcation (Herzfeld 2004). Becoming a builder is also a question of cultivating certain virtues, and through this cultivation, apprentices might also challenge or reshape prevailing norms and expectations as they become members of a "community of practice."[10]

I became aware of this potential for transforming norms and expectations as I began noticing how crews were continuously reorganized at KLAR, which implied that apprentices were paired up with different instructors. This differed from how construction work was normally organized in Denmark, as most construction workers work in fixed, self-managed crews (referred to as *sjak*), that move together as a group between different companies. By contrast, at KLAR, crews were less settled and more dynamic. They varied in size depending on the scale and time perspective of a given project, and the role of the supervisor (*sjakbajs*) also changed. The training of apprentices at KLAR, thus, did not always follow one standardized form of teaching. Rather, apprentices could, for better or worse, learn from multiple builders. Moreover, they were also themselves occasionally appointed as the supervisor of minor projects. The construction administrators often encouraged them to take on this task, because, as Henning said, "Great demands create great people." This was, for instance, the case with the project that I present in the following section, where Astrid was the supervisor.

STEERING THE CONTINGENCIES OF CONSTRUCTION

"Find Astrid," Henning told me one morning when I asked which project I could join that day. He added that she would be working on a project for the next few weeks, which in brief entailed the reinstallation of a ceiling in an office space. I found her standing by the desk in the front room of the workshop. She looked up with a smile. Her hands were fumbling with a piece of paper, as she was making a list of the materials and tools we had to take to the site. Cardboard to cover the floor, a long list of tools, a vacuum cleaner, two portable scaffolds—and coffee, she added. We carried everything to the street, and Bo lifted it into the truck. After a fifteen minute drive through the early morning traffic, Bo dropped us off at the site. We carried everything into the room that we would spend the next couple of weeks renovating. Liv showed up a few minutes later, ready to get to work.

When working in the workshop, the builders had everything at hand. But when the task was the construction of a new ceiling, as in this project for example—or the installation of a new kitchen, a bathroom, a wall, or new floors—construction sites had to be set up before work could begin. Floors were to be covered and doors closed off, and a sign was put up to warn people before they entered the workspace.

Figure 2.2. The framing of a wooden house. Photo by Brian Berg.

Once the initial preparations have been completed, builders take stock of the task at hand. In this case, Astrid and Liv had to decide on the proper height of the ceiling. They began by measuring the walls of the room using a laser distance meter. They stood on the wheeled scaffold, rolling it around the room by pushing on the walls. A wall-to-wall mirror at one end of the room made the procedure difficult as it reflected the laser. Astrid jumped down from the scaffold and looked around with a dissatisfied expression on her face. She was unsure as to whether the new ceiling would be the same height as the window frames. Or whether the measurement would cover the joist in the middle of the room. They decided to do the measurements one more time.

Pencils must be kept sharp at all times, Liv explained. Liv and I got along well, and I often ended up with her as my instructor, whenever we were on the same crews. "Remember to draw the line at the end of the folding ruler," Liv further instructed, stressing that otherwise, the pencil stroke would add to the measurement. One millimeter can quickly turn into ten centimeters if your measurements are not perfect, she explained. Correct measurements were, according to Liv, key to "good craftwork." Yet, precision was also one of the most challenging tasks of craftwork, and Liv continuously struggled to get her measurements precise enough.

It was past lunch before Astrid and Liv had completed a set of satisfactory (according to their standards) measurements of the office space. After having moved around on the wheeled scaffolding in the small space for almost five hours to assess potential challenges which they needed to take into account when determining the placement of the future ceiling, they had finally decided on a height.

For the following weeks, I followed Liv and Astrid's work installing the ceiling. Here, I learned that a ceiling consists of multiple layers of materials. First, Astrid and Liv attached metal studs to the walls of the room. Yet, after having fastened studs onto two of the walls, they began querying the placement of the ceiling, which they had initially decided on. Knowing that they had to add laths and ceiling panels, Astrid doubted whether the finalized ceiling would in fact end above the frame of the windows, as they had initially calculated. They returned to look at their measurements. Perhaps it would be a good idea to raise the studs slightly, to ensure that they would have enough space for the subsequent layers. They decided to do so. After they raised the studs on the walls, they moved on to fasten lateral studs to these. Finally, they had completed the load-bearing construction of the new ceiling. Then, insulation batches were stuffed in between the studs, and fastened laths were attached to the studs to fix the insulation.

As this structure was finished, it was then time to add the panels and thus complete the new ceiling. Consequently, the panels were ordered and delivered on the following day. Yet, contrary to what Astrid and Liv had expected, the panels had a layer of insulation on the back of them. Astrid widened her eyes as she saw them. She had never come across this type of panel before, she explained. She called Erik for advice. He arrived ten minutes later to check on the situation. He had seen this type of panel before, yet he recognized that the layer of insulation attached to them was unnecessary, as Astrid and Liv had already added the insulation batches between the studs. Quick at finding solutions, Erik suggested that they simply remove the insulation from the panels. As Erik left, Astrid turned to me and asked if I could help with that. "Sure," I responded, as I sensed that this additional workload came as a surprise to Astrid, who was probably concerned with whether they could keep to the project's schedule.

It took about a week to finalize the ceiling. Liv was transferred to a different project, so Astrid had to make do with me as her apprentice. In addition to removing the insulation, Astrid further instructed me on how to cut the panels into the right sizes with a circular saw according to her measurements. While I did my best to cut the panels the right sizes, Astrid remained on the wheeled scaffolding, from where she could attach the panels to the laths.

The installation of the ceiling was one of the short-term projects I followed during my fieldwork. It serves as a good example of how even smaller projects moved through different phases, and thus how builders must constantly find ways of steering through the contingencies of the process.

Although the installation of a ceiling might sound like a straightforward task, the challenge is often to make this new installation fit existing spatial structures. This work not only demands meticulousness, as exemplified by Astrid and Liv's dedicated efforts to get the measurements right; it also requires recurrent processes of assessment. Astrid and Liv were highly aware of the importance of this when working on construction projects. In searching for ways to refine this ability, Liv and Astrid had both become inspired by one builder at KLAR, Holger, whose ability to constantly assess the work at hand was supposedly exceptional.

Holger had worked at KLAR for several years and was known among apprentices (and the younger builders) for his calm demeanor, which was reflected in his movements and daily activities. He did not eat during the workday, but enjoyed his coffee in silence during breaks. "You think that he is just standing around, but suddenly all of the work is done," Astrid described energetically. Holger had no formal training, but he learned to build during his many years working as an unskilled construction worker in Denmark and beyond. According to Liv, Holger's most important tools were strings and his eyes. "That's how I would like to work," Liv said, "Although I would have to accept that I need a larger crowbar and to learn how to position my body differently to get the same strength." "You need to train your eyes and hands so they can see if a measurement is right," she further explained. "That's how you become a good builder." Key to Holger's assessment of a piece of work was thus, according to Liv and Astrid, his ability to "see" if a measurement was right with his eyes and hands. Yet, how does one see with the hands?

Heather Paxson (2013) offers a good answer to this question in her study of US artisanal cheesemaking. Here, she extends the concept of "synesthetic reason" "to get at how artisans 'understand' milk and curd by allowing their sight, touch, smell, and taste to register through one another" (Paxson 2013: 131). According to Paxson, a key to such reasoning is a bodily knowledge that emerges from a particular cultivation of the senses and "from learning to act through employing that trained sensory apparatus" (ibid.: 136). She further elaborates that such a form of reasoning is vital to an "artisan habitus," which, according to her, is defined by *sensibility* rather than ability (ibid.: 152). I find Paxson's explanation of the role of sensibility and the "integrated way of thinking-doing" (ibid.) in craft practices instrumental in understanding not only the cross-sensory experiences which Liv referred to above, but also the modes of assessment and action that apprentices such as Liv and Astrid were seeking to cultivate. Indeed, the bodily knowledge and cultivation of the senses that Paxson refers to appeared to be significant skills the apprentices at KLAR were pursuing. As alluded to in their descriptions of Holger, for Liv and Astrid, assessment and subsequent intervention were not only consciously reasoned; rather, I suggest it appeared to be "a reflexive feel for strategic action under contingent circumstances" (ibid.: 136). This ability to steer the contingencies of construction was, in other words, essential for apprentices like Astrid and Liv.

It is the builders and apprentices' positive appraisal of this ability that led me to compare their perception of craftwork with the concept of tinkering. Indeed, tinkering can be perceived as a form of focused and purposeful "attentive experimentation." It might further be perceived as an attempt to work on "what already exists, either transforming a system to give it new functions or combining several systems to produce a more elaborate one" (Jacob 1977: 1163). Tinkering can thus be conceived of as a form of practical, creative, and attentive experimentation that takes what already exists as its starting point. This form of tinkering, I propose, bears a strong resemblance to the efforts of apprentices and builders at KLAR to learn how to act under unpredictable conditions, and thus creatively steer the contingencies of craftwork. While this work at times included verbal interactions, it often happened in silence. In the following section, I pay attention to this silence as I examine the bodily movements and soundscapes of craftwork to shed light on what the builders generally considered the ineffable aspects of the craftwork.

WORKING WITHOUT WORDS

The builders typically listened to music played from loudspeakers during the workday at construction sites. The music was, however, constantly interrupted by the whir and shrill of machine tools, the rhythmic bang of a nail gun or the flames of a blowtorch, which made swooshing noises of fire. As the months went by, I became familiar with most of the sounds, while the loudness of others continually shocked me. Leaving the workshop in the afternoon, I could feel the discomfort of the impact wrenched in my body. Metal grinding fiercely against metal. To protect their ears from such uncomfortable sounds, builders wore hearing protectors most of the time. The protectors created a strange sense of aural vacuum, that often made me feel caught between silence and noise. Verbal encounters could be rare. Shouting was permitted—and preferred by some. But most builders seemed to enjoy the silence; the flow of working without words.

Rather than words, craftwork is about bodily movements. If something has to be corrected at the top of a building or in a faraway corner, builders found a way of getting there. They lifted themselves using the strength of their arms. They balanced on tall ladders (see Figure 2.3), and moved around on all fours when climbing strange surfaces. When working on the outside of buildings or on rooftops, they relied on scaffolds, which provided access to

Figure 2.3. A loft renovation in Copenhagen. Photo by Brian Berg.

all levels of a building from the street level to the top. Moving on a scaffold takes practice. Some parts are more fragile than others and jiggle as you step on them.

The builders mostly worked in pairs. Following the rhythms of others was thus an essential part of the work. The builder Nanna described how the work followed a certain "choreography" that one must learn. "It's like a dance. You can feel it when the work just flows," she elucidated. During my time with the builders, I had to learn this "choreography," which was a challenge I faced from the outset of my fieldwork.

During the first months of my fieldwork, I took part in a project with Sune and Nanna. In brief, the project comprised the production of a large number of soundproof panels from reused materials (primarily old window frames). One morning, Sune asked if I could help him out. I nodded and added a "sure." I followed him into the room with the large circular saw and found a set of hearing protectors. Sune gave me some quick instructions, "Grab the pieces of wood as I push them into the saw—and send the ones in the wrong sizes back to me." Then he started the saw and the loud noise made conversation impossible. I did my best to collect the wood as it passed by the large, fast-moving blade. But I quickly messed up the pile next to me, placing the wooden strips too loosely on top of each other. Sune threw a folding ruler at me and indicated that I should do some control measurements to double-check the size of the strips. I found myself missing a third hand. How was I to organize the strips in a pile, send some of it back to him, and check that the sizes were right? Sune noticed my frustration (or the mess I had made), turned off the saw, and came to show me how to organize the strips in small heaps, before transferring them to the pile.

Like Sune, many builders often refrained from describing tasks in detail. Roar, for instance, a tall, silent man with broad shoulders and large hands, who had worked as a builder for close to twenty years, was known for his reluctance to explain the work in detail. In fact, Roar often appeared rather disgruntled. "Being grumpy and tired has sort of become his identity," Astrid said with a smile as she described him. She explained that there was a certain calmness about his work and added that people get the impression that he is slow. "But he is not," she stressed. Roar was one of Astrid's preferred instructors. He took his time looking at the drawings and rarely made mistakes, she elucidated. Doing things twice was the worst thing he could think of, so mistakes were accepted as long as they were not visible. Builders often jokingly repeated that when Roar was the supervisor, you could only pose three questions a day. He expected others to work on their own. While the most committed apprentices, such as Astrid, were keen to work with him, eager to pick up on his ability to avoid ever making mistakes, the insecure apprentices often ended up confused when in his company. They constantly asked questions about the details of a particular procedure. What is the measurement of this piece of timber? How many screws should I use to fasten the drywall properly? Questions could be endless, but Roar's answers were sparse. Like Roar, Sune also underlined his dislike of questions. During an interview he told me why:

> Many of the new ones ask a lot about all sorts of things. Hell man, you don't get shit out of getting answers now. Just do as I say and stop thinking. But yes, there needs to be room for questions, and it's fine that they ask. Some of the older builders say you have three questions a day. I'm starting to understand why. Because as a supervisor, who are asked about everything, you get annoyed when someone asks about something and often think, 'Why the hell is that relevant right now?' Then I can be a little like, 'I don't know. Just do as you've been told.' But I never feel like I'm coming out with a tone that crosses the line.

Occasionally, I sensed how experienced builders, in accordance with Sune's explanation, got annoyed with apprentices, who were too talkative, asked too many questions, or lacked the ability to take the initiative and put themselves to work. Simply standing around was unacceptable. "There is nothing worse than an apprentice who doesn't work," Sune underlined.

"If you ask for help all the time, you will never learn," Henning explained similarly during an interview. In contrast to repeated questioning, the right way of learning is to look for solutions yourself. If in doubt, you should study the work of others, rather than ask for help. Ingenious apprentices thus rely on their own judgment and try to solve challenges independently.

Many scholars have taken notice of the silence in craftwork and the lack of questions in apprenticeship, but they provide different explanations for this supposed attitude of reticence. Some argue that the logic of language can only partly encapsulate the actions and unpredictability that defines craftwork, as the work is an in-the-moment practice that is not determined by prefigured intention.[11] Interestingly, such arguments seem to mirror the prevailing perception among the builders working at KLAR, as they similarly, yet implicitly, asserted that verbalization impedes craftwork. As Sune underlined, apprentices needed to learn to "stop thinking" when building. Although the builders might have such a belief, it was evident how reflective processes were equally part of the work, as the description of Astrid and Liv's ongoing deliberations in the previous section showed. As such, we must look beyond explanations that simply refer to the nature of craftwork when explaining the prevailing silence in this type of work. In relation to this, Anna Portishch (2011) argues that studies of craftwork that draw on the phenomenological legacy often represent "an implicit reversal of the Cartesian dualism," as "the body, not the mind, is elevated to a status worthy of investigation" (Portishch 2011: 61). Considering such arguments, it seems inadequate to ascribe the builders' reluctance to verbalize their work simply with reference to the nature of craftwork. Rather, we must attend to the cultural belief guiding this reluctance and the social dynamics it engenders.

Focusing on the social significance attached to silence in craftwork, another string of research has argued that silence does not arise because artisans are incapable of verbalizing their work; rather, the verbal ineptitude of craftwork might embody a culturally valued trait of silent action (Kondo 1990). Or, that silence might be imposed to teach apprentices that learning can only be done by stealth and indirection (Herzfeld 2004). While the reluctance to provide verbal instructions among the builders appeared less agonistic than what was seemingly the case, for instance, among their Greek counterparts as described by Herzfeld, it certainly manifested as a hegemonic order. By refraining from providing detailed instructions, the experienced builders not only separated the indolent apprentices from the skilled, they also continuously accentuated self-reliance as a moral imperative in craftwork. The apprentices who succeeded in putting themselves to work and solved tasks independently showed, through diligence, that they were invested in the work, and were thus considered more skillful than apprentices who awaited instructions.

Verbal ineptitude, and the moral imperative of self-reliance that it seemingly conceals, is, as Kondo (1990) notes in her study of a small manufacturing Tokyo firm, also the embodiment of certain masculinized norms. As Kondo vividly summarizes, "A full-fledged artisan is also a full-fledged *man*: able to make a living by his arm, or technique, tough and able to withstand long hours and deprivation, in stereotype and sometimes in actuality, a strong, silent type" (Kondo 1990: 241). I could not have produced a more suitable description of a builder like Roar and the apprentices' (and builders') prevailing perception of him as a prime example of an ideal craftworker. Indeed, Astrid's devoted description of Roar seemed to indicate that she did not find his reluctance to provide verbal instructions discouraging. Rather, and perhaps slightly paradoxically, it seemed as if she was also herself striving to conform to the norm of taciturnity during workdays on the construction sites. Such an inclination seems to suggest, I argue, that apprentices and builders generally had a certain disdain for the spoken word. Rather than relying on language, the builders focused on refining their bodily performance of craftwork.

To engage with these processes of bodily refinement, apprentices had to find ways to handle the physical exigencies of craftwork during their training. By exploring the challenges that apprentices faced in this process, we gain a clearer understanding of the role of the body in craftwork and, furthermore, some of the masculinized virtues, which were perhaps more unattainable for the female builders and apprentices than the silence described in this section.

BODILY DRILLS: RISK, DANGER, AND DISCIPLINE

To overcome the physical strain and discomfort inherent in the manual labor of craftwork, it was clear that apprentices had to learn how to ignore possible pain, while simultaneously assessing the potential risks of the work. My observations from Karl's training session with Sune provide a good illustration of this conundrum.

One afternoon, I followed Sune and the apprentice Karl, as Sune was teaching Karl to install roofing felt—a type of roof covering used on flat roofs or as an underlay beneath slate or tile roofing. Sune began by showing Karl how to unfurl the roofing felt correctly, ensuring that the layers had the right overlap. He explained to Karl where to put the nails to fix the felt to the wooden roof construction. "This is great!" shouted Karl in between the loud bangs as he walked across the roof with the nail gun, clearly excited about this new task. Meanwhile, Sune put on a pair of gloves and prepared the blowtorch. He gave Karl a brief introduction to the procedure: Karl should roll up half of the felt and use the blowtorch to fire into the underside—emphasizing that he had to heat it evenly. He showed Karl how to position the flame of the blowtorch to heat the roofing felt properly. Once the felt was rolled back into position, it would stick to the felt next to it. It was Karl's turn next. He put on the gloves and grabbed the blowtorch instantly, eager to work with fire. He lifted the felt and fired the underside. His first attempt was unsuccessful. The flame was too close and the felt started melting. Karl's frustration and discomfort could be felt as he slapped the melting felt with his hand. Sune repeated his instructions. Karl tried again, but without success. Sune corrected him, "The flame is too big." Karl tried again, but he was impatient. Sune told him to slow down, "You'll learn it. Don't worry." "You know me, Sune. I'm too eager to learn," Karl responded while preparing for another try.

As Sune and Karl completed the first section of the roof, they came down and went for a break in the sun outside the workshop. I followed along and asked Karl whether he was still fond of the work. "It isn't easy," Karl said disappointedly and showed me his burned thumb. "I thought it was tricky to begin with too," Sune added encouragingly. "You constantly need to have a sense of the softness of the felt." "But you seemed to have fun?" I asked and looked at Karl. "Yes, it was great. There is fire and felt," he responded with a smile, seeming to forget about his injured thumb. "It's risky. Everything risky is also fun," Sune added with a wry smile.

Like Sune and Karl, many builders seemed to enjoy the risky elements of craftwork. Playing with fire when installing the roofing felt was only one example. Climbing on scaffolds or rooftops similarly caused excitement and laughter. But risky situations could also change rapidly. One day, for instance, when Sune was lifting some heavy timber off a truck in the forklift, the weight of the timber suddenly caused the back part of the forklift to lift off the ground. Peter—the humorous apprentice with the unpredictable temper—and Tage—a hardworking builder in his late fifties without any formal education—rolled around on the ground laughing as they took pictures of Sune in the flying forklift. To begin with, Sune seemed nervous, obviously afraid that the forklift would tip up. But as soon as the forklift stopped moving, he joined the laughing crowd.

While this situation was benign, other occurrences had enduring outcomes. Minor accidents were recurrent incidents on the construction sites. Screws would accidentally pass through a builder's finger, leaving them with an open wound or a nail split apart. Or someone would slice their fingers or hands with a utility knife while cutting drywall. The builders would occasionally share stories of more severe incidents, describing how a builder was almost overthrown by a hoist; how a large piece of timber had fallen from a framing construction leaving a builder with a broken nose; or how a fall from a roof or scaffold had left a construction worker injured for life. The builders discussed such situations with gravity. They knew about the high number of work-related accidents occurring in the construction industry, and that accidents could have lethal consequences in the gravest situations. Work-related accidents in construction and safety practices and discourses more generally form a complexity of issues that have received extensive scholarly attention in Denmark (e.g., Baarts 2004; Ajslev et al. 2013; Arnholtz, Krause-Jensen and Juul 2015; Grynes 2018).

Yet, I found it noteworthy that the builders generally associated the physical toll of construction work with accidents—that is, to certain events, as the above examples also reveal—rather than with the mundane physical strain of the work. Part of the explanation for this was probably that the repetitive movements and strenuous aspects of the daily physical work had not yet left physical traces on the bodies of the younger builders and apprentices. Or, in accordance with a prevailing perception in the Danish construction industry, they might consider such physical deterioration an unavoidable condition within construction work (Ajslev et al. 2013; Ajslev et al. 2017). They therefore rarely questioned whether or how to organize their work differently to minimize any physical strain.

In this regard, the apprentices at KLAR had to accept that arduous toil is part of the work. They had to learn—in the words of Patrick McNaughton (1988)—"to master pain." In his study of Mande blacksmiths, McNaughton explains that: "Before the neophyte [Mande blacksmith] can master techniques and form, he has to master pain. He begins at the bellows, where he spends many hours each day" (McNaughton 1988: 24). Yet, to master such pain they were also required to learn to distinguish between different forms of danger.[12] As we saw in the example of Sune and Karl's roofing felt installation, Karl simply accepted that burn injuries were part of the work and thus did not classify this as a danger. In fact, he even seemed to understand this potential suffering as part of the risky and thus exciting aspects of the work.

An appetite for risk and the acceptance of arduous toil has historically been associated with masculinity; an association that remains today.[13] These imperatives could thus potentially put the female builders and apprentices in an ambiguous position. Yet few builders spoke openly about this ambiguity or more broadly about gendered differences in the physical performances of craftwork. One day I asked one of the experienced builders, who had been involved in the training of several female apprentices, whether their performance differed from their male colleagues. He hesitated for a moment, before coming up with a wary reply. "You can't be a gentleman. You have to keep yourself from helping them out. They have to learn how to perform heavy lifts. It's part of the work," he said. "But I would not expect them to carry the same as a male apprentice." In contrast to this reluctant reply, a younger builder openly criticized his female colleagues during an interview. He often thought they were a danger to themselves, as they were too busy proving their worth.

While the female apprentices and builders would object to such allegations, they were aware that they sometimes struggled to conform to the physical demands of the work. Astrid explained, while we were drinking coffee in the sun during a break, that from the beginning of her training, "I wasn't sure whether I would be capable of performing the same tasks, because I'm simply smaller than many of the others." But, with time, Astrid had learned that physical strength was not always necessary to become a good craftworker. "Gradually, I have realized that the work is not only about [physical strength]," she elaborated. "Of course, it's frustrating when I can't carry the same weight as others. But then I can contribute with other things." Like Astrid, Liv was also convinced that female builders could contribute something different to the work exactly because they were less prone to rely on physical strength. Despite her conviction, Liv had realized during training that her physical capability could also be restrictive. After having worked hard on a project that included highly repetitive procedures, her lower back had started to ache. To begin with, she tried to ignore it, eager to continue the work and to complete her apprenticeship. But she slowly realized that the discomfort simply would not disappear. During the following months, she tried different treatments. While at the beginning it felt like they only worsened the ache, they nonetheless with time made her injury bearable, although the discomfort never completely disappeared.

In a gloomy way, Liv's story reveals that the body might at times strike back, complicating the disciplining projects pursued by apprentices and builders working at KLAR. Her story, I suggest, thus provides us with some important insights into the role of the body in the craft practices of the builders. As described in this section, the physical bodies of apprentices (and builders) were constantly at stake in the work they undertook. Not only did they have to overcome momentarily bodily pains, like when Karl burned his thumb; they also exposed themselves to attrition, as the work tends to leave deteriorating marks on the physical body, as in Liv's case. In seeking to manage the physical demands of the work, control, perseverance, and endurance were important virtues that apprentices had to learn to cultivate.

Yet as I talked to Liv about her injury, I realized that the bodily hardships of the work also served other purposes. While the situation had been rough on Liv, as it had made her reevaluate her passion for craftwork, it had also carried a striking lesson. In her own words, Liv had recognized that she could simply not continue, "to do as the men do," as she put it, but had to find her own path in order to refine her craft skills. She elaborated and explained that her situation had made her realize that she sometimes had to ask for help, thus realizing that achieving complete independence in craftwork was perhaps improbable and quite possibly undesirable. Liv's injury had neither made her give up on her passion for craftwork nor made her reconsider her decision to become a builder; rather, her experience of bodily setbacks had made her reconsider some fundamental life orientations and decisions. Her bodily impairment, therefore, somehow conveyed a more profound meaning for her. It had made her question the independence she had seemingly longed for.

I suggest that Liv's story provides us with some important insights into the significance that many of the builders at KLAR ascribed to the corporeality of craftwork. Indeed, her story reveals how the bodily intimacy of craftwork was considered a vehicle for self-reformation and transformation. In coercing their bodies through the strenuous yet stimulating work of construction on a daily basis, the apprentices experienced new forms of engagement with, and gained different perceptions of, their bodies in an effort to, among other things, achieve new forms of self-awareness. Here, I argue, it becomes clear that while the builders were busy learning the ability to tinker on the construction sites, they were also engaged in a more reflexive and embodied tinkering of themselves.

CONCLUDING REMARKS

Craft practices are currently undergoing a renaissance across Euro-American contexts as they have taken on renewed significance in an era of globalized industrial capitalism. KLAR has become a front runner in this development in Denmark, as the builders working at the co-op have sought to bring renewed attention to the possibilities of choosing a professional path in the skilled trades. Because of this development, a multitude of apprentices have begun to apply for training placements at the co-op. To explore why many of these apprentices and builders have come to perceive craftwork as a liberating and creative form of work, and furthermore how they come to draw meaning from their daily craftwork, I foregrounded Liv's claim that craftwork is about "freedom" in this chapter. Tracing the work of apprentices like Liv showed how diverse apprentices seek to conform to the dominant norms and forms of "good craftwork." Yet as we saw in Liv's case, these diverse apprentices might only partially succeed in conforming to these professional norms, as they are often guided by gendered expectations. Although Liv's injury had made her reconsider the form of independence she was longing for, it had seemingly not made her question that independence was achievable through the hardship of craftwork. The "freedom" of craftwork that apprentices like Liv were seemingly pursuing was thus not a question of attaining a state of refuge from external forces, exemplified by the prescribed forms and norms of craftwork in this case; rather, it appeared to be about exposing oneself to these forces to seek out possibilities for self-reformation and transformation.

While the symbolic significance of craft practices might currently be changing, contemporary craft actors remain captivated by the material and embodied aspects of these practices. A "reversal of the Cartesian dualism," as Portishch (2011) noted, might come to shape not only certain scholarly accounts of craft practices, but also contemporary perceptions of craftwork. This was perhaps also the case among the builders at KLAR, who often elevated the status of bodily performances and abilities, which in their view represented more reliable pedagogical and transformative potentials, compared to intellectual and verbal activities. Words can be manipulated, the builders believed. But so can bodies, as we have seen in this chapter. Through the authorized models of embodied behavior, apprentices not only learn the practical skills of craftwork, but they also cultivate certain embodied virtues such as endurance, diligence, self-reliance, and meticulousness. Virtues that everyone might strive to acquire, yet which are often more attainable to some than others, as we saw with the female apprentices and builders. Together, these virtues culminate as a version of tinkering, since they guide the builders' attention toward the ever-growing possibility of a practical, creative, and attentive experimentation that takes what already exists as its starting point.

In this chapter, we have further begun to see the contours of the kind of political subject which the builders at KLAR seek to cultivate. This is a self-reliant and agentive subject capable of tinkering not only with the external world, but also with oneself. The subsequent chapters of this book are dedicated to unfolding how the builders transpose this ability and aspiration to tinker to other social domains. Exploring this transposability will also provide more insights into the characteristics of tinkering as a transformative action. In the following chapter, we begin by examining why the ability to tinker becomes relevant in relation to cooperativism in the first place.

NOTES

This chapter includes ethnography previously published in Danish in: Maia Ebsen (2021). Køn, kroppe og kontroverser i håndværksfagene. *Økonomi og politik*, 94(1), 16–26. In this article, I present a more comprehensive and critical analysis of the female builders and apprentices' marginal position within the Danish construction sector as a whole.

1. See, e.g., Kondo (1990) or Paxson (2013) for elaborations of this argument.

2. For a discussion of the historical evolution of vocational education see, e.g., Fode, Møller and Hastrup (1984), Juul (2013) and Jørgensen and Bøndergaard (2018). For a detailed presentation of the craft guilds in Denmark see Dübeck and Dybdahl (1983).
3. See Jørgensen (2018) for a more elaborate comparison of vocational education in the Nordic countries.
4. See Jørgensen (2018) for a detailed presentation of the reforms in the 1990s and 2000s.
5. Half of all the 109 vocational training programs are dominated by either men or women (Jørgensen 2018). For discussion on the gendered division of the Danish labor market see, e.g., Larsen, Holt and Larsen (2016).
6. The number of training placements which an individual enterprise has to offer is settled through a tripartite agreement negotiated between employer organizations, labor unions and the state that regulates the Danish labor market (see announcements and reports at the Danish Ministry of Education, e.g., Praktikpladsafhængigt AUB-bidrag 2018). Apprentice salary is settled through a similar agreement and depends, among other things, on the age and living situation of the apprentice. The co-op disregards the age question and provides the highest rate of payment for all apprentices who have moved out of their parents' home.
7. See, e.g., Fode et al. (1984) or Juul (2016) for historical discussions on the hazing of apprentices.
8. Heather Paxson (2013) makes this assertion as part of her attempt to develop an *anthropological theory of craft* in her work on American artisanal cheesemaking. Contemporary craft practices, Paxson shows, join subjective sensory apprehension and tactile bodily knowledge with the rational objectivism required to carefully observe how raw materials behave under specific circumstances (Paxson 2013).
9. Jean Lave has also addressed the lack of focus on individual struggles, controversies or relations of power in the context of learning in *Situated Learning* (see, e.g., Lave 2008).
10. I draw on Saba Mahmood's distinction between "inculcation" and "cultivation" here (Mahmood 2005: 152–53).
11. Charlotte Baarts (2004) makes this assertion in her study of workplace safety in the construction industry in Denmark (Baarts 2004).
12. Regine Grytnes (2018) makes this point in her study of carpentry apprentices in Denmark.
13. See, e.g., Ajslev et al. (2013), Kyed (2014) and Grytnes (2018) for examples from the Danish context.

CHAPTER 3

THE "FAMILY" OF KLAR

Generational Continuities and Ruptures in Cooperativism

If you walk past the KLAR office building and through the gate, an alley will take you directly to the main entrance of the co-op's workshop. The workshop consists of three larger and several smaller rooms. Construction materials and tools, carefully organized into boxes and sections, take up most of the space in these rooms. While dust, noise, and construction work fill the workshop during the day, this area also constitutes an important social space at KLAR. The builders usually gather here on Friday afternoons to mark the end of another five-day work week. Work experiences, political opinions, and other stories are exchanged during these gatherings. Several of the conversations that I present in this chapter took place during such get-togethers in the workshop, including the following vignette.

At the end of one of my first weeks at KLAR, I joined the informal Friday afternoon gathering in the workshop. I had just opened a beer when Gerda grabbed me by the shoulder. "Actually, I don't know why you're here," she said and looked at me curiously. I stood in silence for a second, compiling my thoughts so that I could give her a coherent answer. Gerda's question came unexpectedly, as I had already talked to her on a few occasions. I gave her a vague answer, highlighting my interest in the current resurgence of cooperativism in Denmark—and added that I would follow the daily work of KLAR over the next few months. Gerda told me about a conversation she had with a good friend the other day. Her friend had asked whether she was planning to stick around at KLAR until she retired. "Yes, I probably will," she said as she recounted their conversation. There is always a lot of work to be done, she explained, and sometimes it can be a bit too much. Nonetheless, Gerda felt as though she belonged there. "It's like we're a family," she said and took a sip of her beer before continuing, "I think, you need to figure out what this is in your project. Yes. You need to find the spirit of KLAR."

Gerda was not the only builder who used the notion of *ånd* (spirit) when describing KLAR. While the use of this term might not be extraordinary in descriptions of social communities, accounts such as Gerda's continuously reminded me that for some builders, KLAR did not simply constitute a workplace. The co-op was far more than that. To get a better understanding of this, I usually asked members to describe KLAR during interviews and asked them to elaborate on their motivations for working at this particular organization. While practical considerations evidently shaped their decisions regarding work, close to every builder stressed that they had actively pursued jobs at KLAR as they consider the co-op to be different from other construction companies. When I asked what the difference was, most highlighted KLAR's cooperative organization or equal pay for everyone, highlighting that they did not like to "beaver away so that some random master tradesperson could drive around in a large Mercedes." Bo often repeated this phrase when we talked about the social life of KLAR. When I met Bo during my fieldwork, he had worked as a builder at the co-op for close to ten years. He offered me a ride to a construction site on one of my first mornings. At first glance, Bo might seem apathetic about the work and political aspirations of KLAR, as he is typically in a grumpy mood during the workday. This was also true that morning, although a few dry humor jokes did escape his lips as we made our way through the bustling morning traffic. I later learned that Bo, like Gerda, was more talkative after a few beers on Friday afternoons. During conversations on such occasions, he would always proclaim with certainty that a co-op is the only right place to work.

Some builders' strong devotion to KLAR was a source of doubt for other builders. They speculated whether KLAR was in fact different from conventional enterprises and, as such, whether the organization deserved such strong devotion. During lunch breaks in the construction trailer, a builder would occasionally air skeptical remarks such as, "we're simply wage slaves like everyone else," and thus question the "alternativeness" of the co-op. Skeptical comments on the current form of KLAR often came from younger apprentices and builders, who had been employed at KLAR for a while. These comments clearly exposed an internal division within the co-op.

In popular and certain scholarly accounts, horizontal unity is often envisioned as an essential feature of co-ops. Internal divisions and power relations have thus figured prominently in ethnographic accounts of co-ops and similar associations, as scholars have sought to challenge idealized images of co-ops (e.g., Kasmir 1996; Narotzky 2007; Rakopoulos 2018). In this chapter, I build on this long-standing focus on stratification in relation to cooperativism. However, rather than examining stratification as a corollary of different structural positions within the organizational framework of co-ops—often referred to as the emergence of a managerial regime in scholarly accounts—I explore stratification as the result of the varying motivations and aspirations that the builders have in relation to their investment in the collective projects. I attend to these motivations and aspirations as products of historically contingent cultural processes,[1] which implies that they change over time. In this chapter, I explore this change by examining how the entrepreneurial ethos of KLAR as defined by the founding members has been renegotiated through encounters with the builders who have entered the co-op during recent years. I mostly focus on the builders who belong to a "younger generation," with special emphasis on their understanding of and moral-cum-political assessment of the entrepreneurial ethos of KLAR.[2] By comparing the perspectives of the younger generation of builders with those of the founding members, whom I will refer to as "the older generation," this chapter sheds light on a "generational gap" at KLAR.[3] Attending to the intergenerational dynamics shaping this gap shows, I shall argue, how the meanings of entrepreneurial and cooperativist practices are constantly renegotiated.

Ethnographically, the chapter brings together insights from the two previous chapters, as it compares the perspectives and perceptions of the founding members of KLAR and the builders who have subsequently entered the co-op. As in many other organizations, new people enter the co-op on a regular basis, while others depart. As transience generally marks employment in the Danish construction industry, this labor shift is by no means abnormal. Yet, when taking the supposed particularities of KLAR into account, it is pertinent to examine how the entrepreneurial legacy is renegotiated through these transitory encounters. By focusing on these transitions along with KLAR's ongoing changes in the composition and organization of the co-op's workforce, the chapter sheds light on the complexity of social continuity and the elusive nature of cooperativism. In this regard, the chapter also unfolds some of the reasons why constant social tinkering is demanded when practitioners, such as the builders at KLAR, seek to realize their cooperative aspirations.

FROM EIGHT FOUNDING MEMBERS TO SEVENTY BUILDERS

Five years after the eight founding members launched KLAR, more than twenty builders worked at the co-op. At their tenth anniversary, the workforce had increased to more than fifty people, and a few years later to one hundred. At this point, however, the members began questioning the growth rate. "At some point, we realized that we couldn't be that many," Frode mentioned during an interview. "People didn't know each other's names, who they were, what they were doing, or how long they would stay. It changed the atmosphere." Crossing the line of one hundred people had therefore reminded the members about the importance of also looking inwards. "People want to work here because of the atmosphere," Frode explained, "so we had to find a way of maintaining that." To Frode, this had been a turning point, as employing more than the one hundred members had changed the spirit of solidarity at KLAR. At this point, the builders thus decided that the workforce of the co-op should be reduced. As they held back on recruitment, by the late 2010s, KLAR consisted of seventy people—a size the builders were determined to retain.

Expanding the workforce at KLAR had never been directly related to concerns of economic growth, although this had become a precondition for the expansion. Rather, the creation of jobs had become a key concern to the founding members, Erik, Frode, and Henning stressed. During the years, the builders' aspiration to offer work opportunities had increasingly become targeted at people who had previously found themselves on the edge of the Danish labor market, owing to illnesses, disability, or personal circumstances, all three emphasized. Getting a job at KLAR helped provide them with an opportunity not only to participate in the labor market, but also to secure them an acknowledged position within the contemporary configuration of the Danish state, which was increasingly defined by a shift from "welfare" to "workfare," as outlined in the Introduction. Because of this shift, having a job has increasingly become important to access welfare benefits. According to many of the builders, ensuring jobs for people otherwise excluded from the labor market was also one way to adhere to the principle of solidarity, often promoted as a key concern in cooperativism. Offering work opportunities had thus emerged as a high, if not higher, priority than maximizing wealth. Many of the builders underscored during interviews that they had come to view these goals as mutually enhancing.

At the end of the 2010s, the workforce of the co-op was made up of a wide variety of people. Ensuring a sense of commonality and solidarity across the workforce had been an ongoing concern to the founding members since the inception of KLAR, as Frode's explanation also illuminated. Many builders shared this objective. In their portraits of KLAR, they would thus foreground the positive aspects of social life at KLAR. This was often articulated through the use of kinship idioms, including the term "family."

THE KLAR FAMILY

Kinship idioms often appeared in conversations related to the builders' aspiration to craft a community that spans different age groups. This aspiration—and the obligations it implies—was, for instance, articulated during a discussion on the strenuous challenges of construction work, which occupied the agenda of a few assemblies at KLAR during the spring of 2019. The debate was sparked by discussions on retirement regulations in Denmark, which had emerged as a core topic of concern for political campaigns during the Danish general election held in the early summer of 2019.[4] At the core of these discussions was the question of whether worn-out workers should be offered early retirement or not. The debate took a more practical turn among the builders, as they were primarily concerned with what kind of tasks they might be capable of offering to builders who would at some point no longer be able to complete a full day of work on construction sites. Knowing that a few of the builders belonging to the older generation were already struggling to keep up with the work, the members knew that they had to come up with something to offer them. As Erik said, "We can't have that many people sitting in the office." At two assemblies, the builders therefore discussed different solutions to the problem at hand. They came up with ideas ranging from educational activities for "maladjusted young people," to launching a store where they could sell repurposed construction materials. The question of responsibility across generations was an important concern to several of the builders. As Henning said at one of the above assemblies, "People should not feel like they are losing their value just because they are getting older."

The builders' emphasis on securing jobs for worn-out coworkers was part of a wider aspiration of ensuring that the workforce of KLAR consisted of people from various age groups. Henning, for instance, emphasized that a certain "age fascism" ruled in many other construction enterprises. But for him, it was important that the youngsters working at KLAR also got the chance "to drink a beer with somebody who is not their age." Liv also spoke to this issue. During her apprenticeship, KLAR had increasingly come to occupy an important position in her life. During an interview, we talked about her commitment to the co-op. "I've had a great desire to come and be a part of KLAR," she said, "but it's just as much because I feel like it's my new family. It's great to find a place where I can be who I am." Liv's perception of KLAR as a "new family" was thus clearly loaded with positive connotations. Her statement even indicated that she highly valued the familial intimacy that seemingly defined the atmosphere of KLAR, as it, according to Liv, enabled her to find out "who she is." More than that, the familial discourse utilized by Liv and other builders hinted that the builders had come to envision KLAR as a space for making kin-like relations.

The builders' inclination to draw on various kinship idioms when describing or debating the form of commonality which they were seeking to create at KLAR is mirrored in the greater Danish society. As in many other places, "family" generally acts as a strong metaphor in Denmark, and one that Danes draw on to describe close emotional and unbreakable ties to other people

(Mogensen and Olwig 2013). However, the category "family" further occupies a peculiar position in tales of the Danish nation, as expressed, among other things, through the customary kinship idiom *Familien Danmark* ("The family of Denmark"). This idiom, which depicts the Danish nation as one big family, conveys a sense of national unity, solidarity and security (Knudsen 1996). Such "kinship images" that portray the national community of Denmark as a "happy and safe family" have increasingly come to dominate public discourses in Denmark, introducing and legitimizing a distinction between a majority of "real" Danes and a minority of "not-quite-real" Danes (Rytter 2010). Such insights seem to draw attention to a proclivity among Danes to apply kinship idioms when outlining the symbolic order of "imagined communities" such as nations.[5]

Looking at the builders' description of KLAR as a family, a similar propensity seems to be at play in the co-op. Yet, while a discourse of family is used to draw distinctions between different groups of people in the context of the Danish nation-state, inclusion seems to be at the core of the builders' use of kinship idioms. Although these idioms were evidently associated with divergent sentiments, such as intergenerational bonds, a form of intimacy, and a source of commitment, as Gerda, Henning and Liv's explanations show, they were all characterized by a certain positivity and inclusivity. This indicates that the builders generally value relations of intimacy, affection, and responsibility, which they seemingly associate with family ties.

However, looking across the literature on craftwork and cooperativism, kinship generally seems to occupy more ambiguous or even adverse positions in many contexts.[6] Prior studies of the symbolism of family and kinship in cooperativism in Denmark have similarly shown how kin relations can be positive and harmonious as well as ambiguous and conflict-ridden.[7] This suggests that we must look beyond the positivity of the kin idioms applied by the KLAR builders in order to probe and better grasp the more subtle dynamics of the familial discourse unfolding at KLAR.

Yet rather than moving directly to questions of ambiguity and dynamics of inclusion and exclusion, I center my analysis on the productive as well as constraining aspects of the symbolic order implied in the builders' kinship idioms. I thus approach the familial discourse used by the builders as a complex structure of sentiment and power that simultaneously creates and constrains the builders' lives within KLAR.[8] To shed light on this complex structure, we must examine the builders' everyday contests over the meaning of "family" and cooperativism, which I do in the following sections.[9] Exploring these internal contests also allows me to question the continuity often assumed in (idioms of) kinship by asking "why and (and which) members of lineage care about the continuity of these social collectives" (Yanagisako 2002: 85). In asking this question, I am concerned with how the younger builders at KLAR respond to the entrepreneurial and cooperative vision passed on to them from the founding members of KLAR. In the following section, I address this question as I examine the younger builders' motivations for working at the co-op. My focus is on the more politically inclined builders and apprentices, as they had, like the founding members, deliberately pursued a job at KLAR because of its framing as a politically motivated organization. Some of these builders include Astrid, Une, and Sune. Although these builders have already appeared in earlier chapters, I give a more thorough introduction to each of them in the following section. These will allow us to explore in more detail their motivations for becoming builders and applying for jobs at KLAR.

THE YOUNGER BUILDERS AT KLAR

From the first time we met, I was mesmerized by Astrid's amicability and perseverance. She was curious and laughed with an irresistible charm, and she was liked by most of the builders. Astrid grew up outside of Copenhagen, but started traveling regularly to the city in her late teens as she was having troubles in school. Astrid had never really felt comfortable in educational settings. "I was bad at having routines, and I've always found it difficult to have a boss," she explained with a wry smile on her lips. "I was often involved in a conflict of some sort, if a teacher wanted to make too many decisions, or if there were parents who wanted to decide everything." Astrid said that she typically felt like doing the opposite of what she was told. Skipping class had thus felt like the right decision. Hence, it surprised her that she had succeeded in sticking to a seven-to-three job for the past few years. "I'd never had a job before," she said with a laugh. "It was a random choice to begin with," she explained when I asked her why she had decided to become a builder, "I was just planning to take the first period in school to begin with and then leave." Astrid had come to enjoy the practical work and the collaborative aspects, as the builders always worked in pairs or crews. She had grown fond of craftwork and her dedication seemed to rub off on others.

The lack of interest in school was a common story among the builders. Most said that they had in some way or another disliked being at school. This was also the case with Sune. Like Astrid, he had arrived at craftwork by coincidence. But, in contrast to Astrid, this was not the first educational process Sune had embarked on. He had completed his training as a graphic designer some years ago, but he disliked the work environment of design companies and quickly decided to leave the industry. After a period of traveling, he started working at a construction company. They offered him an apprenticeship as a bricklayer, but he was reluctant to accept it. An injury forced him to quit work for a few months, after which he decided to resume traveling. He worked a number of random jobs upon returning to Copenhagen, but when one of his friends embarked on vocational education as a carpenter, Sune decided to follow suit. "Why not? I thought," Sune said, shaking his shoulders. "It sounded like fun. I always liked working with my hands and to do physical work." Sune had managed to complete this second educational process, although he was not fond of school. "I never felt comfortable in school," he explained. "Already in primary school, I thought that we had to learn things strangely." Sune, like other builders, attributed his failure to advance within the school system as having a difficult time learning. Sitting on the same chair for an entire day was too great a challenge. "The ones who sit nicely and do what they are told without asking questions get the good grades," he elaborated, clearly indicating that he did not feel like he belonged to this group of students.

This common dislike of school brought the builders together across generations. Henning also touched upon this dislike during an interview as he proclaimed that he had never understood why adults made the decisions in school. "It's the kids who have to learn something," he stated questioningly. Henning himself had left school decades ago, but he remembered feeling unease. "The teachers weren't allowed to hit students anymore, but that was a fairly new thing, so some of them had forgotten about it," he said without providing any extra details. He added that, "I found some people whom I got along with, and I managed to complete primary school." Immediately after primary school, Henning had started an apprenticeship and had not once considered going to college.

A few builders, however, had continued onto university before they had begun doubting whether an academic career was truly what they were looking for. "I could not see myself sitting in front of a computer screen 99 percent of my working life," one builder said as she explained why she had left the university shortly before she was to finish her degree. Another explained that he grew tired of academic work, "It was too abstract," he explained. "I thought there was too much theory and too much hot air." Several builders stated practical concerns about their future jobs as a reason for embarking on a vocational education; yet, in many cases their decisions had also been politically motivated. As a builder mentioned during a lunch break in the trailer, "Our society needs people who can do more than read books."

Une, who had recently finished her apprenticeship, was of a similar belief. Her choice to become a builder was further guided by a strong urge for independence, as she described during an interview:

> Well, I just think it is a romantic, but also idealistic anarchistic idea that we should do things ourselves, and we should do things together, independently of economic means and the state and such, yes. We should be able to support ourselves. And that also includes being able to build our own houses. And I actually think that this has been the case for a long time.

For Astrid, learning the skills of construction work had similarly felt empowering. Like Liv, Astrid wanted to learn how to build a house. "I'll be capable of building my own house when I've completed my training," she explained. "It feels empowering. It makes me feel independent." Une, Astrid and Liv had thus come to associate the manual work of the skilled trades with a certain *uafhængighed* (independence).

THE CONUNDRUMS OF COMPROMISES

Builders from the younger generation shared their aspiration for independence with the founding members and other builders at KLAR. Similarly, they also considered craft skills a means through which "independence" could be achieved. However, during my fieldwork it became obvious to me that the builders ascribed different meanings to their search for independence. The founding members' search for independence was guided by a rather optimistic belief that "everything is possible," as described in Chapter 1, while the younger generation of builders were more skeptical toward the prospective emancipation. They were less convinced that the independence they were searching for was achievable through endless entrepreneurial adventures. The younger builders' doubt was fueled by concerns about global environmental destruction and economic collapse. Particularly Astrid was deeply distressed about these multiple "crises," as she termed them. During an interview, she described how and when her attention had been drawn to these pressing societal issues:

> Our interest probably emerged around the time of the financial crisis [in 2008], as waves of protests developed to an extent we hadn't seen before in our lifetime. For me, it was also, I think, connected to the question of climate change. This was probably where my interest emerged from. I became interested in questions related to climate change and began to read a lot about how climate change affects our ecology, which makes me kind of depressed. It's simply too big and too obscure, and it's a huge problem—what should we do about it? At one point, I got really frustrated about how often rebukes are made to the public that turns this into an individual responsibility—"Remember to turn off the light"; "Don't prepare more pasta than you can eat so we avoid food waste"—phrases like these. At the same time, you can read about how the oil industry is allowed to increase its production without being held accountable. They are the biggest offenders in my world. ... There is simply a disproportion in relation to who is and who should be held accountable. At that point, I started to think of this as more of a political question, a question about economic power structures in the world—it's these questions that we have to confront.

In Astrid's view, the pressing societal challenges of today are all tied to questions of "economic power structures." In other conversations, she often referred to these as "capitalism." Overcoming these pressing issues was for

Astrid, therefore, a question of finding alternatives to capitalism; a quest she has dedicated herself to. Together with a friend, she had traveled the world to visit people who, in various ways, organize their lives according to different economic ideas. Astrid's urge for developing alternatives to capitalism and inspiration from her travels abroad had initially attracted her to KLAR. Yet, during her apprenticeship, she had been obligated to work full-time, which had made her realize that this was not the kind of work-life balance she wanted. She wanted to have more time for exploration. I asked her what her dream work-life balance would look like, to which she responded: "My dream work-life would probably be to work part-time, so I would have the freedom to run off and find people whom I find inspirational, and not be too tired to even read the newspaper. It would be good for me. I believe it would be great for everyone."

Astrid was thus skeptical of whether the kind of work-life that KLAR offers—a full-time job—is in fact right for anyone. She elaborated on this remark later on in one of her critical analyses of KLAR, in which she stated that "KLAR is based on the premise that work is a good thing as a job gives you access to a meaningful community." While Astrid supported inclusion in workplaces, she was also critical of the kind of politics promoted by this idea. "I would rather minimize the need to work," she argued. She explained that, for her, this was an inherent problem in social co-ops. "Sometimes, I have internal conflicts. I can feel that I disagree with attitudes of the older builders on the extent to which you have to follow the terms of the market," she elucidated, "because KLAR works on the premises of the market. That is a defining characteristic of social co-ops. And, I'm not sure, I ... You have to make a lot of compromises and that's frustrating." For Astrid, KLAR was inherently a compromise, which she found problematic. While Astrid is supportive of the basic ideas of KLAR, such as equal pay and collective ownership, her critical approach to work made her question the logic shaping these ideas.

Not all of the younger builders were as articulate as Astrid about their concerns with the political ideas guiding KLAR. But many agreed with elements of her analysis and similarly questioned the emancipatory potentials of cooperativism as pursued by KLAR. So, while the founders had found some sort of liberation in work, Astrid and many of the younger builders had a different set of beliefs. Several of them strove to create a life for themselves in which work played a minor role. These divergent perceptions of work were essential to the intergenerational dynamics, differences, and bifurcations shaping KLAR. On various occasions, they produced frictions among the builders. For instance, this was the case in a complex discussion of so-called *arbejdsdage* (work parties), which flourished in the early months of 2019.

WORK PARTIES: THE TRIALS OF SHARED OWNERSHIP

I joined my first work party on a Saturday in March. When I arrived at KLAR a little before nine in the morning, only Henning, Erik, and two apprentices had shown up. During the regular Monday morning meeting, Erik had informed everyone that a work party would be convened the following weekend. “It won’t take long if a lot of people show up,” he stressed, doing his best to encourage people to join. However, only a few seemed to have embraced Erik’s encouragement. We spent the first half hour eating and chatting in the common kitchen area, while a few more people arrived. Subsequently, it was time to get to work. Coffee mugs were refilled before heading to the workshop.

Work parties were, in brief, assemblies organized outside formalized work hours, where the builders convened to solve specific tasks. Normally, such tasks included cleaning the workshop, preparing the collectively owned summerhouse for a new season, or working on specific construction tasks for social projects in the neighborhood or projects instigated by grassroots organizations. Yet during the early months of 2019, the work parties at KLAR were assigned a new purpose. In the fall of 2018, a review of the accounts of the co-op indicated to the builders that KLAR might finish the year with a deficit. To prevent this from happening, Erik and the other construction administrators took on additional projects. One of these was the production of a large number of soundproof panels from reused materials, which I presented briefly in the previous chapter. According to Erik, the project presented an innovative collaboration with an architectural company. While the task at first seemed straightforward, the preparation of the reused materials turned out to be a time-consuming task. Whenever a deadline approached, the builders were thus asked to spend extra hours on weekends to help with preparing the materials.

Preparing the reused materials was also the main task at the first work party that I joined. The task was straightforward: wooden pieces from old window frames had to be painted. Before the work party, tools and paint had already been primed. Most of the builders there were acquainted with the work, so no further instruction was needed. Two people took turns pushing small pieces of timber through an outdated paint machine; the rest of us collected the pieces as they exited the machine to dry off any excess paint gently. The work slowly progressed, while music played in the background and remarks about soccer, music, and politics were exchanged. A few hungover apprentices arrived after a few hours, increasing the size of the crew to close to ten. Several of the builders had commented that the atmosphere was different at work parties than during regular workdays. I also sensed that. As I picked up yet another piece of timber from the paint machine, Erik casually asked me how my writing was going. I shook my shoulders, "Okay, I guess." He jokingly replied that I should join KLAR instead. "That's easier," he said, smiling. After a few hours of work, the pallets of timber pieces that had to be painted were emptied, tools and materials were stowed away, and someone found a few packs of beer in the fridge.

This was neither the first nor the last weekend where the builders met to prepare materials for the production of the soundproof panels. The announcement of yet another work party became a recurrent event at the regular Monday morning meeting during the winter and early spring of 2019, as the builders tried to keep up with the pressing deadlines of the project. However, during these months, internal tensions also grew as critical discussions on these seemingly voluntary workdays began to surface. The extent to which these were "voluntary" was indeed a central point of discussion. When I asked Liv whether anybody kept track of the participants at work parties, she replied ironically that no one took notes, but Erik always remembered who had been there. While some of the younger builders were skeptical of the changing purpose of a work party, many of the builders from the older generation seemed more indifferent. Several of them did not appear to give it much thought. Henning and Erik took part in most of the work parties, while Frode and Torsten, another founding member of KLAR, rarely seemed to be present. When I asked Torsten why he did not join the work parties, he told me that he had withdrawn for a while because of some personal issues.

At a social gathering with builders from the younger generation, the increasing number of work parties was brought up for discussion. One apprentice explained that he had not been able to participate in many of them, yet no one seemed to care about this. Another said that a *svend* (journeyperson) had stressed that he had joined all of the work parties back when he was an apprentice. A third highlighted that they all felt responsible for helping out as a deficit would affect everyone working at KLAR. A fourth joined the conversation and added that some challenges could perhaps be solved if the purpose of the work parties was explained. "Of course, we want to help out if the project is flopping in some way," he said. Astrid and a few of the others subsequently voiced their concerns to Erik at an assembly. It was not the first time Astrid aired doubts regarding the work parties, as she had previously questioned the necessity of these additional workdays. At this assembly, Erik responded by explaining that they had to take on additional projects to improve the accounts, and thus avoid forcing anybody to work during the winter break.[10] Erik further explained to those gathered, "This is how it is when you have your own business." This was a statement that Erik often resorted to in discussions regarding additional work hours; however, this argument triggered a strong reaction among some of the builders from the younger generation. “It’s a wrong way of talking to us,” one of them said during a more informal conversation we were having along with a few others over a cup of coffee in a construction trailer one Friday morning. He added that:

> This idea that we [the new ones] should consider ourselves as owners of the co-op, that we have to dedicate ourselves to KLAR to the same extent as the founders do. Their heart’s blood is written into the co-op, whereas we are completely new. Suddenly we have to dedicate our body and soul to this project.

This statement seemed to encapsulate a core issue in the discussion that unfolded among the different builders. What did their collective ownership of KLAR in fact imply? And, would it ever be possible for new generations of builders to “own” KLAR to the same extent as the founding members?

Erik later elaborated on some of these issues in an interview. It turned out he had lots to say about it. How could they run a co-op, if only a few people cared to join the work parties, he pondered. “People have to understand that everything we have—our shared car, our summerhouse, our parties, and our yearly company trip—it’s our voluntary work, our enthusiasm and activism that makes this possible,” he explained. To Erik, these work parties were a necessity if people wanted to work at KLAR. “If people want an eight-to-four job, they have to go somewhere else, because here you sign up to become a co-owner. Owning a business requires work,” he stated. Although Erik knew that some builders were prevented from participating in the work parties because of personal issues, he was genuinely disappointed with the commitment of many of the builders, particularly since he knew that several performed *sort arbejde* (black work) on weekends.[11]

Work parties were evidently not simply about solving a particular practical problem. Indeed, as other studies of work parties and related activities in co-ops in Denmark have shown, socializing is often considered the primary purpose of these activities, whereas the actual work done is of secondary importance.[12] At KLAR, more complex questions of ownership, commonality and solidarity also seemed to be at stake in the builders’ discussions about these events. Although it might seem as if different perceptions of formalized work arrangements were at the core of the builders’ divergent perceptions of work parties, their discussion of these recurrent events equally constituted an ongoing negotiation of the social obligations and commonality (supposedly) inherent in cooperativism. While the actual work done at the work party described in this section unquestionably made a difference to the specific construction project, the builders’ participation in these events was also, particularly for Erik, about actively taking part in the shared ownership of KLAR. “Owning a business requires work,” as he said. While many of the younger builders shared a commitment to the KLAR project, they also appeared to be critical of the idea of shared ownership. As the younger builder said above, their "blood" is not "written into the co-op" to the same extent as the older generation. These divergent perceptions of ownership not only animated the builders' ongoing discussions about work parties, but they were also at the core of the intergenerational dynamics currently shaping KLAR.

The changing purpose ascribed to work parties during the spring of 2019 became a source of discord among the builders. The social tensions produced by this discord as well as by other disagreements were curtailed during the many social gatherings, parties, and celebrations continuously organized at the co-op. Indeed, while the work parties divided the builders at KLAR, the social gatherings after work hours united them. Exploring these numerous celebratory events convened at KLAR might thus also help us understand how a sense of commonality was negotiated and recreated among the builders. Doing so will also take us back to the place and social context where this chapter started: the workshop.

PARTIES AT WORK: THE VOLATILITY OF COMMONALITY

Palle, a new apprentice, interrupted a conversation that Gerda and I were having while hanging out at the bar during a party in the workshop in the late spring. Palle's gaze was fuzzy. He looked like he had had his share of the evening's offerings and was then, apparently, heading home. Palle turned to Gerda to say goodbye. The two of them began talking about the upcoming company trip—an annual event. Gerda insisted that Palle should go. That was the only way he could get to know everyone, she said, adding, "It's an amazing trip" (they were heading to a destination in Southern Europe). "You have to talk to Erik on Monday," Gerda said, "he might extend the deadline." Palle seemed a bit reluctant. He only knew a few of the people going, he muttered. "You just have to go for it. You need to show up at work, participate in as many of the voluntary events as possible, and go on the summer trip," Gerda encouraged him, clearly trying to help this new apprentice gain a foothold in the KLAR community.

I did not get the same message as Palle when I started my fieldwork at KLAR. But I slowly became aware of the many activities taking place outside regular work hours at the co-op. The end of a project was celebrated with a few beers; trips were organized to see finalized construction projects or other remarkable craft productions; and, on Fridays, when the work finished at 2:30 p.m., builders stuck around for a couple of beers. In the summertime, people gathered outside in one of the alleys close to KLAR hoping to catch the last rays of sunlight, while they huddled up in the workshop on workbenches and piles of wooden boards during the winter months. During one of my first weeks at KLAR, I was standing outside with some builders on a Friday afternoon as they were drinking a beer and discussing the pros and cons of different safety shoes. Henning came out to join us. As he saw me, he started laughing. "When in Rome, do as the Romans do," he said, and told me to remember to take notes. "Sune just opened his third beer. His balance is slightly affected. Now, he is falling. Now he is lying on the ground," one of the others said, imitating what he seemingly thought would be included in my notes. Everyone laughed.

The Friday afternoon gatherings in the workshop could head in two directions: either people left after a few hours, or the evening turned into a long drinking session with beers constantly arriving. The builders described the latter as a proper *værkstedsbrandert* (workshop drunkenness). Conversations and games were a central part of these gatherings. The opening chats typically revolved around work; one of the standard questions being, "where have you been today?" referring to the different construction sites. As the number of beers consumed increased, conversations loosened, and people moved on to discuss political issues, jokes, music, and travels. The less talkative builders sometimes moved to the corners to play darts. Friends of the builders occasionally joined these gatherings. If the crowd became large, loudspeakers were set up, music was turned on and a dancefloor was opened.

Apart from the regular yet spontaneous Friday afternoon gatherings, the builders also had several pre-organized social events. These events consisted of a number of ritual celebrations that were generally practiced among craftworkers in Denmark. For instance, there were *indkitning* (kick-off) and *udkitning* (farewell) ceremonies. These ceremonies took place when new people were employed (*indkitning*) or when somebody left a construction enterprise (*udkitning*). The builder who was either entering or leaving the enterprise was supposed to provide beers for everyone on these occasions. Moreover, there were *svendegilde* (a celebration of somebody who has finished his apprenticeship) and *rejsegilde* (topping-out ceremonies). There were also a number of annual celebrations, such as summer and Christmas parties, and a party after the yearly general assembly. These events typically took place on Saturdays, and they often began with a collective meal. After the communal meal, music would be turned on and the dancefloor was set up. Sometimes, the rumor of a party traveled beyond KLAR and people from the neighborhood snuck in to take part in the festivities. This was also the case with the summer party convened during the early fall of 2019. During the afternoon and night, a few hundred people congregated at the co-op. And, as usual, the party continued until sunrise.

Varying social activities evidently took place at KLAR; nonetheless, they also shared certain features. First of all, the majority of the builders ascribed great importance to these gatherings. They would often stress that they brought people together across gender and age differences. The intergenerational dynamics thus became less significant during these events, where everyone joined to eat, drink, chat, and dance together. Second, a particular kind of commonality seemed central to these events as relations were seemingly created and sustained. Common ideas and opinions circulated and were reinforced, and new people were drawn into the group. Much like Gerda's advice to Palle, newly arrived builders were encouraged to make an effort to get to know others—and to let others get to know them—by participating in these events. Participation in these social activities after work was thus presented as an imperative.

Taking these points into account, the many celebrations convened at KLAR easily lead to an analysis of ritual practice. Indeed, these celebrations could readily be understood as a form of 'anti-structure' that provided the builders with a sense of 'communitas' as they, during these events, could disengage from their regular positions within the co-op, such as the position of daily manager, in Erik's case, or positions such as apprentice and instructors.[13] This would also explain why the intergenerational divides often withered during these events. Indeed, the experience of being a "family," recounted by Liv and others, seemingly appeared in its fullest during these gatherings. Following this line of analysis of rituals thus suggests that the key purpose of the numerous celebrations convened at KLAR was to enhance the sense of collective identity among the builders. The events, in other words, provided the builders with a space in which they could perform the commonality/community of KLAR and display their shared solidarity. In this regard, the celebrations also represented an idealized form of sociality highly valued by the builders.

Yet analyzing ritual practice also requires attending to the more subtle dynamics of these practices. In the case of KLAR, this implies asking what or who is not included in the commonality performed during these celebrations. Many builders had come to consider these social gatherings as a prerequisite to working at KLAR. As such, only a few builders uttered critical comments about these events, and no one ever questioned the necessity of the many social gatherings. However, during my fieldwork it became clear to me that there were a few builders who rarely joined these events. When I inquired during interviews and one-on-one conversations about why they never participated, some explained their lack of participation by mentioning family obligations. Others provided more scattered explanations, in which abstinence from alcohol, engendered by personal circumstances or choices, often figured in one way or the other. Such explanations underscore the importance of alcohol consumption at the celebrations convened at KLAR, as also conveyed in the descriptions of the events above, where the consumption of beer was a common theme. As other studies of similar drinking activities in Denmark have shown, the consumption of alcohol, and beer in particular, is associated with a specific form of commonality and egalitarianism in the Danish context (Madsen 2018). This also appeared to be the case among the builders at KLAR, who often had a joyous time during the celebrations.

However, the frequent drinking and partying unfolding at the many celebrations also sparked other social outcomes. While new social relations emerged between some builders, other relations were broken as verbal disagreements occasionally arose when alcohol levels increased during the late hours of the night. In rare situations, some of these also turned into physical confrontations. I never witnessed any of these incidents during my fieldwork, but I heard stories about them. These stories were often told in fragments by individual builders and were rarely brought up in everyday conversations. I occasionally became aware of these incidents—such as when a builder was suddenly transferred to a different crew, or when a builder was banished from the co-op after they had gone out of control on a late Friday night. Taking the Scandinavian context into account, it is perhaps no surprise that these stories only circulated informally among the builders at KLAR. Indeed, ethnographic accounts of Scandinavia have often stressed that open and personal conflicts must be avoided at any cost.[14]

A certain competitiveness and tension thus also characterized the social activities convened at KLAR. The celebrations were, in other words, also marked by a form of rivalry.[15] Indeed, a coexistence of conflict and commonality seemed to animate the celebrations at KLAR. Social alliances were, in brief, built and broken during these celebrations, and the internal groupings of the co-op were thus renegotiated. Although the purpose of these events was to craft a sense of commonality among the builders, they simultaneously emerged as arenas of ongoing negotiation and struggle over the internal social composition of KLAR. These negotiations and struggles, indeed, disclosed the volatility of the commonality pursued by the builders.

CONCLUDING REMARKS

Mainstream accounts of co-ops often ascribe great significance to the shared and impersonal ownership, which in their view characterizes cooperativism. This idea also circulates in current discussions of cooperativism in the Danish context. Advocates and activists propose that the co-op ownership model could be a key solution to the "great transition" of the Danish corporate sector that will take place as the baby-boomers retire and thousands of enterprises change hands in the next ten years (Bennedsen and Meisner Nielsen 2014). It is argued that employee-owned enterprises are generally more sturdy and stable than so-called conventional corporate structures; hence, they provide a longer-term solution (Jørgensen 2020: 91–95). Stability rather than volatility is thus promoted as a key feature of cooperativism. Yet such accounts of cooperativism assume that legal continuity also produces social continuity. However, the question of social continuity is more complex. To understand how continuity is created or disrupted, we need to unfold the range of desires, sentiments, and motivations that are invested in ensuring the social production and reproduction of social collectives, as I have done in this chapter.

To many of the builders working at KLAR, cooperativism was about "independence" and "freedom." They drew on these notions when they described their motivations for joining the co-op. Yet, while a language of "independence," "freedom" and "autonomy" bound the different builders together, they also ascribed divergent significance to these notions. For the founding members, notions of "independence" and "liberation" were drawn from the economic and political transformations of Danish society in the 1980s; a decade when they learned how acting, creating, and mobilizing can lead to societal change. For the younger generation of builders, the meaning of and struggle to achieve "independence" has become more complicated because of the global "crises," as Astrid termed them, currently unfolding around them. Many of the younger builders were keen on learning from the founding members' political trajectories; however, some were skeptical of whether a formalized work arrangement could have any emancipatory force. Although many of the younger builders enthusiastically joined KLAR, they simultaneously questioned the entrepreneurial legacies and obligations passed on to them. The younger builders' moral-cum-political assessment of the entrepreneurial ethos of KLAR underscored how the meanings of cooperativist practices were far from stable; rather, cooperativism constituted a heterogeneous practice among the builders at KLAR. Hence, the builders' commitment to cooperativism simultaneously united and divided them across generations as they often disagreed about how to practically realize these ideas. This reveals that cooperativism must be approached as an elusive project that demands continuous renewal, rather than an ostensibly fixed organizational form or an all-or-nothing proposition. Moreover, it also underscores that internal stratification cannot be fully accounted for by analyses focusing on different structural positions within the organizational framework. Rather, stratification might also arise due to the varying motivations and aspirations that cooperative practitioners invest in these collective projects.

Constant labor is thus demanded to ensure a sense of continuity and commonality within a co-op. As we shall see in more detail in the following chapter, the builders at KLAR engaged with a form of social tinkering in their attempt to accomplish this undertaking, as they were constantly looking for possibilities to practically, creatively, and attentively experiment with various cooperative activities, such as the assemblies continuously convened at the co-op.

NOTES

1. As in Chapter 1, I draw on Yanagisako's (2002: 10–11) explanation of sentiments here.
2. Here, I follow the seminal work of Karl Mannheim (1972 [1928]), who defined "generation" as a "historical community" consisting of individuals who have come to share specific historical experiences by, inter alia, taking part in the same historical events, thus becoming in Mannheim's terms "a generation in actuality" (ibid.: 303).
3. I borrow the term "generational gap" from Margaret Mead (1978).
4. It is generally expected that the age of retirement in Denmark will increase gradually in line with the general life expectancy. Retirement thus depends on year of birth. Today, the average pension age is 66.5 years. It is currently expected that it will reach 72 years by 2050.
5. The term "imagined communities" is borrowed from the work of Benedict Anderson (1991).
6. As Herzfeld (2004) shows in his study on artisanship in Crete, kin relations are often considered a source of conflict among the artisans, and partnering with kin members is generally avoided because of fears of the exploitation of kinship norms. Likewise, in the Sicilian agricultural co-ops studied by Rakopoulos (2018), cooperativism is generally idealized as an anti-mafia endeavor disassociated from kinship, although locals often entered the co-ops through channels of kin.
7. In her study of housing cooperatives in Copenhagen, Bruun (2013) shows how the inhabitants drew on the symbolism of family and kinship when describing their co-ops. Bruun proposes to approach such kinship formations through the notion of "house relatedness" (ibid.: 168). Drawing on earlier anthropological discussions on kinship (for example, Peletz 2001), Bruun's analysis emphasizes how kin relations can be positive and harmonious as well as ambiguous and conflict-ridden.
8. In making this assertion, I draw inspiration from Sylvia Yanagisako's (2002) approach to kinship as a complex structure of sentiment and power.
9. Here, I draw on Dorinne Kondo's (1990) study of workers in a family-owned confectionery factory in Tokyo. Kondo examines everyday contests over the meaning of "company" and "family" to show how "company-as-family" idioms create and constrain the workers' lives within the factory (ibid.: 161).
10. It is customary in several trades that craftworkers are fired during the winter as many projects are put on hold during these months. KLAR has done this on a few occasions, but they generally try to avoid doing so or limit the use of "winter breaks" to those craftworkers who prefer to take time off during these months.

11. While the builders rarely talked about "black work"—that is, undeclared or "under the table" work—I knew from conversations that some of them at times increased their income by taking on additional work, particularly on the weekends. This is quite normal in Denmark. A recent study estimates that 20 percent of Danes are engaged in various forms of undeclared work (Bentsen et al. 2018).
12. In an analysis of similar work parties at housing cooperatives in Copenhagen, Bruun (2011) shows that socializing is considered the primary purpose of work parties, whereas the actual work done is of secondary importance. Taking into account that the Danish notion of *fællesskab* (community) etymologically refers to "the sociality that comes from taking care of common property together," this might not come as a surprise (ibid.: 74).
13. Asking questions about ritual practice in an anthropological study opens up an array of different analytical approaches. An obvious first choice is to turn to Victor Turner's (1969) seminal work on the rituals of the Ndembu in Zambia. In this specific analysis, I draw on Turner's outline of the ritual process as a movement from "structure" to "anti-structure" and back to "structure," and his concept of "communitas." According to Turner, a sense of communitas emerges in the transitional phase (the anti-structure) of the ritual process, as the temporary disintegration of a social group generates a lack of positions, which creates a form of all-leveling sociality or equality (ibid.: 98–99).
14. This argument is repeated in several ethnographies of Scandinavia, but it figured prominently in the work of Marianne Gullestad (1990).
15. This kind of rivalry in ritual practice could be compared to the one described by anthropologists in studies of Indigenous peoples of the Northwest Coast of North America. In his writings on the famous potlatches among the Kwakiutl, Franz Boas (1897) shows that although these gift-giving ceremonies were concerned with the reaffirmation of family, clan and intergroup relations, they were also considered a method of acquiring rank. I find Boas's description of rivalry and commonality instrumental in understanding how these two can coexist in ritual practice. In drawing on these descriptions, I am aware that "potlatch" has a checkered past and that writings, such as Boas's, to some extent constitute a misrepresentation as the notion in fact covers a range of different ceremonial exchange complexes (Schulte-Tenckhoff 2001).

CHAPTER 4

TINKERING WITH DEMOCRATIC FORMS

Negotiating Cooperativism at Assemblies

"You're turning me into an employer and yourself into employees," Erik said with equal parts dissatisfaction and distress during an assembly convened at KLAR in the late winter of 2019. He looked around at the crowd of builders who had congregated in the workshop with a serious look on his face. I lifted my gaze from my notebook, where I had jotted down Erik's statement, to see how the builders responded to his claim. Many stared blankly into the space of the workshop or lowered their eyes to the ground. While they appeared indifferent, I had a feeling that many felt stung by his words, which lingered in the air. After a while, Erik continued speaking. Later in this chapter, I shall return to recount what he said and what he implied with the above statement.

The builders at KLAR convened for briefings, meetings, and assemblies on a regular basis. Every Monday morning, they congregated at 6:30 a.m. to go through the practicalities of the construction projects running at the co-op; moreover, in the afternoon of the first Thursday of every month, they met to discuss the operations of KLAR. After having completed a day's work on different construction sites, builders returned tired to the main office at KLAR on these days. Most would grab a cup of coffee or a soda and gather outside the office building while they waited for the assembly to begin. Cigarettes would be lit and quiet conversations hummed, before Erik called everyone together and asked them to congregate in the common kitchen area. As detailed in the organizational outline of KLAR presented in Chapter 1, assemblies such as these were from the outset considered key to the cooperativist structure of the organization.

Assemblies were not only a recurring phenomenon during my fieldwork; many builders ascribed great significance to these events. Indeed, several builders continuously stressed the importance of these gatherings, which, for them, were crucial to the *medarbejderdemokrati* (industrial democracy) of the co-op. I was continuously reminded about this on Thursday afternoons as I sat among the crowd at the co-op assemblies together with many of the builders, who seemingly prioritized joining these events month after month. Yet, as we shall see in this chapter, this dedication also became a source of frustration to some of the builders. In brief, their frustration revolved around the question of whether or not the assemblies constituted *demokratiske møder* (democratic meetings), and thus whether they contributed to or inhibited the democratic control of the organization.

Negotiations regarding assemblies and the industrial democracy of co-ops more broadly—the involvement of workers in decision-making processes—has been a key focus for scholars working with such organizations (Rakopoulos 2020). Several researchers have stressed that the collapse of the industrial democracy in co-ops is often connected to the emergence of hierarchical relations, contending that institutions such as states (Narotzky 2007) or markets (Kasmir 1996) impose this stratification from above or from outside the organization in question. Recent contributions have challenged such accounts, arguing that the cause of internal stratification must be found in the broader social relationships in which cooperators are embedded (Rakopoulos 2018). Nonetheless, the causes of this trajectory remain located *outside* the cooperative framework, and assemblies or similar actives are thus typically omitted from ethnographic accounts of cooperativism.[1]

Yet omitting the assemblies from the ethnography of KLAR would seem like a strange choice, considering their recurrent nature and the builders' emphasis on the importance of these events, an importance which indicates that, to the builders, the assemblies contained an "epitomizing potential" (Strathern 2017: 198). Exploring these gatherings might thus provide significant insights into the builders' efforts to handle the elusive nature of cooperativism. Indeed, social activities such as assemblies "are not just instances that exemplify broader issues, but key sites through which social, political, temporal, spatial, and material circumstances are constituted and transformed" (Brown, Reed and Yarrow 2017: 11). Accordingly, assemblies, such as the ones convened at KLAR, might even be considered productive arenas in which social realities are made and remade.

In this chapter, I follow this line of inquiry as I explore not just what the assemblies at KLAR set out to achieve, but rather what was entailed in doing so (Strathern 2017). Rather than passing judgment on the democratic nature of these assemblies, I approach these meetings ethnographically, seeking to understand, describe and explain how the builders perceived their own involvement in this mundane and recurrent form of social activity. In doing so, I am particularly concerned with the constitution of participation and attendees at the assemblies. I thus examine the kinds of subjects that the assemblies pre-supposed and the modalities by which the participants inhabited and converted these (Brown et al. 2017).

To shed light on the social reality made and remade during the assemblies convened at KLAR, the ethnographic accounts of this chapter stay close to these events. More precisely, the ethnography is organized around the progression of the specific assembly introduced in the opening of this chapter. Although this particular assembly was framed as extraordinary, as I shall show, it serves as a starting point for examining the social activities that shaped these gatherings. I thus examine segments of this assembly piece-by-piece in order to analyze the particular activities that unfolded in detail. From this fine-tuned attention to the specificities involved in such meetings and assemblies, I argue that wider empirical and conceptual insights can be derived (see also Brown et al. 2017). Indeed, the detailed presentation of the specific assembly will show that the builders continuously came up with new suggestions for how to reorganize their assemblies in their efforts to cultivate the "democratic" nature of these events. Or, as I shall suggest in this chapter, they continuously sought to *tinker* with the practical organization and operation of the assemblies. I return now to the assembly convened at KLAR in the late winter of 2019 to examine how this was unfurled.

ASSEMBLING

As I entered the changing room that Thursday afternoon, I immediately knew that this assembly would be more crowded than usual. Copious safety shoes and sets of dirty workwear were lying around in large piles. I left my work clothes and bag in the cubicle that I normally used and continued to the common kitchen area to grab a cup of coffee. A few people were chatting at one of the corner tables. Where were the rest, I wondered, as I took a seat on the bench in the back. Henning showed up after a while to inform us that today the assembly would take place in the workshop and not in the common kitchen area, as it usually did. I followed the others to the workshop, where we encountered everyone else. The space had been re-arranged for the day's event. Tools, machines, and materials had been removed, leaving space for tables and chairs. I found a chair at the middle table and counted the number of people gathered: there were approximately fifty-four builders, which was definitely above the average attendance. And even more people continued to show up. Close to all of the builders at KLAR were therefore suddenly present, sitting tightly together in groups of five to six people at the tables set up for the event. However, Erik had also stressed at the Monday morning briefings preceding the assembly that everyone should join as they had to discuss the current state of affairs of KLAR. More precisely, they had to review their financial situation, as a number of construction projects were not progressing as planned, which was beginning to show in the accounts. I heard from a few builders that Erik's announcement had created a nervous atmosphere during the days leading up to the assembly, as some worried that the supposed economic decline would require a collective reduction in wages.

Erik did not normally communicate the agenda of assemblies in advance. As a result, the builders often seemed unacquainted with the schedule of the Thursday afternoon assemblies. The topics discussed at the events usually varied greatly, ranging from the evaluations of construction projects to the yearly company trip, financial issues, and political issues of the day. In contrast, the weekly Monday morning briefings always followed a fixed agenda. This was probably a good thing since some builders seemed half-asleep when Erik opened these meetings at 6:30 a.m. The builders who managed to get there before time, grabbed a cup of coffee and some slices of bread with cheese. Some engaged in quiet conversations, before Erik opened the meeting with a loud "good morning." First on the agenda was the introduction of new people or interns if there were any new faces in the room. Then, Erik moved on to the list of construction projects currently running. Practicalities were discussed and coordinated to ensure that projects could progress as planned during the week. Subsequently, Erik asked if there had been any problems with the company cars or bikes in the past week. Occasionally, somebody mentioned a minor incident—perhaps a broken side mirror. Next up was the work environment and health and safety. Here, people had a chance to bring forth accidents that had occurred during the past week on the construction sites. Last, Erik reminded people of upcoming social events and future assemblies, before closing the meetings with a loud, "Have a great week."

Although the content of assemblies and meetings varied, assemblies generally followed a recurrent and thus specific cultural script. Builders convened, Erik made the opening remark, the floor was open for talk and discussion, and as the meeting was winding up, Erik would make some final remarks, often regarding practical issues, and the meeting would end. Because of this distinct nature of assemblies, scholars have been inclined to consider them ritual events and, in doing so, stressed that they contain meta-communicative commentaries on social life in associations such as co-ops (Bruun 2012). Yet although a ritual discourse and documentation might be adopted to legitimize and give credence to the purpose and activities of assemblies and meetings (Abram 2017), I would be reluctant to classify them as ritual events because, in doing so, attention is primarily directed at the contexts generated and represented through these events. This would deflect attention from the routine procedures and forms through which context is constituted at meetings and assemblies (Brown et al. 2017). Rather than defining the assemblies and meetings at KLAR broadly as ritual events, I thus attend to the forms, concepts, and assumptions that assemblies work through. In the following section, I employ this approach by providing a more thorough introduction to the intended design of the co-op's assemblies as well as the builders' internal discussions about how to practically realize this design.

THE INTENDED DESIGN: DELIBERATIVE DEMOCRACY

Henning provided me with some valuable insights into the intended design of the co-op's assemblies when we discussed the details of these events during an interview. According to Henning, the assemblies were generally modeled on a version of *konsensusdemokrati* (consensus democracy) or deliberative democracy. For Henning, this implied that the builders sought to make decisions collectively by talking together. "We don't vote on decisions. No, we sit and talk about it," he explained and added that, "It takes enormous discipline." He stressed that deliberative democracy evidently requires that people agree, "If you persistently stick to your own opinion, you block the decision-making process. So, people have to be flexible, right?" He emphasized that the strength of such a form is that collaboration and agreement ensure that the majority does not simply overrule the minority by formally voting on a decision. In his view, such an approach would be non-democratic as it implied that the majority would simply overrule the minority. Rather, everyone should agree—or as a minimum accept decisions made collectively, he underlined.

Henning's interpretation of deliberative democracy largely reflects a more general perception of such a democratic form in Denmark and, moreover, of social movements associated with the alter-globalization or global justice movement.[2] Official representations of the so-called Danish variety of democracy accentuate that consensus is an important feature of democratic practice as "major political decisions are made in broad agreement, and good political craftsmanship is measured by the ability to gather broad agreement on important decisions."[3] This perception of democratic practice is also common in other institutional settings in Denmark.[4] As such, a general preoccupation with democratic practices that goes beyond formal acts of voting seems to dominate in the Danish context. Indeed, ideas of consensus, compromise and unity have historically been key to the ideological formation of the Danish welfare state (Jöncke 2011). Based on this, it is perhaps unsurprising that many of the builders expected that deliberation, an activity which Henning also highlights, would be key to the assemblies convened at KLAR.

Yet, in the view of many builders, deliberation rarely took place during the assemblies, which disappointed several of them. In their view, such verbal exchanges did not take place since Erik simply did most of the talking. The lack of discussion at the assemblies implied, they asserted, that there was no "democratic control" in the co-op, and the organization was thus in reality simply run by Erik. This assertion was only confirmed by the fact that Erik had remained the daily manager of KLAR from the early years, which, for them, implied that this position was de facto not up for election at the yearly general assembly, which was otherwise a key principle of the co-op. Moreover, the influence of "the council" (the group that should supervise the daily manager's work) had seemingly diminished, as nobody appeared to know when the council met or what they discussed. In sum, this all revealed, several argued, that KLAR was not a democratically controlled enterprise as it claimed to be, and its status as a co-op was therefore also, some contended, debatable.

During my fieldwork at KLAR, several builders repeatedly related this line of argumentation, as they pondered, queried, and criticized the assemblies convened at the co-op and Erik's leading position in the organization. Yet why did Erik take up so much space at the assemblies and what did he tell the builders during his talks? To investigate this question, I approach Erik's speeches as a form of political oratory. I thus explore some of the questions often examined in anthropological studies of oratories: How are his speeches made authoritative? How do they narrate what is going on? And how do they address the audience?[5]

THE OPENING: THE POWER OF ORATORIES

Shortly after 4 p.m., Erik took the chair. "It shouldn't be a secret that I'm not happy with my job as a daily manager at the moment," he informed the crowd. His voice quavered slightly. Everyone was listening quietly. He took a breath before he resumed by recounting that he had been in a meeting with a potential client together with Henning the day before. The meeting had continued until 9 p.m. "Is it fair that I have to spend my evening working?" Erik asked. "No, but that is how the industry works." He looked around at the crowd before he continued. "But why should I do it, if no one else stays for a few extra hours when they made a mistake or when they are falling behind on a project's schedule?," he said in frustration. He had begun questioning whether he wanted to continue as the daily manager of KLAR. He did not feel happy when he left for work in the morning. "I feel like some of you are making a joke of our collective project," he said with frustration.

Erik provided a few more details on the meeting he had attended with Henning, before he turned and pointed at a few words he had noted in advance on a blackboard. *Rettigheder* (Rights) and *pligter* (Duties) it stated. Erik underlined that, for him, people seemed more concerned about "rights" than "duties." "People rarely enter the door before they claim some sort of right," he said, "but duties are something individual—rights are something we fight for." He continued by emphasizing that this was exactly the type of argument critical voices would use when assessing KLAR; people like the builders "consider society to be one large cake from which you can eat as much as you want," he said in a strict tone.

Erik is a passionate speaker. This was not the first time he took the chair and filled either the workshop or the common kitchen area with frustrations, anecdotes, or encouragements. In fact, the assemblies at KLAR always opened with some kind of declaration made by Erik. The topics of his talks varied greatly. Sometimes he reminded everyone to pay more attention to traffic to avoid car accidents; other times he stressed that the builders overfilled their waste bags, thus not respecting the unskilled hands responsible for picking up waste. He might repeat that it was important to return tools to their proper places in the workshop, or that everyone should help with cleaning up after parties. Erik's talks were often both sincere and humorous, as he did his best to convey messages appropriately and capture the attention of the builders. Although the topics of his talks differed, they always, as in the above situation, directly or indirectly addressed a lack of engagement or attentiveness among the builders. Hence, they served as a kind of reminder of the collective project at the heart of KLAR. Erik, in other words, continuously urged builders to renounce any traces of individualism and instead orient themselves toward the collective.

In the situation above, he did so by introducing the notions of "rights" and "duties." These terms have a distinct historical trajectory in the Danish context, as they invoke long-term historical debates on the moralizing aspects of the Danish welfare state and its dependence on a particular type of citizen, who readily fulfills their duties while voluntarily restraining their claim to rights.[6] While I do not assume that all builders knew this, Erik's (intentional or coincidental) use of these terms nonetheless serves as an example of his occasional use of formulaic language.[7] Moreover, his talks were rarely directed toward particular builders. Rather, Erik often seemed to be deeply concerned that the builders had come to separate individual responsibility and commitment from collective achievements. By not investing in the collective project of KLAR, the builders were, according to Erik, reducing themselves to "regular employees," as we heard him say in the opening of the chapter.

As Erik wrapped up his talk, he returned to his frustrations regarding the increasing number of slips and faults at the co-op. He was frustrated that people often came to him instead of dealing with their difficulties on the construction sites. He wanted people to reflect upon their own efforts and contributions. That is, he wanted them to consider the balance and distribution of "rights" and "duties" in the co-op.

Henning had been standing next to Erik throughout his talk. Henning rarely said much during the assemblies, except for a few comments or practical details now and then. But that day he followed suit. Henning underlined that he shared many of Erik's frustrations. He described KLAR as a long elastic band and added that, "It's close to breaking." Those at the front had to lower their speed, or those in the rear had to run faster. "We don't know where the chain will break," he added. "You have to act responsibly when you're in charge of a project." They needed to find a way to avoid deficits on the construction projects underway at KLAR, but Henning was running out of suggestions. "There is no enterprise anymore if we run out of funds," he finished.

As the accounts from this particular assembly demonstrated, Erik (and on this occasion Henning also) took up a lot of spotlight during these events. With his strong oratory skills, Erik often came to occupy a role as a charismatic leader in the Weberian sense during the assemblies. Accordingly, it was not necessarily Erik's structural position as the daily manager of the co-op that provided him with a privileged position at the assemblies, but his individual abilities and oratory skills. In fact, one could speculate whether these skills had paved the way for Erik's leading position in the co-op in the first place.

Yet the emergence of charismatic leaders in settings that are supposed to be egalitarian poses certain challenges as it stimulates a certain power concentration, which is generally associated with a transition from egalitarian to hierarchical social contexts (Boni 2015). Several of the builders at KLAR shared this interpretation, as Erik's extensive talking, in their opinion, undermined the democratic nature of the assemblies convened at KLAR. Several often said that it implied that "nothing happened" at the assemblies. During most of the assemblies I participated in at KLAR, I unconsciously acknowledged the premise put forward by these builders in their interpretation of these gatherings. Consequently, my attention was directed toward what Erik was saying and his words thus also figured widely in my field notes. Yet, at some point, I began turning my attention to the crowd at the assemblies instead to see what they were in fact doing while Erik was talking.

IN THE MEANTIME: THE SILENCE OF THE BUILDERS

A quick glance at those gathered for the Thursday afternoon assemblies reveals that most builders sat through the meetings with red cheeks and drowsy eyes. Many, including myself, were often tired at this time of the day after having worked on the construction sites since 7 a.m. Erik and a few others stressed that this was one of the reasons why participation was often low at the assemblies; low in the sense of the number of builders present at the assemblies, but particularly referring to the limited involvement of those gathered.

Attendees at meetings or assemblies more generally often resent the minutes and hours that meetings take up, complaining that they can, for instance, be dull or boring (Brown et al. 2017). The work of assembling can even be perceived as exhausting. While such exhaustion can be seen as "a vacuum enabling the appearance of novel social and political roles" (Jiménez and Estalella 2017: 110), this did not always seem to be the case at KLAR. At most assemblies and meetings, most builders seemingly took up their usual roles as tired attendees.

Despite this collective tiredness, several builders told me that they had in fact tried to be attentive during the meetings in their first months at KLAR. At some point, however, their concentration started to slip, they explained, as they came to consider Erik's talks tedious and slightly repetitive. Although this was seemingly the case, a closer examination of their facial expressions during the assemblies occasionally indicated otherwise. As I began to study the reactions of builders during Erik's talk, I spotted rolling eyes or the shadow of a smile when Erik, once again, reminded them of the importance of keeping the workshop tidy. Many were, it seemed, paying attention; yet, while there may have been faint traces of attentive interest in the room, rarely did anyone contribute with comments or questions. Indeed, when Erik opened the floor for a plenary discussion after his speeches, only a few builders typically voiced questions, comments, or concerns. Many, furthermore, seemed to withdraw whenever complicated questions were brought up. This was, for instance, the case during the general assembly convened at KLAR. An external accountant presented the financial statement of the year to the crowd. Step by step, he walked us through the numbers. I concentrated to keep up with the presentation, not knowing much about "assets" and "liabilities." My impression was that many of the builders faced a similar challenge. Nonetheless, Erik stressed that everyone had to take part in the general assembly. "You probably think numbers are boring, but financial statements are about the balance of power. Everyone needs to know the numbers," he underlined as he opened the general assembly.

Overall, I never got the impression that anybody tried to interrupt Erik's talks. Even the most dedicated and politically motivated builders seemingly kept quiet. Bo, the builder who was often in a grumpy mood during the workday, but who was often more talkative after a few beers on Friday afternoons, provides a good example here. As described, Bo has worked at KLAR for close to a decade, and although I never noted down the names of attendees at the assemblies, I know that Bo was present at all of them; yet, I never heard him say a word at any assembly. Like most of the builders, he simply remained silent.

Academics are liable to read silence as evidence of a lack of awareness, although it might, particularly among craftworkers, carry very different meanings. Indeed, the builders' silence during assemblies at KLAR was not merely due to, I believe, the absence of communication. However, grasping exactly what they expressed through this silence remains a tricky task. Indeed, tracing modes of silence in social life also means embracing the multivocality and unintelligibility of silence itself (Dragojlovic and Samuels 2021). Although it might be alluring to simply conclude that silence was imposed on the builders by Erik as he did most of the talking, I think it is more instructive to examine whether their silence also conveyed other meanings.

Indeed, wordless participation in the assemblies also appeared to be a deliberate choice made by many. While their silence seemingly challenged the idea of verbal exchange as key to the democratic practice of the assemblies, it was nonetheless a professional virtue, as silence was valued and cultivated during the daily work on construction sites. Asking builders to discuss, question, or criticize clearly speaks against this virtue. Indeed, when apprentices learn that they can only ask three questions a day, according to the builder Roar's mantra, how were they to recognize when they could openly engage in discussions during the assemblies convened immediately after the workday? The norm of taciturnity cultivated at construction sites might in this regard pose a serious challenge to the politics of oratory and rhetoric defining deliberative democracy (Jiménez and Estalella 2017). This shows that it can be a challenge to reconcile the norms of "good craftwork" and cooperativism. While silence is, in the builders' view, a prerogative in craftwork, it poses a fundamental challenge to their perception of deliberative democracy as a guiding principle and practice of assemblies, and thus also of cooperativism.

Only the very skilled builders, I realized, were capable of navigating the different realms of craftwork and cooperativism within the same social context. Accordingly, it was primarily some of these apprentices and builders who openly expressed their frustration at the lack of conversation and discussion during the assemblies. Acting on this frustration, some of them had suggested that they introduce a new type of assembly at KLAR, which they named the "discussion group." They proposed that this particular forum should be a place for discussion, in which no decisions, the consequences of which extended beyond the discussion group itself, could be taken during meetings. Erik and the other builders immediately supported the idea.

Erik, in fact, initially shared some of his concerns regarding the current state of affairs of KLAR at a meeting in the discussion group prior to the assembly detailed in this chapter. The meetings in the discussion group had been running for about half a year at this point. After some of the builders had shared information on a few projects they were working on during this specific meeting in the discussion group, Erik took a firm grip on the discussion. He told the attendees that he was tired of the *lønmodtager-attitude* (wage-earner-attitude) that many of the builders had, according to him, developed. Erik exemplified his views with reference to the numerous faults and deficiencies in the construction work. "Why don't people stick around for a few hours to correct the mistakes they make," he asked rhetorically. "Some projects are in the red after only two days of work." Erik considered KLAR *demokratisk* (democratic), but this was no longer the case in relation to the work effort. He stressed that the co-op helped people in so many ways—providing apprentices with a high salary, contributing financially toward various medical treatments for the builders, and so on—but when it came to the work itself, many seemed to have other things they would rather do.

As Erik spoke, the air slowly grew thick with unease. Everyone could sense his disappointment. Gro, one of the younger builders, was the first to react to Erik's frustrations. The deficit was new to her, but for Gro, money was not the only concern—the physical work environment was equally important. Many of the builders had years left on the labor market and had to take care of their physical well-being. Erik immediately agreed, "Money is not a goal in itself, it's simply a means." Others subsequently joined the conversation with remarks and questions. Several builders stressed that the number of newly arrived builders had increased during the fall, highlighting that onboarding of these new builders had caused certain challenges. Following the no-decision-dogma of the group, the discussions remained open-ended as the meeting ended. Yet they agreed that it was perhaps pertinent to discuss some of these challenges at the following Thursday assembly.

During my fieldwork, it came to my attention that the builders had divergent opinions about this novel discussion group format. Astrid stressed this as we talked one afternoon over a cup of coffee in an urban park located close to KLAR. Astrid was one of the initiators of the group format. She wished more people would join the meetings, but she also knew that this was impossible. "We're a diverse group," she described, "I know that a large part of the workforce simply doesn't care about joining such activities." Nonetheless, Astrid had come to enjoy the openness and conversations at these meetings, as it was easier to take part in the discussions than during the regular assemblies. Speaking with other builders and apprentices about the new initiative reminded me of Astrid's remark on the differing views of the discussion group. A couple of apprentices told me that they had quit the discussion group after they had participated on a few occasions. "I participated in a meeting once," one said, "but I didn't say anything. I didn't really know what I could contribute with." Another highlighted that Erik did most of the talking anyway and ironically denoted it "the listening group."

Accommodating the various needs and aspirations of the heterogeneous groups of builders at KLAR was seemingly a complicated task. While some, like Astrid, wished they could have more lively discussions during the assemblies, others, like Bo, probably welcomed Erik's speeches, as it meant that they could sit in silence. What solutions could solve the tensions between these positions? Could the heterogeneous group of builders possibly find a way to practice deliberative democracy in such a silent polity?

SPLITTING INTO GROUPS: COMPOSING THE SOCIAL "DIVERSITY" OF THE CO-OP

At the assembly convened in the late winter of 2019, Erik and Henning had come up with one possible answer to these conundrums. After their respective speeches, they invited the crowd of builders to do something they rarely did. To ensure that everyone took part in devising potential solutions to the current challenges of KLAR, they proposed that the builders divided into groups. I asked the builders sitting at the same table as me if I could take part in their discussions. "Sure," Rune—a younger, but experienced builder—replied. Two apprentices and Torsten were sitting at the same table.

This particular assembly took place in the workshop instead of the usual common kitchen area of the co-op. Consequently, the builders could not sit at the same tables or in the same subgroups as they usually did for assemblies. This was a peculiar situation, as the subgroups were normally close to being set in stone. Indeed, Erik once told me that he gets a laugh out of telling newcomers simply to choose a seat when they join an assembly for the first time, as he knew they would end up taking someone else's chair. For Erik, it was a puzzle as to why the builders always sat in these seemingly fixed subgroups. In contrast to Erik's puzzlement, most of the builders appeared to take the social subgroupings of KLAR for granted. When I asked a few how they knew which group they supposedly belonged to, most looked bemused and explained that they simply enjoyed the company of some more than others. A few builders elaborated that the subgroups had highly different preferences in music. This might sound shallow, but music was an important aspect of sociality among the builders. Some play in bands or attend concerts and festivals together. Based on the builders' lack of reflection around the organization of the subgroups at KLAR, it seems as if many considered these subgroups naturally occurring social entities. Looking closer at the organization of the groups, it further seems as if these groups were organized around perceived social similarity.

Strong awareness of social similarity has been a central theme in the anthropology of Scandinavia. Ethnographers have repeatedly shown that an interactional style that emphasizes similarity and downplays difference tends to dominate social life in Scandinavia.[8] Looking at the above outline of the subgroupings at KLAR, this interactional style also appeared to be a guiding social principle at the co-op, as the builders seemingly associated with people they considered similar to themselves. By organizing according to perceived similarities, the builders clearly made social differences more subtle and hidden, as they seemingly distanced themselves from people who they considered different from themselves. It further, I suggest, enables the builders to avoid conflicts, which was a general concern.[9] Henning openly described this sentiment during an interview. He explained that he does his best to avoid conflicts. "I hate conflicts," he stated. "I hate it if I have to correct people. Or fire somebody, that's the worst ... It's not because I can't handle conflicts, but I would rather that they didn't exist," he told me and added that, "There is nothing worse than people who constantly have to air conflicts." Like Henning, Erik also expressed his concerns regarding conflict. During a meeting in the aforementioned discussion group, he explained, "There are probably around twenty-five different cultures in this co-op, and I am the one that makes sure that all of them are kept together." He added, "I—and maybe Henning and Torsten—we can sense all of you." Erik's remark revealed that he was very aware of the internal social divisions of the co-op.

I returned to this question during a follow-up interview, where Erik and I talked about the employment strategy of the co-op. Here, Erik stressed the importance of "diversity." He explained that if the organization had just hired "four middle-class boys in their twenties," they had to look for other types of people in subsequent recruitment processes. For Erik, it was important to keep such a "balance" in the social life of KLAR. In Erik's own words, they had to ensure that the co-op did not "capsize" by employing too many seemingly similar people. Henning in many ways shared this view, as he similarly stressed the importance of "diversity" at KLAR. He argued that it is important that people with a university degree and people with a criminal record could work together at the co-op. "Diversity is good for everyone," Henning explained, "even if it requires everyone to go a little extra." Erik and Henning were apparently concerned with making sure that none of the subgroups became a majority within the co-op.

This focus on "diversity" and the social composition of the workforce reveals that builders like Erik and Henning also had an educational aspiration for KLAR. They aimed to teach the builders how to be part of socially diverse groups. As Henning said, "diversity is good for everyone." This principle was not only employed to enhance the social life within the co-op, I suspect, but also reflected a broader vision for society, where social diversity should be encouraged.[10] Assemblies were seen as one potential venue for pursuing this aspiration. Indeed, meetings are often imagined as spaces where people confront and resolve differences, whether social, epistemological, political or otherwise (Brown et al. 2017). In their effort to promote their aspiration for social diversity, the assemblies at KLAR effectively miniaturized society, becoming spaces for social training that the builders deemed important for the broader society.[11]

Yet reinforcing the social "diversity" at KLAR was not a straightforward task. If we return to Erik's description of KLAR as a diverse place with a potential for social discord if he (along with Henning and Torsten) were not there to manage, this statement not only brings attention to the social heterogeneity of the co-op; it also reveals that Erik considers himself (and Henning and Torsten) as key and responsible for the social cohesion and equality of the organization. Rephrasing his argument, he seemingly suggests that to avoid internal hierarchies and thus uphold egalitarian relations at the co-op, he had to, rather paradoxically, take up the role as "spokesperson." In this regard, Erik seems to argue implicitly that to ensure the democratic control of the co-op, he in fact has to take up a leading position. Some form of hierarchy was apparently, in Erik's view, necessary to ensure social equality at KLAR.

Yet this stance was exactly what many of the builders objected to when they criticized Erik's dominant position during assemblies. For them, this was, as we have heard, an obstacle to the deliberation that they consider key to democratic practice. However, during the assembly convened in the late winter of 2019, the builders did in fact attempt to instigate deliberation. Let us return to the workshop to examine what the group I joined ended up talking about during the group discussion.

"BUILDERS VOTE WITH THEIR FEET": THE LACK OF VERBAL EXCHANGE

Back in the workshop, the conversation flourished. The group I sat with turned directly to discuss the practicalities of the workday. Someone suggested that everyone should turn up for work on the construction sites earlier. Another said that they should keep track of the breaks, which some tended to prolong. Torsten argued that they could reduce wastage on the individual construction sites if they were more attentive, and added that they could relieve the pressure on construction administrators by ordering materials on the sites too. The group discussion ended with a longer talk about apprentices. Did it take too long to instruct apprentices? Should they reduce the number of apprentices? One of them added that they could generally be better at correcting each other's mistakes. An apprentice jumped in. He explained that he had felt excluded from the first crew he worked with. The others appeared to be displeased with his work, but nobody explained why. The supervisor of the next crew had been more direct and told him to concentrate on and increase the speed of his work. Rune concluded that perhaps they had to be more forthright with each other's performances. The time for group discussion then ended.

One by one, the different groups presented their conclusions to the rest of those gathered. It turned out that most groups had centered their conversations on the practicalities of daily work on the construction sites. Many repeated the challenges and solutions that we had discussed in our group—ranging from the length of a break to more frequent evaluations of the progression of construction projects. Although only representatives from the groups took the floor during this plenary discussion, it appeared that the majority of the builders present at this particular assembly had participated in the discussions in their respective groups. In this regard, Erik and Henning's quest that everyone should participate in devising potential solutions to the current challenges of KLAR appeared to be a success.

Contrary to this, Henning told me during an interview that they had previously tried to implement group discussions in an attempt to foster more engagement and supposed democratic participation at the assemblies, but the initiative had failed. I decided to share some of my reflections with him and told him that I had heard many of the builders criticize the lack of discussion at the assemblies. "Yes, it might become a bit like North Korea sometimes," he responded ironically and added that there were several reasons for that. "It's important with meetings in a democracy," Henning underlined, "but there have to be limits." Back when KLAR was launched, the builders met up every Monday morning from 7 a.m. to 9 a.m., he explained. "So, we didn't do any work for those two hours," he stated. "You can't pay yourself for participating in meetings." They had therefore decided to relocate assemblies to after work hours and change the Monday morning meetings to a briefing session. "I think we're challenged by the fact that it would be great to work in a place where you can take part in decision-making processes. But nobody really cares to say stuff, because it's simply easier to let somebody else do it," he explained. So, for Henning, it was about ensuring the right amount of talk during a meeting. “Some like to participate in these meetings, but others don’t,” he explained. “There has to be room for everyone.”

Henning, it seemed, proposed that talk and discussion were not always the right methods to make decisions. In fact, his explanation seemed to indicate that if there was to be “room for everyone,” that is if everyone was to be included, it was sometimes necessary to limit the amount of discussion at the assemblies.[12] Yet, if we remember that Henning had explicitly stated that decisions should be made by “talking about it,” there seems to be a certain ambiguity in his descriptions of the assemblies at KLAR. In fact, it seems as if he is suggesting that talk and conversation can be both liberating and oppressive, depending on whether individual builders were willing to engage with exchanges of words and opinions. In this regard, his explanations also seemed to deviate from his initial emphasis on deliberative democracy, as he—with these claims—rather seemed to compare the internal democracy of KLAR with recently described forms of participatory democracy. That is, forms of democracy that emphasize the importance of self-governance, as decisions should be made by those actively involved in each matter.[13]

Erik typically made a similar shift in his depiction of the assemblies at KLAR, as he also at times stressed that perhaps participatory democracy was a more suitable solution at KLAR than deliberative democracy. During an interview, he underlined that he doubted whether activities such as group discussions could strengthen the democratic culture in the co-op, since he knew that some of the builders hated them. For Erik, it was important to take these different preferences into account, as he was determined not to let those who were willing to speak up make all of the decisions. Although some might feel uncomfortable talking in larger crowds, their voices should be included, he argued. Moreover, Erik knew that although some refrained from expressing their concerns and asking questions during the assemblies, this did not imply that they supported the decisions taken during these events. “Builders vote with their feet,” he told me; builders merely show their dissatisfaction by subsequently refusing to comply.[14] Hence, one should not interpret lack of verbal protest as a sign of support.

Erik was right. Even though the builders were reluctant to show dissatisfaction or engage with disagreements during the assemblies, they often did so during secluded conversations while driving to construction sites, during breaks or—most frequently—at parties, where tongues wagged freely. It was also in these instances that builders would air critical remarks regarding Erik’s claim to authority or forge critical evaluations of the supposedly failed assemblies continuously convened at KLAR. In these clandestine conversations, the builders expressed their moral evaluations of other people working at KLAR, or more generally of the co-op’s governance structure.

Gossiping, such as during the private conversations among the builders, can relieve frustrations in social contexts where one is, as described earlier, expected to evade social differences.[15] Through discussions on matters typically omitted from the assemblies, the builders could gain relief from their frustrations that arose from conflicts and other sensitive issues. Gossiping was thus not only a social activity among the builders, but also a loophole that allowed them to let off steam and frustration. However, such acts of gossiping also undermined the open and inclusive conversations which several envisioned as essential to the industrial and deliberative democracy of KLAR since the builders would rather share and debate conflicting views and opinions in spaces beyond the assemblies. Yet, this only raises the question of why the builders, despite their strong talkability outside the assemblies, nonetheless continued to silently attend these gatherings? Let us return, for one last time, to the assembly convened at KLAR in 2019 to examine this question further.

THE END OF THE ASSEMBLY: THE ETERNAL WORK OF TINKERING

After the group presentations, the floor was returned to Erik. He repeated one of his recurring messages: being self-employed and owning your own business takes time and effort. He hoped that the builders understood that everyone had to take responsibility for cleaning the company cars, the workshop, and the common spaces. He then finished off with an optimistic remark, as he thanked everyone for joining the assembly and added that he was sure they could solve the problems they were currently facing together.

In his brief recap of the meeting, Erik thus somehow ended up answering the queries that he himself had presented at the opening of the assembly. In his opening speech, he stated that he felt like some of the builders were currently making a joke of their collective project and thus disregarding their responsibilities, or "duties" to use his phrasing, toward the collective. His response to this conundrum was to remind the builders, once again, that everyone should contribute to solving what we might describe as the "household" tasks of KLAR.

When Erik had wrapped up the meeting, the builders went to have dinner together as they always did after the Thursday afternoon assemblies. Tables and chairs were collected and put away in a storage room, and the workshop returned to its normal state. Everything was, in other words, brought back to normal. Hence, it appeared that this supposedly spectacular assembly, which from the outset had been framed as an extraordinary meeting where the builders needed to discuss the current affairs of KLAR, had no immediate implications.

Yet this was not quite the case. A few days afterward, I talked to a younger builder about the event. It had in fact left him quite frustrated. According to him, the assembly had only reinforced a division among the builders between those who supported and those who were critical of Erik's methods of management. As I resumed the conversation with this builder some weeks later, it turned out that he and a few others had aired their critical reflections on the assemblies to Erik during a meeting in the discussion group, which I unfortunately had not attended. The group had subsequently decided that perhaps they should try to restructure the practical organization of the assemblies, letting a few of the younger builders take turns acting as moderators during the meetings.

This specific solution reminded me of the strategies normally pursued by the builders at KLAR in relation to their engagement with craftwork and cooperativism more broadly. Despite the discord and disagreements that the assemblies seemingly produced at KLAR, and the builders' ongoing criticism of the perceived efficacy of these events, they paradoxically continued to convene, participate in, and change the practical organization and operation of these events. That is, although they often depicted the assemblies as unsuccessful in achieving the tenet of democratic control, they still somehow believed that this form of control could potentially occur every time they congregated at these events. Rather than abandoning the assemblies, several builders continuously came up with new suggestions for reorganization in an effort to make them "more democratic." When some builders requested more discussion, while others preferred to reduce meetings to a minimum, they invented the discussion group. When they wanted more conversation at the assemblies, they split the builders into groups. And when they agreed that Erik's role had perhaps become too dominant at assemblies, they decided on introducing a moderator. These were just a few of the adjustments introduced during my fieldwork at the co-op.

These ongoing experiments serve as prime examples, I suggest, of how the builders continuously sought to tinker with the practical organization and operation of their assemblies in an effort to instantiate the idea of industrial democracy at the co-op. Applying the trope of tinkering in this case allows us to see how the builders' ongoing work with adjusting the organization and operation of their assemblies often took the shape of a form of practical, creative, and attentive experimentation. However, even though they persistently seemed to believe that their suggested adjustments of the assemblies would in some way increase the "democratic control" of the co-op, they never appeared to arrive at any final solutions. Democracy can indeed be hard work, not least because the constant consideration regarding correct procedures is both tiresome and necessary (Abram 2017). Tinkering is also hard work. And, when seen from the perspective presented in this section, it might also appear as a never-ending effort.

CONCLUDING REMARKS

In this chapter, I have challenged the inclination to omit assemblies and meetings from ethnographies of co-ops and similar organizations, by presenting an extended ethnographic account of one assembly convened at KLAR in the late winter of 2019. Rather than excluding the messy accounts from these gatherings, which many ethnographies of cooperativism seemingly do, I have detailed the builders' ongoing critical, yet engaged, efforts to tinker with the practical organization and operation of these events in accordance with their principle of industrial democracy. In doing so, I have attended to assemblies not merely as "indicative but also as generative of socio-political transformation" (Brown et al. 2017: 15). The detailed ethnography revealed the complicated social negotiations and unstable dynamics of power that continued to interfere with the tenet of industrial democracy in cooperativism at KLAR.

Narratives of democratic control in cooperativism, and the unity and solidarity they imply, are often ambiguous. This was also the case at KLAR. Yet in illuminating the social negotiations and dynamics of the assemblies at KLAR, I have argued that the assumed horizontal unity of cooperativism was not only disrupted by social forces existing outside the cooperative framework. Rather, as we have seen, the internal heterogeneity and mundane messiness at KLAR make realizing the ideal of industrial democracy in cooperativism an ongoing challenge. Ensuring allegiance to the cooperative project of KLAR thus takes constant work and negotiation. During the assemblies, events that should supposedly epitomize the tenet of democratic control, builders occupy different positions as some talk while others remain silent, which complicates the basic idea of verbal deliberation as a means through which equality can be achieved. A recurrent challenge was that a large proportion of the people present seemingly insisted on remaining quiet. In depicting the builders' silent participation in the assemblies, this chapter has illuminated some of the reasons why excessive verbalism, such as the dominating vocal presence of Erik, and not only silence, might also take the shape of hegemony. By unfolding how the professional virtue of silence in craftwork interferes with the principles and practices of deliberative democracy, which the builders consider one of the key tenets of cooperativism, this chapter has shown that reconciling the norms of "good craftwork" and cooperativism can be a challenge. This shows that the various political projects of KLAR do not always neatly coexist. In fact, they might at times work against each other.

When engaging with a phenomenon like cooperativism, which we have by now established is characterized as elusive in nature, a form of attentive, practical, and persistent engagement is required. The builders' efforts to repair, refine, recalibrate, re-model, or simply renew—that is tinker—with the practical organization and operation of assemblies, were thus ways to tame this elusive nature of cooperativism.

Engaging with this elusiveness might be particularly challenging in a context such as Denmark, where cooperativism is not strictly envisioned as an oppositional activity to either the state or the market. This chapter has largely omitted the builders' engagement with these external forces due to my strict focus on the internal dynamics at the assemblies convened at KLAR. However, I take heed of these forces in the following chapters, where I return to the construction sites and workshops at KLAR to examine the builders' efforts to alter the material and political economy of contemporary building in Denmark by searching for ways to tinker with the regulatory frameworks for construction and, moreover, with capitalism itself.

NOTES

1. In his ethnographic accounts of Sicilian agricultural cooperatives, Rakopoulos explicitly states that he omits "the typical and typified decision-making processes in cooperatives [from his] ethnography" (Rakopoulos 2018: 89). Maja Højer Bruun's (2012) work on housing co-ops in Copenhagen provides an exception to this tendency.
2. In his comparative account of meetings in recent social movements, Stefano Boni (2015) explains that actors in these movements are focused on collective processes aimed at producing consensus rather than voting. As he states with reference to the work of David Graeber and Marianne Maeckelbergh: "While voting produces factions, consensus tends to balance the satisfaction of the different needs and thus be collaborative, inclusive, and participatory: several contemporary social movements thus refute elections and representation" (Boni 2015: 15).
3. The official representation of the so-called Danish variety of democracy, which I refer to here is *demokratikanon* (The canon of democracy) (Jespersen et al. 2008: 10). The aim of this canon was to "identify key events, philosophical currents and political texts that have contributed to the debate and influenced the development of freedom, rights, and democracy in Denmark" (ibid.: 97).
4. For example, anthropologist Sally Anderson (2008) provides an informative analysis of how voluntary sports associations in Denmark are envisioned as key sites for the democratic enculturation of children. Popular reports on cooperativism in Denmark today make a similar point, since they likewise stress that the cooperative

focus on involvement in decision-making processes can contribute to the wider development of democracy in Danish society (Pelle Dragsted in Gjerding and Rask 2021; Jørgensen 2020). In a similar manner, Stine Krøijer (2011), in her work on left radical activists from *Ungdomshuset* (The Youth House) in Copenhagen, stress that activists pursue consensus decision-making and self-organization as they consider these practices "to hold out the promise of true democracy, more so than the representative democracy praised in parliamentary politics" (Krøijer 2015: 83).

5. Maurice Bloch's anthology *Political Language and Oratory in Traditional Society* (1975) is considered one of the seminal contributions to this literature. I recognize that there were accounts of political oratories before this particular anthology was published, as David Parkin (1984) also underscores. Yet, this seminal anthology nonetheless marked an important contribution to this particular field of study.
6. See Petersen (2014) for an elaboration of the concepts of "rights" and "duties" in the Danish welfare state.
7. Studies from Bloch's anthology on political oratories, inter alia, encouraged scholars to look for contrasts between formulaic oratorical language, in which customary and unquestionable verities are phrased, and a freer, less predictable everyday language that is best suited for suggesting pragmatic political decisions.
8. See Bruun, Jakobsen and Krøijer (2011). Marianne Gullestad (1992) also advanced this insight in her seminal study of urban living in contemporary Norwegian society, where she, among other things, examined the Norwegian definition of equality as a form of "equality as sameness." According to Gullestad, this form of equality is sustained through an interactional style that highlights sameness and plays down difference, a situation further reinforced by avoiding contact with people who are considered "too different" (Gullestad 1992: 174).
9. Gullestad (1992) stresses that in Norwegian society, the perception of equality as sameness is not incompatible with hierarchy, as egalitarian relations are simply maintained by avoiding unequals. Yet, as Gullestad notes, this only functions up to a certain point. According to the author, social life in Scandinavia is also characterized by a certain conflict avoidance. More precisely, Gullestad argues that "a withdrawal from the relationship often occurs in situations where differences are felt to be 'too great'" (Gullestad 1996: 193).
10. This attentiveness to the composition of social life has been a recurrent issue in ethnographies of Scandinavia, which have shown how Scandinavians commonly believe that "community" must be "created" (Mogensen and Olwig 2013: 12) or "produced" (Bruun 2012: 193), and have emphasized that sociality, in the Scandinavian context, is often an object of constant speculation and reflection (Bruun et al. 2011).
11. Marilyn Strathern (2017) makes a similar assertion based on her reading of a chapter by Corsín Jiménez and Adolfo Estalella (2017).
12. The use of such spacious metaphors are common in the Danish context and are generally applied when describing shared ideals of public sociality (Krøijer and Sjørslev 2011).
13. Participatory or autonomous democracy have, inter alia, been advanced in many of the writings of David Graeber and of Francesca Polletta on contemporary social movements (see, e.g., Graeber 2009; Polletta 2014).
14. This phrase is also used in other accounts of meetings. In his ethnography on Kalahari village politics, Adam Kuper (1971), for instance, notes that accord is

achieved through collective dialogue; those dissatisfied with the outcome may "vote with their feet" by simply refusing to comply.

15. From an anthropological perspective, gossiping can be considered a powerful tool through which the social and moral order of a community is manipulated either to maintain the unity of a group (Gluckman 1963) or to forward and protect individual interests (Paine 1967). In the Scandinavian context, gossiping is also a well-documented social activity. Among villagers in northern Norway, gossiping is indeed so interwoven in the daily affairs and interactions between people, that it can be viewed as an institutionalized means of communication used to, among other things, keep newcomers in the village at a social distance, yet all the while it is also publicly disapproved (Andreassen 1998).

CHAPTER 5

CRAFTING AGAINST THE STANDARDIZATION OF CONSTRUCTION

Reckoning with Regulation

A couple of builders had spent a few days preparing the large wooden construction, which they were now about to incinerate in a large facility located about an hour south of Copenhagen. The wooden construction had been placed on a mobile rack, which was subsequently connected to the end of an apparatus reminiscent of an oven, with both elements sealed off properly. Inside the oven, flames slowly began to consume parts of the wooden construction. A couple of builders, including Erik, stood around and watched with serious expressions on their faces. The wooden structure, towering and intricate, was a testament to the builders' labor and strong belief in "good craftwork." They had spent days putting together the construction. Now, they were witnessing its incineration. Embers from the wood roared as the oven was opened after a set amount of time, casting shadows that flickered across the ground. The crackling sound of burning timber filled the air. The builders and a few technicians watched as the oven was fully opened, revealing how much of the builders' construction had been reduced to ashes. A strong sense of relief spread in the large facility as it became evident that the core of the construction had withstood the power of the flames.

The burning of the prefabricated wooden construction was a decisive moment for the builders at KLAR. I was later told that they had been waiting for this moment for months. I did not witness the burning myself, but I saw the video recording that subsequently circulated. The above description is based on this recording. On the day the burning took place, I was at a bar with Astrid, Liv, and Yrsa—a builder who started working at KLAR briefly after I finished the formal part of my fieldwork at the co-op. Our conversation had started out quietly as the three of them gave me an update about life in and outside the co-op. However, the conversation quickly took an unexpected turn. Yrsa checked her phone and exclaimed a loud and enthusiastic, "Yes! We're winning," and threw her hands into the air. The three of us—Astrid, Liv, and I—looked at Yrsa with surprise. What were we winning? Yrsa explained that she had received a text from Erik, who was currently surveying the burning of the prefabricated wooden construction. In the text, Erik stated that the burning of the construction had passed the required ninety minutes, making Yrsa shout in excitement.

At first glance, the burning or destruction of objects appears futile. Why would the builders invest time and effort into building a wooden construction, only to burn it down? Anthropologists have devoted extended attention to such acts of destruction, often approaching them as different kinds of sacrifices. In its most basic form, sacrifice implies "the idea that something must be destroyed to create something new" (Mayblin and Course 2014: 309).[1] To unleash such transformation, a rupture from reality is needed, which, in the view of some, turns sacrifice into an "act of revolution" (Düzel 2024: 510). In certain ways, the builders' burning of the wooden construction described above could be approached as such an "act of revolution." A crew of builders had invested a solid amount of time in the construction, knowing that the end result of this work would be burned. Yet as they monitored the burning, they were also awaiting the emergence of something new. The innovation that the builders were seeking to create, however, was more complex than an initial interpretation of the event might reveal. In showing that their wooden construction could withstand a fire that extended beyond ninety minutes, the builders were hoping to disprove dominant voices in the construction industry and authorities in Denmark, which have for years questioned whether wooden structures could live up to the Danish fire regulations. To prove their point, the builders had, for reasons I shall elaborate on later, decided to pay for a comprehensive fire test themselves. They had, in other words, decided to sacrifice their time, labor, and money to challenge existing conventions in the construction industry and thus pave the way for change.

The builders' efforts to prove the value and validity of timber in construction were part of a larger mission to rebuild the value and meaning of craftwork. In this way, they also sought to challenge the uneasy position ascribed to artisans or traditional craftworkers in industrial societies. In the Cretan context, for instance, artisans and traditional handicrafts are often associated with an incurable "backwardness," as they "are treated as the last bearers of true tradition" (Herzfeld 2004: 30). Yet artisans also take part in this historical trajectory as they themselves "write craft culture and make their own history through texts—written, visual, and performative" (Terrio 2000: 7). As we shall see in this chapter, the builders at KLAR similarly attempt to redefine the significance of craftwork, and thereby contest the historical inequalities that have come to dominate perceptions of craftwork in Denmark as in many other countries.[2] From the builders' perspective, construction work has become overly constrained by abstract calculations, uniformity, and regulations. This interpretation evidently repeats a familiar narrative of how ideas of techno-scientific progress and industrial production have increasingly shaped the construction industry since the postwar building boom.[3] In this process, skilled workers and craft practices, virtues, and traditions more generally have increasingly become perceived as archaic and irrational.

This misrecognition and devaluation of craftwork has recently become the object of attention in the Danish construction sector, as discussions on *bæredygtigt byggeri* (sustainable construction) and the environmental impact of construction have flourished in Danish society more widely. While the builders have become greatly concerned about the problem of carbon emissions in the construction sector, they distrust the models and measures implemented by authorities to solve this problem. For them, the environmental impact of construction will not be reduced by turning abstract calculations into regulations. Rather, it is, as this chapter will demonstrate, about trusting the embodied knowledge of craftwork; it is about believing in one's hands—a creed that the builders and other craftworkers in Denmark refer to as *kloge hænder* (wise hands).[4] However, convincing authorities and other construction professionals about the validity of such knowledge is a complicated task. In seeking to solve this task, the builders have sought ways in which they could politicize questions of materiality and methodology in contemporary construction and thus challenge the standardization imposed by prevalent building conventions. To understand how the builders simultaneously sought to comply with and contest building conventions and regulatory frameworks, this chapter explores what I call *the material politics of construction work*.

In this chapter, I examine the work at construction sites to show how the builders at KLAR engaged with cooperative craftwork as a source of critical resistance to hegemonic regulatory and political structures in the Danish construction sector. First, I examine the builders' evaluations of specific construction materials and techniques. Subsequently, I explore how the builders connected materiality and politics in construction work, and how craftwork in this process emerged as an ideology among the builders. Last, I show how they sought to alter the material composition of contemporary building in Denmark by searching for ways to change—or, in the words of this book, *tinker*—with the regulatory frameworks for construction. In this chapter, we thus see how the builders at KLAR transposed their ability to tinker onto social domains outside KLAR, such as regulatory struggles.

THE BASIC BUILDING BLOCKS

Construction sites in Denmark range from sites for full-scale development projects to minor sites established, for example, when a kitchen needs to be refurbished in an apartment. Despite variations in size, an array of materials can be located on every site, each required to bring structures to life. Wooden planks are stacked high, ready to be transformed into sturdy frames and floors. Windows and doors are often packed up carefully and placed at the corner of sites. Wires might snake through the site, ensuring that electricity can flow seamlessly throughout the finished structure. Drywall might be prepared to create smooth surfaces for rooms and hallways. Screws and other fasteners are meticulously organized, ready to hold everything together with precision. Each of these materials plays a crucial role, brought together to build new spaces or renew old places.

The builders at KLAR mostly worked at smaller sites, yet the types of projects they worked on varied greatly. While a variety of materials were employed in some projects, certain procedures and materials dominated others. When retrofitting apartments, drywall was often unavoidable. When building new kitchens, timber in various forms was typically used. And when the builders occasionally got the chance to craft saunas, shelters, or similar structures, they often turned to refurbished timber (see Figure 5.1) or to biodegradable materials. Despite this diversity, the builders' choice of which materials to use in each project was never random. Whenever a new customer approached KLAR with a potential project, Erik, Henning, or one of the other construction administrators assessed the project, looking into the material composition, particularly in cases where this had already been determined. In this process, they would stress the importance of taking the environmental impact of the materials into consideration. Since the builders considered timber products as an essential means to lower the environmental impact of construction, they often suggested using these materials. In their view, timber was not only the longest-standing construction material in existence; it was also the building material of the future, as Erik and the rest of the builders would loudly express whenever they got the chance. In doing so, they join a growing chorus of craftworkers, architects and researchers who similarly stress the value of wood in construction (e.g., Pedersen, Dyck-Madsen, and Jarby 2020).

From a craft perspective, wood is not simply wood. Any builder would argue that it constitutes an extremely versatile material that comes in

Figure 5.1. Refurbished wood. Photo by Brian Berg.

numerous varieties, which each carry distinct properties. Pinewood or spruce, for instance, are prevalent choices for framing, while oakwood is a preferred choice for flooring and tabletops as its durability makes it particularly apt for surfaces exposed to intensive wear. Yet oakwood is also an expensive choice, so certain kinds of pinewood can also be used as an option for indoor flooring if costs have to be kept low. Moreover, various innovations are being introduced, where timber products are turned into insulation products, finish materials, or exterior cladding.

When working on projects with wood, the builders were often interested in inspecting the type and quality of the material. To begin with, they would look for ways to identify the specific type of wood. While certain visual traits can be useful to determine the type—such as the direction of the fibers, vessels, and rays—builders often relied on tactility. They would slide their hands across the surface or take a firm grip to get a feel for the density of the sampled material. The builders' reliance on tactile gestures when identifying a specific type of wood was especially noticeable during one of the projects I followed. The project, in brief, entailed the construction of a number of small rooftop houses made from different kinds of wood (see Figure 5.2). The hallmark of the project was the use of recycled materials or factory rejects. The boarding used for the houses, for instance, consisted of

Figure 5.2. Rooftop houses made from refurbished wood. Photo by Brian Berg.

discarded wood from a Norwegian sawmill. This included a variety of types and sizes of boards ranging from soft pinewood to jatoba wood (a dense tropical wood). In contrast to the regular chemical treatment, all of the boards had been treated with furfuryl alcohol—a byproduct of sugar production. After applying this sugary substance to the surfaces, the materials were heated to a temperature of around 100 degrees Celsius. This treatment increased the weight and density of the wood which would prevent it from cracking, while also coloring it light brown and giving it a smooth surface. Many of the builders were unfamiliar with this treatment. When newcomers joined the crew, they often inspected the boards by touching and smelling them. As one builder said, the boards appeared as if they had been "caramelized." I could not provide a better description myself.

Many of the builders were quite fond of the project with the rooftop houses. Apart from the enjoyment they associated with building with wood, many were also enthusiastic about the use of (mostly) recycled materials. I realized as I joined the work that building with such materials was different, as they did not fit into a predefined system. As a result of the diversity of the materials used, the architect behind the project had merely told the builders to install the boards as closely together as possible, adding that the surface was intended to be "playful." Accordingly, the builders had to constantly grapple with getting the different forms and types of planks to match when decorating the rooftop houses. During a break, I asked Astrid and Sune what they thought of this task. Sune explained that normally they would follow a certain system when boarding a construction, highlighting that they typically used clapboard siding, channel gap, or board-and-batten. He therefore considered the aesthetic of the boarding on the rooftop houses messy. Astrid, on the other hand, was quite fond of the work. She described how it sparked her curiosity as she had to think about how to combine the different boards, which she enjoyed. "You have to think more. And make decisions," she said. Like Astrid, many appeared to enjoy the trials of working with such variability, as it forced them to find ways of working with rather than against the varieties of construction materials.

The challenge of variability, which many of the builders seemingly enjoyed, was a more pronounced feature for wood compared to other construction materials, such as drywall, which comes in standardized and uniform sizes. Even though wood is cut into beams and planks before it is delivered to construction sites, these are usually inconsistent regarding their strength, even sometimes within the same piece, although they may appear identical from a distance. The size and density of wood fluctuates, as does its appearance, lending to its charm, but also bringing potential challenges. The builders rarely explicitly evaluated these features; rather, they appeared to continuously take them into account intuitively. When I paid attention to the bodily actions of builders on projects, such as during the construction of the rooftop houses, I observed how they continuously followed the movements of a material to get a sense of it. They studied the lines of planks to determine how to position them. If a board was crooked, they pushed it in certain directions to prevent it from twisting while they fastened it to a construction.

The builders' diligent attention to construction materials seemed to provide them with a form of "material consciousness"; that is, a form of "rapt attention" and curiosity about the material at hand (Sennett 2008: 119).[5] When they relied on tactility in identifying a type or quality of wood, they mobilized their senses in order to pay close attention to the shape, movement, and variety of materials. This work continuously strengthened their "sensory reason" (Paxson 2013: 136). It also taught them that materials are not functional tools that are easy to control. Rather, their intimate engagement with materials such as wood led them to consider materiality as shifting, changing, surprising, and adaptable. It is this diversity that they sought to bring back into construction and craftwork in Denmark. The form of bodily attention required to work with such material diversity, furthermore, seemed to be key to the tenet of "wise hands" employed by the builders at KLAR. A goal of this tenet was to rebuild trust in the embodied knowledge of craftwork.

Yet the builders' strong belief in wood also produced, to a certain degree, certain paradoxes. Vagn, a construction administrator at KLAR, introduced me to some of these concerns during an interview. To begin with, he told me that wood constitutes a "sustainable material" because of its "naturalness."

Vagn further stressed that he always looks for "natural" building materials as these "do not pollute." When I asked him to elaborate, he expounded, "The ones that contain a minimum of chemicals. They should be as pure as possible." Vagn's explanation was intriguing. "How would he define 'pure'?" I asked him. "Well, the materials that are natural. I mean, the ones you can simply extract from the soil," he explained. "That would be the purest form of sustainable construction. It would mean that they hadn't been processed in any way." "Naturalness" was key to "sustainable construction materials," as Vagn argued, and it was an inherent feature of wood, which, in his view, made it an apt material for future environmentally friendly constructions.

While many of the builders would, I believe, agree with the thesis put forward by Vagn, it was also evident that several of the types and cuts of wood that they used in their projects were the results of industrial production. Indeed, laminated wood—beams assembled by gluing wooden boards together—is key to larger timber frame constructions. Although such methods evidently challenge Vagn's definition of "natural" construction materials, many of the builders did not consider this an inconsistency. Indeed, several stressed the advantages of such prefabricated structures and argued that the fabrication process in fact reduces waste since the beams are made from smaller pieces of wood.

The question of "naturalness" in construction materials is thus complex. Vagn also touched upon this and thus on the paradoxes produced by this category as he further explained that it would be impossible to build with only "natural" materials. "You want a window in a house too, right, so you can look outside and get some daylight inside. But it is no secret that producing window glass is a really CO_2 intensive production," he elucidated. "There are certain things where you can't make compromises." Rather than being a strict criterion, "naturalness" was, it appears, a guiding ideal in the builders' evaluation of building materials; a criterion that at times had to be negotiated. These negotiations became particularly prevalent when it came to the intersection of different types of materials.

COMBINING THE BLOCKS: THE INTERPLAY BETWEEN MATERIALS

Building a basic external wall in any construction project in Denmark includes putting together several different building materials. The exterior layer—or facing—of a building is usually built from bricks, wood, slate, or similar materials. This layer is intended to block out sunlight from the wind barrier membrane—the adjacent layer of the wall. The wind barrier (also referred to as a rain barrier or house wrap) is then installed to protect the insulation material from moisture that condenses on the backside of the facing. Subsequently, the insulation material is installed behind the wind barrier.

A vapor barrier then follows which is used for damp proofing as it stops the diffusion of moisture through the interior wall. The vapor barrier is typically made of plastic or foil sheets. Then, another layer of insulation is added, before the interior layer is installed. In the Danish context, this would usually consist of drywall. Wallpaper is applied, before the interior wall is painted.

Many of the builders at KLAR find this material composition odd and artificial. Particularly since this implies that they primarily work with materials such as plastic, insulation, steel, and drywall when building walls, which, in their view, has nothing to do with the "naturalness" they seek to introduce into contemporary building construction. "[Conventional construction] creates a bad indoor climate. People get water in their lungs. And mold grows," Lars stated one day during a morning break in the break-room container, as we were drinking coffee and eating sliced bread with cheese. One of the other builders, Carsten, was explaining a project that another crew of builders were currently working on at the outskirts of Copenhagen. That house was made entirely from timber products and was thus made from a different composition of materials than the one described above. Wood fiber insulation would be blown into the construction, Carsten said, once they had completed the frame. "Our summerhouse is built in the same way," he added. Une joined the conversation adding how annoying it is to install vapor barriers. "If you do it slightly wrong and don't use all their specially produced items, they just say it's installed incorrectly," Lars confirmed. Une added that the production of all of these artificial materials must pollute extensively.

The builders' critical conversations on conventional building techniques and materials would often proceed in this way. In these conversations, they would further underscore that they had not imagined that they would be working with plastic, steel, and drywall when they decided to specialize in carpentry. Sune made this clear one afternoon at a construction site when he loudly proclaimed, in pure frustration, "I did not become a builder to work with plastic." Like Sune, the builders often aimed their frustrations toward the required plastic layer—the vapor barrier—which in their view was the most peculiar element. Why is it a good idea to wrap a building in plastic, many pondered. One day Liv jokingly added that it was like dressing houses in waterproof clothing.

Rather than fully sealing off buildings with plastic, houses should be constructed as *åndbare bygninger* (breathable buildings), the builders at KLAR argued.[6] Many of the builders have become fond of this specific technical model of construction, as it could, in their view, be key to the future of environmentally friendly construction. Breathable buildings are also known in the trade as structures that are "open to diffusion." This means that their walls must be constructed from material layers that allow the passage of vapor without the use of electrical ventilation. Put differently, materials must be assembled so that humidity can move through the entire construction without the accumulation of moisture. According to the builders, the technique requires that the different materials used in construction should work with and not against each other. Applying this technique further limits the number and variety of materials required in contemporary building techniques, and thus reduces what the builders perceived as excessive use of materials in construction.

While many of the builders were strong believers in the technical model of the construction of "breathable buildings" and more generally in material diversity, they rarely had the chance to try this themselves. When working with urban housing construction in Denmark, it can be challenging to get the opportunity—and permission—to build according to experimental ideas. A recurring challenge to the builders was the Danish building regulations (see Box 5.1).

Box 5.1: The Regulatory Framework for Construction in Denmark

The first national regulatory framework for construction was introduced in Denmark in 1961 (Engelmark 2014). Since then, regulations have continuously been revised. Today, The Danish Transport, Building and Construction Authority is responsible for developing the regulatory framework of construction work with support from research institutions specialized in construction. The framework consists of a legislative framework (*byggeloven*) and a set of technical regulations (*bygningsreglementet*), which outline the general technical requirements for new buildings. The requirements are based on so-called performance-based criteria. Hence, they outline how a final construction must perform and not how it should be built. When determining whether a given material performs according to these criteria, construction professionals draw on guidelines developed by the Department for the Built Environment or standards developed by committees organized by Dansk Standard (Danish Standards).[7] These committees consist of industry actors, researchers and representatives from interest organizations. Overall, Danish building regulations are considered among the strictest in Europe (Gram-Hanssen et al. 2017).

When building for someone else, the builders had to follow the strict conventions and regulations for construction in Denmark. This meant that they had, like all other craftworkers, to build walls from plastic, insulation, steel, and drywall. For some of them, this was a source of frustration, partly because it implied that they had to work with materials they were uncomfortable with. This was particularly the case with insulation materials.

THE INVISIBLE ELEMENTS OF CONSTRUCTION

During the daily work on construction sites, builders often suggested that I help with cutting and stuffing insulation materials. This is the perfect task for an untrained apprentice, as the procedure is fairly simple. The soft, yellow material is cut into the right size using a custom-made knife, which looks like a breadknife. Subsequently, the material is squeezed into the framing, finally ensuring that no ends of the material stick out.

Insulation material serves several purposes and is an important part of practically all the construction aspects of walls. Apart from preventing noise and fire from moving through buildings (one of the most important features), the material also contributes to thermal insulation. That is, it keeps buildings warm. Insulation materials have emerged as a key focus in contemporary discussions on how to improve the energy efficiency of the built environment. These discussions typically focus on the consumption of energy in construction and operations. So far, efforts to reduce this consumption have primarily focused on the thermal insulation of buildings (Gram-Hanssen et al. 2017). As a consequence, insulation has turned into a highly regulated and standardized area in construction in Denmark (Jensen 2014).[8] Insulation materials and techniques are therefore ubiquitous for the builders at KLAR.

During the time I spent on construction sites, I primarily came across one kind of insulation material: mineral wool.[9] Mineral wool comes in large batches tightly wrapped in plastic. The shape of the batches is similar, but the thickness of the insulation materials inside them varies, as diverse constructions require different amounts of insulation. Overall, the thickness depends on the function of the construction: Is it a wall or a ceiling? Is it an outer wall? What does the fire regulation specify? Does it have to be soundproof? These questions are typically evaluated and answered by an engineer or construction administrator when they outline the details of a given project.

To the untrained eye, pieces of insulation may look like pads of soft cotton. The fine fibers make them appear fluffy, and their pale, yellow surface somehow resembles the color of wood. However, after running your hands over this seemingly harmless material, you may notice a burning sensation on your skin. This experience might be supplemented by an itchy sensation in your eyes or a tickle in your nose that makes you sneeze more than usual if you engage with the material for longer periods.

The first time I assisted with an insulation installation, Liv and Astrid ensured that all three of us dressed up in safety wear to minimize bodily contact with the material. Although they did not say it directly, I got the impression that they wanted me to wear the entire outfit, which is in fact required when working with mineral wool. As such, they pulled out protective goggles, gloves, facemasks, and protective suits. They also opened doors and windows to ensure significant ventilation while we completed the installation. As we got dressed, I felt like I was dressing up in a plastic bag. The two of them explained that, in their experience, only a few construction workers take the necessary precautionary measures when working with insulation materials, as they do not like to waste time dressing up in safety wear. In most cases, many simply ensured that their regular workwear covered their exposed skin, and thus only occasionally wore protective goggles, gloves, and face masks. Upon completing the work, many would, however, rinse themselves with cold water (warm water opens the pores of the skin to the fibers of mineral wool) and perhaps change their T-shirt or sweatshirt.

Given the builders' mixed attitude toward the dangers of working with mineral wool, one could wonder whether all of these precautionary measures were important or whether some of the builders were overreacting. Various stakeholders in the construction industry—union representatives, the Danish Work Environment Authorities (DWEA) and similar institutions in other European countries—have debated this question for decades. In these discussions, it is generally argued that while working with mineral wool has historically caused harm to construction workers, contemporary materials do not pose similar health risks (see Box 5.2). However, over the past few years, the DWEA has changed its position. Its shifting stance has caused the unions to publicly declare that the organization is strongly influenced by industry lobbying (for example, Westh and Rebouh 2018). The builders at KLAR were, like the unions, skeptical of the declarations made by the DWEA. For them, past incidents have revealed that health implications resulting from exposure to certain materials might not become discernible until much later on.

Box 5.2: Mineral Wool

Mineral wool is produced from glass or rocks. It consists of mineral fibers—also referred to as synthetic vitreous fibers. When workers install mineral wool products, mineral fibers of varying sizes are released. The larger fibers can cause itching and rashes as they scratch the skin or irritate the eyes. The smaller fibers can block the nose and cause pain in the nose and throat. New regulations are currently being introduced in Denmark, which stress that specific precautionary measures must be taken when working with mineral wool installed before 1997, as older installations might be carcinogenic; and further, that alternatives to mineral wool should always be considered in any future construction projects (Beskæftigelsesministeriet 2021).

Such divergent perceptions of risk can be found in most contemporary societies (e.g., Douglas and Wildawsky 1982; Beck 1992). Risk assessments are not determined by "scientific monopoly," and there is thus "rarely expert agreement either on what constitutes acceptable risk, or on how it may be managed" (Caplan 2000: 3). As risk assessments often include biases, significant disjuncture can exist between community risk perceptions and official risk evaluations (Checker 2007). Rather than alleviating the risk of toxicity for communities, risk mitigation initiatives thus often end up reminding people of the toxic environment in which they live or work (Little 2012). As I think back to the day when Liv, Astrid, and I dressed up in safety gear, the latter also seems to be the case among the builders at KLAR. Apart from being an uncomfortable practical reality, the safety gear also served as a sort of mnemonic device that reminded the builders of the potential risks of working with hazardous materials like mineral wool. The outfit symbolically expressed how humans must keep a distance from these risky materials, which is at odds with the perceived material intimacy of woodwork discussed above.

These latent dangers present at construction sites were an ongoing concern to several of the builders who were worried about the long-term effects of working with hazardous materials, although some of them were occasionally hesitant to take the precautions stipulated by the regulations. The most cautious builders constantly paid attention to their own bodily reactions when interacting with these materials. Tracing their changing bodily reactions made them question whether the materials they were forced to work with when following the Danish building conventions and regulations could in fact be trusted. In this way, these builders drew certain connections between questions of materiality and politics in construction, thus engaging with what I recognize as *the material politics of construction work*. These builders turned their critical attention not only toward insulation materials, but also toward the general work conditions at construction sites. Consequently, even a material like dust became a question of politics among these builders.

THE POLITICAL ECONOMY OF DUST

Construction sites are dusty and dirty. Anyone who has been on a site knows this. Keeping sites organized and tidy is thus a Sisyphean task. Nonetheless, upholding cleanliness is an important precautionary measure, which alleviates the possible health implications of spending day after day in these environments. When cleaning construction sites, one must follow certain rules, which I had to learn as I began working there. Birger, one of the experienced builders at KLAR, came to my rescue one day, as I was close to breaking one of the most important rules.

Birger and the rest of the crew had worked on a project for about five months, which in brief comprised the retrofitting of a shelter, when I later joined them. As the project entailed the construction of a number of rooms, one of the main tasks was to install drywall, which is a rather straightforward job. First, walls, floors, and ceilings were measured to determine the position of the wall. Then, horizontal steel studs were attached to the ceiling and floor. Subsequently, studs were installed vertically between the horizontal studs with a 30 cm distance between each of them. Drywall was attached to one side of the studs using screws, and insulation was filled between them. Then, the second layer of drywall was attached to the other side of the studs. Finally, screws were placed every 15 cm at the top, bottom, center, and along the sides of the drywall. The process would then be repeated. Steel studs, drywall, insulation, drywall, screws, and so on. Some builders seemed to enjoy the repetitive procedure of this installation, while others considered it tedious and exhausting, as it was physically demanding to carry and install the 90 cm x 240 cm drywalls. Moreover, they disliked working in spaces filled with dust from the plaster of the drywall. Une described with a sense of concern how the dust made her hands and eyes feel dry, and added that she constantly had a dry taste in her mouth, as the small plaster particles pierced her mucous membranes.

"What to do with the anthropologist?" Birger wondered out loud as we walked around on the site together on one of my first mornings there. He soon realized that I was incapable of putting up drywall by myself, so he decided that I could help with the cleaning, which was necessary to reduce the dust from the plaster and fibers from the insulation material on the site. Birger pointed at one of the newly built rooms and told me that I could begin there. Lacking experience, yet doing my best to display an enthusiastic approach to the task assigned, I grabbed a broom and began to sweep the room. A few minutes later, Birger walked past the room where I was in the midst of sweeping. "You should never use a broom on a construction site," he said as he crossed the threshold into the room. Confused, I looked at the broom I was holding. I assume Birger noticed my facial expression as he anticipated my unarticulated question and added, "I don't know why we have a broom on this site." He explained that dust contains small particles, which can cause chronic obstructive pulmonary disease (COPD)—a lung disease characterized by long-term breathing problems and poor airflow. He added that brooms are banned from construction sites as they make dust swirl around. The only proper method of cleaning is, I learned, vacuuming.

While it has often been ignored or simply considered an unavoidable part of construction work, dust is, in fact, one of the most hazardous materials found on construction sites. Several of the builders working at KLAR were aware of this. Like Birger, they did their best to keep construction sites clean by organizing waste and vacuuming. While this reduced the amount of dust, it did not eliminate it. Knowing this, the builders were attentive to how these invisible materials affected their bodies. One day, for instance, Astrid initiated a conversation about dried mucus ("boogers"). While a blocked nose is customary when working on construction sites, Astrid asked me if I had ever looked at the paper after blowing my nose and noticed the small black lumps in the mucus.

On a more serious note, I got into a conversation with Sune about "Stone lungs"—a Danish expression for the condition of asbestosis—one day as we were driving back from a construction site. In a concerned tone, he asked if I had ever heard about the condition. I nodded and looked at him. "One of the older builders has it," Sune responded, keeping his gaze at the road. "Have you heard him cough? He sounds like a man in his eighties." I knew that the builder Sune was referring to was only close to turning forty. I had not heard him cough myself. But, knowing that he had worked as a builder for years, I was not surprised to hear that his health was in decline. Similarly, I also talked to Une about the health implications of working on construction sites. Une was particularly worried about what the exposure to certain materials, particularly insulation materials, might entail in the long term. "I can see the splinters in my finger," she said, "But I can't see the fibers in my lungs." The invisible fibers of mineral wool seemingly made her more uncomfortable than the perceptible sawdust produced from wood.

Yet, for many of the builders at KLAR, the potential health implications of working with the materials used in contemporary construction were not simply a question of the risks at work. One morning, Sune asked rather worryingly, "How can we make people live inside these materials when we have to dress up in safety gear every time we touch it?" Sune's intimate encounters with these materials—or his attempts to avoid such intimacy by wearing safety gear—had thus also made him question why housing constructions are built from these materials in the first place. Ruminations such as these made me realize that the builders connect their experience of potentially hazardous work environments on construction sites to a more general skepticism of contemporary building construction.

One of the younger builders, Stig, who has worked at KLAR for several years, drew my attention to this during an interview. I asked him whether the daily work of construction was different from what he had expected when he initially decided to undertake a vocational education in the skilled trades. "I was stunned at how dirty and contaminated the work environment is," he immediately replied. He was reminded about the hazards every time he was forced to wear masks, safety glasses, and other means of protection when working. He felt lucky that he was working for an enterprise that paid attention to these risks. "My impression is that only a few companies are concerned about these issues," he explained. Nonetheless, the risks of working in these environments made him reconsider whether he actually wanted to work in construction in the long run. "I have so much mistrust in the construction industry," he told me. He added that he did not want our talk to be "too political," but for him this mistrust was essentially about capitalism. "Capitalism is simply everywhere. Everything is about profit," he explained. As he elaborated on this reply, he told me that he had a strong disbelief in the manufacturers of construction materials. "Only a few suppliers are concerned about the safety of the worker or the work environment. They just have to make money, so they develop some great construction materials, which are also extremely toxic for the builders to be around," he explained. "Although they are newly developed products, they might contain some substance, which—in ten to twenty years—we'll realize that they were made out of some fucking crap," Stig said in an angry tone. "It's such a polluting industry, the construction industry. It bothers me a hell of a lot."

While few were as outspoken as Stig about their concerns, several builders seemed to share his critical reflections. Astrid, for instance, similarly stressed, on several occasions, that "capitalism" was the determining factor in construction. She explained that industry interests ultimately guided even the training of apprentices at the state-run technical schools, as they only learned to build with certain materials. During dinner after a Thursday afternoon assembly, another builder similarly argued that construction was all about "capitalism," as we discussed why certain products were used in contemporary masonry over others.

In the invisible particles and fibers often found on construction sites, Stig and other builders apparently saw the contours of an economic and political system that, in their view, determined the structure of contemporary construction. For them, the pursuit of profit had essentially destroyed the work environment for construction workers and building construction more generally in Denmark, as the industry was beholden to certain interests. This vigilance further fueled a general mistrust toward the entire construction industry.

Critical analyses of the work conditions at construction sites circulated among the builders in various forms. Newcomers were taught to ask critical questions about vapor barriers and to identify capitalist inequalities in the dust at construction sites, thus learning to make certain economic and political connections from the volatile conditions of construction sites. Their daily embodied experiences at construction sites became the source of the builders' social critique. These experiences allowed them to think about political economy on the ground in the context of changing regulatory power due to an intensified focus on the environmental impact of construction, and more generally shifting implications of capitalism. The builders' daily work at construction sites emerged as a heuristic through which they could grasp and analyze the historical inequalities that have come to define craftwork in Denmark, as in many other countries. In this way, their material and bodily engagement with craftwork at construction sites, and the contradictions, ambiguities, and inequities they faced as part of this work, also turned into an ideology as it provided them with an entry point for ordering their individual and collective conceptions of the world and the large-scale power structures that encompass these conceptions. To object to these contradictions, ambiguities, and inequities, the builders were constantly on the lookout for ways in which they could contest the standardization and uniformity imposed by prevalent building conventions, and perhaps even for ways in which they could transform the regulatory frameworks themselves.

TRANSFORMING REGULATORY FRAMEWORKS

Defining the contours of contemporary regulatory frameworks can be tricky. To better understand how regulatory frameworks were produced, I interviewed researchers, participated in public events, and took a course on the production of standards. This course took place in the headquarters of Dansk Standard, which is located in Copenhagen's Nordhavn district. This area, once an industrial port, had recently transformed from construction sites to a lively waterfront area with modern residential and business spaces. As I arrived at Nordhavn, I took the elevator to the top floor of one of the renowned buildings in the area where the course was being held. I was welcomed with fresh coffee, along with a folder of collected materials that was intended to showcase how important standards were to our everyday lives. The material included an image of stairs with steps of an unequal height and an image with different shapes and sizes of credit cards. In simple terms, the images underscored how challenging life would be in the absence of standardized systems. I spent the afternoon delving into these materials and the perception of standards implicitly guiding them, together with new employees from various large-scale companies. A few of them represented some of the manufacturers of construction materials, who I knew the builders were critical of. I could not help but think that the setting and content of this course was somehow worlds away from a construction site.

The course and the other activities mentioned above provided me with a deeper understanding of the importance that some actors ascribe to standardization. They also offered an overview of the different institutions and actors involved in producing and revising various elements of the regulatory frameworks for construction. Understanding how the interplay between research institutions, policymakers, and private actors have shaped regulatory frameworks in construction is a complex task. As an anthropologist, I am not an expert on building regulations; however, neither are the builders at KLAR. When I returned to the co-op after my excursions, I would, encouraged by builders like Astrid, share reflections or insights from these events and conversations. This also happened on the day I describe below.

One early morning, the slow conversation in the car heading toward a construction site on the outskirts of Copenhagen somehow ended up focusing on the regulatory frameworks for construction. Sune was driving, and I sat next to him in the front seat, while Astrid and an apprentice drowsily rested in the backseat. My eyes were focused on the mug of hot coffee in my hands. I did my best not to spill it, while Sune speedily steered the large truck through the narrow streets of the city. Sune asked what I had been doing for the past few days. I told him about the course that I had taken at Dansk Standard. Astrid interrupted from the backseat, "What is Dansk Standard?" I turned my head and told her briefly about the organization and the forty-six committees they facilitated, who supposedly produced standards for construction materials. I added that, "It seems like three of them are working on insulation directly or indirectly," assuming that she would be interested in knowing this. "You're an anthropologist. Why are you interested in this?" Sune asked, as the truck hit the gravel on the construction site. "Because it matters to you," I responded, unsure whether he could hear my reply through the noise of the car tires crunching through the gravel.

Our fleeting conversation in the car had sparked Astrid's curiosity. She returned to the topic several times during the day while we worked together. Excited about the turn my research was, in her view, taking, she wanted to know more about the production of standards in relation to construction materials. "Can you present some of it at one of our collective events?" she asked. Maybe, I responded, unsure what she was expecting. "People have a difficult time grasping all of these technical details," she stated. "It's simply too difficult. But it has such a great impact. It defines our work."

Like Astrid, many of the builders were keen to find ways to better understand the governmental regimes for contemporary construction. However, the builders also continuously grappled with apprehending and defining the contours of these regimes. The relations between the state authorities, research institutions, and industrial interests that seemingly shape these regimes were often the locus of intense speculation, as the builders debated how and why regulations require certain solutions and not others. A recurrent concern aired by builders was who and what in fact determined the building regulations in Denmark. Like Astrid, in the situation depicted above, and Stig, in the conversation I recounted earlier, builders would often speculate about the medley of political and industrial interests affecting the content of these regulations, which, in their opinion, promoted the use of certain construction materials over others. For the builders, these regimes seemingly appeared nebulous, and finding the right place for intervention was difficult. Indeed, how does one contest the configuration of capitalism that builders such as Stig identify in the dust on construction sites? Frustrated by the lack of discussion on the political aspect of regulatory processes, the builders often organized workshops, and invited researchers and other building professionals to give talks at the co-op. They wanted to mobilize these various actors in a common struggle against the increasing standardization and uniformity determining building regulations. Moreover, they occasionally addressed disputes with individual contractors directly. This was what happened in the case of the fire test that opened this chapter.

After Yrsa's outburst of excitement, we all sat in wonder. None of us had heard about the fire test nor about the specific project which had seemingly instigated the test. The project, which in brief entailed the construction of a recreational center, had been presented as ambitious from the outset, Yrsa explained. The client and contractor had enthusiastically agreed to build the entire construction from wood, including the insulation in the walls, where the builders had used wood fiber insulation (one of the materials they were currently trying to introduce instead of mineral wool). However, after the builders had completed the project, both the client and the contractor grew uneasy, questioning whether the construction truly complied with the fire protection measures detailed in Danish building regulations. Yrsa had followed the project during the entire construction phase, and had been part of the subsequent dialogue with the contractor and client. Discussions had moved back and forth for some months. At some point, Erik had resolutely decided to order a test that would assess the composition and qualities of the material and its suitability for use in construction according to Danish building standards. The builders' dispute with the contractor and client of this specific project had turned into a matter of principle regarding the use of wood fiber insulation in construction. With his tenacious attitude, Erik had apparently not seen any solution other than getting KLAR to pay for a validation test to calm the nerves of the contractor. By doing so, the builders also hoped to obtain evidence that could finally support their (and others') claim that wood fiber is a safe, effective, and sustainable insulation material. The builders had subsequently reproduced a subsection of the construction so a technician could test how long the construction could withstand fire.

Disputes like this between clients, contractors, subcontractors, and similar stakeholders are mundane occurrences in the construction process, as the different parties debate questions of risk and responsibility unremittingly. Yet, I find the builders' toil with this particular project illuminating for understanding how they turned their ongoing engagement with the politics of materiality in construction into action. Rather than merely engaging in verbal contests, which they evidently did too, they also sought to alter the very regulations that determined their choice of materials in construction projects through specific encounters, such as the one narrated here.

In situations like these, the builders deliberately sought ways of testing the premises and boundaries of the regulatory frameworks for construction. In doing so, the builders, I argue, deliberately engaged with a form of attentive and meticulous experimentation—that is, they tinkered not only with novel building materials and techniques, but also with the regulatory frameworks and prevalent building conventions in Denmark. This demanded that they engage with the constantly shifting asymmetrical fields of power that characterize the Danish construction industry, with its multiple actors and stakeholders, and reconfigure their strategies and actions in accordance with these. Hence, they had to navigate the various governmental fields that characterized the apparatuses of power typically faced by contemporary resisters.[10] In this process, the builders had to engage with the kind of practical, creative, and attentive experimentation under contingent circumstances that inherently characterizes their aspiration and ability to tinker.

CONCLUDING REMARKS

This chapter has traversed the vast material and regulatory terrain of construction in contemporary Denmark to explore how the builders at KLAR worked on politicizing materiality in building construction. For them, construction materials were not simply about the composition of buildings; they also impacted their daily work environment and, furthermore, were key to limiting the future impact of the built environment on climate change. When evaluating the quality and environmental effect of materials, the builders drew on their intimate bodily encounters with the materiality of construction. They relied, in other words, on their "wise hands" and the bodily knowledge that they gained from tactility. Their daily craftwork taught them that materials are not merely functional tools that are easy to control; rather, their intimate engagement with materials such as wood led them to consider materiality as shifting, changing, surprising, and adaptable. It is this attention to diversity, I argue, which they sought to bring back into construction in Denmark. In doing so, the builders faced the uniformity that has increasingly defined housing construction since the postwar building boom and which has somehow turned the standards of craft and the standardization of construction into an oxymoron. Whether or not it is possible to alter the historical trajectory of construction is a complicated question. Yet, for most of the builders working at KLAR, it nonetheless seemed worth trying as they determinedly sought ways to tinker with the construction industry and bring back attention to the possibilities of craftwork.

Working with construction in Denmark implies operating in complicated legal and economic terrains. Technical and regulatory disputes over building construction are, for the builder, envisioned and enacted as political struggles. While the strict regulatory frameworks for construction evidently complicate these struggles, they also provide the builders with technical tools and ideas through which they can challenge prevalent conventions in construction. Counter to general perceptions, advanced legal and regulatory frameworks like Danish building regulations do not always prevent grassroots actors from intervening. At times, they also provide a direction or resource through which these very same frameworks can be contested and rethought. As the builders resolutely decided to order and pay for a fire test of their wood construction, they used regulations and associated test practices as a transformative opportunity that had the potential to make other types of regulation possible.

The builders' attempts to change regulatory frameworks for construction have thus shown how the builders at KLAR engaged with cooperative craftwork as a source of critical resistance to hegemonic regulatory and political structures in the Danish construction sector. To the builders, craftwork was not just a technical activity; it also involved reflecting on one's role within larger societal structures. In this regard, it also emerged as an ideology among the builders. The builders' everyday encounters with the contradictions, ambiguities, and inequities that have historically come to define craftwork allowed the builders at KLAR to understand and sometimes subvert the systems they were a part of, leading to personal and collective transformation. It was through such operations that the builders sought to turn KLAR into a "power base," as Henning said in the Introduction.

A central aim of this chapter was to show how the constantly shifting asymmetrical fields of power in which the builders work has led them to reconfigure their strategies and actions. It is this kind of collective, practical, and creative experimentation under contingent circumstances that I seek to grasp with the notion of *tinkering together*. In the following chapter, we shall see how the builders similarly put their ability to tinker to work in the entangled collaborations, complex supply chains, and ever-evolving urban political economy defining construction in the city.

NOTES

1. Early anthropological studies focused on the ritual form of sacrifice and the gift-giving logic of this form. More recent contributions question the idea of a universal sacrificial logic and have, instead, proposed to approach sacrifice as a "near-universal phenomenon" (Hubert and Mauss 1981).
2. The builders at KLAR might not be fully comparable to artisans, such as French chocolatiers (Terrio 2000) or US artisanal cheesemakers (Paxson 2013). Yet their search to redefine the meaning of craftwork in contemporary construction includes attempts to reintroduce techniques and materials previously used in construction, such as clay, wood and lime. In this way, their practices carry elements of artisanship.
3. As World War II ended, Denmark—like other European countries—faced a significant lack of housing, as construction projects were halted during the war, while urbanization simultaneously accelerated. To deal with this situation, policymakers sought to redefine construction in the early postwar years. As Danish engineer Sven Bertelsen (1997) explains this decision implied that so-called planning engineers increasingly took control of projects and their efforts to "rationalize" increasingly guided building construction, which, inter alia, entailed an increase in the use of prefabricated elements (Bertelsen 1997). As others have argued, this amplified what is generally described as a "path dependence" in construction, which implies that the use of specific materials and building techniques came to define other decisions beyond the building process (Jensen 2014). During the 1950s and 1960s, standardized products and predetermined supply chains thus became fundamental to construction in Denmark, which changed housing construction radically—not only materially, but also in terms of the organization of the work, as craftworkers were demoted from the overall planning and practical stages of work on projects.
4. The expression "wise hands" (*kloge hænder*) is used broadly in educational and professional contexts related to craftwork in Denmark. In 2013, the Danish politician Mattias Tesfaye published a book entitled *Wise hands: In Defense of Craftwork and Professionalism* [my translation]. It is debatable whether or not the expression was coined by Tesfaye for this particular publication.
5. In a similar vein to Sennett, Timothy Ingold describes the skilled maker as "one whose movement is continually and subtly responsive to the modulations of her relation with the material" (Ingold 2000: 357). More specifically, Ingold proposes that we think of the maker as "a participant in amongst a world of active materials," and in the process of making "he [*sic*] 'joins forces' with them, bringing them together or splitting them apart, synthesizing and distilling, in anticipation of what might emerge" (Ingold 2013: 21).
6. This particular model of construction is still rare in Denmark, but is beginning to emerge in certain parts of the country. In discussions on this topic, the builders would typically refer to one house in particular, completed in 2015.
7. Danish Standards is the national standardization organization in Denmark. They contribute to the work of the European and the International Organization for Standardization (ISO).
8. Energy conservation in the built environment has been a concern in Denmark since 1973, when the global energy crisis hit Denmark. This sparked a golden age for insulation materials. In 1979, an amendment was added to the Danish building regulations, which for the first time in history specified regulation of the use of insulation

in construction (Engelmark 2014). Energy conservation was, as scholars have noted, from this moment on, defined as a matter of design and not a matter of housing operation (Jensen 2014). From the 1970s onward, discussions on energy conservation in construction have only intensified. Today, it is well-known that building construction and operations account for 36 percent of global energy use (IEA and UNEP 2018). In Denmark, the building regulations' energy provisions have been continually tightened over the course of almost four decades. This has turned insulation into a highly regulated and standardized aspect of construction work (Jensen 2014). Yet the aforementioned framing of energy conservation as a matter of design and not housing operation is currently being re-evaluated. Research has shown that estimated energy savings are not met, as projections are based on non-realizable ideals. This finding indicates that design and operation have to be reintegrated in order to find new ways of evaluating energy consumption in construction (see, e.g., Birgisdottir et al. 2019; Gram-Hanssen et al. 2020).

9. While Danish companies producing these materials offer sophisticated products and reliable production, they also, according to some scholars, managed to influence the writing of regulations and standards significantly. According to Jesper Holm and Inger Stauning (2007), since the introduction of the aforementioned amendment in building regulations in 1979, preferential treatment has been given to mineral wool and thus limited the possibility of using other products, such as cellulose insulation (paper), which is typically used in Sweden, and expanded polystyrene, typically used in Germany.
10. In his comparative account of Burmese grassroots activists and Rohingya civil society actors, Elliott Prasse-Freeman (2020) makes this assertion as he seeks to develop a conceptual framework for attending to how contemporary subjects navigate the various governmental fields that characterize contemporary apparatuses of power.

CHAPTER 6

TINKERING WITH CAPITALISM

The Production of Value in Construction Projects

The builders have taken part in countless construction projects since KLAR was launched in 2001. In the main office of the co-op, one finds a range of colorful, large-scale pictures of selected projects, including pictures of wooden buildings bathed in a sunset glow, refurbished apartments in bright colors, newly made balconies or rooftop terraces bursting with green plants and urban wind turbines moving in the wind. On a few occasions, some of the founding members made references to some of these or other past projects. Some projects were, for various reasons, more memorable than others.

This was, for instance, the case with a project Henning mentioned in a passing remark during a social gathering one afternoon. He explained that the builders had bought a house in the suburbs of Copenhagen shortly before the financial collapse in 2008. They had intended to retrofit the entire building and turn it into four modernized apartments, which they could subsequently sell or rent to a housing collective. A disappointed smile appeared on Henning's face as he revealed that the project had turned out differently than expected. First, the building license had been delayed, which had postponed the project for months. Second, the costs of the remodeling had exceeded the initial budget. "We ended up selling it to some random people in the middle of the crash," Henning explained, adding, "We lost so much money on it."

Listening to the builders' stories about past building projects drew my attention to KLAR's diverse project portfolio. Rather than dedicating themselves to one specific task, as most other construction enterprises do, the

Figure 6.1. A customized storage solution in wood. Photo by Brian Berg.

builders had evidently taken part in a variety of projects. Henning's tale of the above project further made me aware that they had also occasionally taken on the role of contractors and investors in projects. In fact, I realized during my fieldwork that the building with the bright colored facade—the main building at KLAR—was not the builders' only property investment. The co-op also owned two buildings and a few workshops in the metropolitan area of Copenhagen. They further controlled the tenancy agreements of several housing units in the city, which provided affordable housing opportunities for younger people working at KLAR. During an interview, I asked Erik about the co-op's real estate portfolio as I wanted to understand how he differentiated between KLAR's property investments and real estate investments made, for instance, by investment funds. The conversation went like this:

Maia: I've been wondering what role profit plays in your enterprise?

Erik: Profit is both good ... Something can be profitable. The word in itself isn't bad, if we understand profit as what's left when everything else is paid off. It's basically what you're left with, it's what you've earned. It's the blood that all companies need. But what do you do with the profit? Do you withdraw it from the company or do you reinvest? Profit is part of the drive. It's like there is an ecological balance, where you cultivate the land and add nutrients so you don't deplete the soil. The economy is similar to this. It's a mechanism that you have to feed. Speculation is to withdraw value from those who have created it. You release value from things, giving you a value without a source, an unrestrained value, which you can invest in something new. All of these buy-out activities in Copenhagen and the world, that is the equity funds draining value. At some point, they withdraw when the surplus is at a maximum, and then they simply leave houses and buildings and people with a huge debt.

Maia: I remember that it surprised me that you also own quite a few properties?

Erik: It's called a property portfolio.

Maia: Would you call that speculation?

Erik: Yes. A kind of. But again, the word has different meanings. The reason why we invested in property is that we didn't want to pay installments on other people's loans. If you're leasing, you pay for other people's loans and after thirty years you'll have paid the piper and they get the entire surplus. Profit and speculation need to benefit the collective. I would rather have seventy people own this property than one person. I often have to explain to people that we live in a capitalist treadmill. We can dance attendance and choose any name we like. But it is the daily operations that count. I have to get inside the head of these people every single day, so we can act like them. We can't run a co-op in a capitalist society without thinking like that.

In this brief exchange, Erik answered several questions that I had pondered for a while. First, he explained that words such as "speculation" and "profit" evidently have multiple meanings. For him, the significance of these concepts depended on whether they were targeted at collective or individual gain. Second, he also hinted that, in his view, certain solutions and decisions were inevitable if the builders wanted to succeed in running a co-op. In his words, the builders had "to think" and "act like [capitalists]" if they want to "run a co-op in a capitalist society."

A key aim for the builders at KLAR and other contemporary cooperative practitioners and advocates in Denmark was to contest what they described widely as "capitalism." This might not be a surprise. Cooperative practitioners in Argentina, for instance, similarly present cooperativism as a counter logic to neoliberal capitalism (Faulk 2008). The question of whether or not cooperativism constitutes an anti-thesis to capitalism has also been a returning issue among scholars. As mentioned in the Introduction, Marx was one of the first to raise this concern as he debated whether co-ops represent "the first sprouts of the new," or if they simply reproduce "the shortcomings of the prevailing system" (Marx, *Capital III*, in Bottomore 1991: 112). The questions initially raised by Marx have since been debated. To verify the former claim by Marx, scholars have presented co-ops or similar associations as attempts to create enclaves of "good" economic practice or "islets of benign capitalism" in what cooperative practitioners and advocates often perceive as "a sea of sociocultural malice" (Rakopoulos 2018: 4). Yet this assertion has naturally been debated, as scholars have questioned whether you can in fact "seal out economic life from the social fodder it is embedded in" (ibid.).[1] While this chapter and the book as a whole similarly aim to explore the relationship between cooperativism and capitalism, the analytical focus applied in this chapter in particular departs from this scholarship.[2] Rather than questioning whether these organizations provide an alternative to capitalism, I seek to understand how the builders at KLAR themselves reflected upon and sought to understand the relationship between their cooperative craft endeavor and capitalism.

Throughout the chapters of this book, the builders have brought up concerns related to capitalism in various contexts, ranging from climate change to dust at construction sites. The builders' diverse depictions of capitalism indicated that, like other political activists studied by anthropologists, they perceived capitalism as pervasive, persistent and "intrinsic to all relations," which implies that "there is, so to speak, no Archimedean point from where capitalism can be perceived and attacked in its totality; rather, it demands constant work to keep the encroachment of capitalism at bay" (Krøijer 2015: 54–55). In this chapter, I home in on the constant work that the builders had to perform "to keep the encroachment of capitalism at bay." To do so, I take Erik's assertion that cooperative practitioners, like the builders at KLAR, have to "act *like* capitalists" as a starting point. Interestingly, his words seem to indicate that the builders' cooperative endeavor is in fact an attempt to imitate the workings of capitalism. That is, rather than seeking to battle the capitalist market system, they try to imitate its logics deliberately with the goal of managing and perhaps eventually ending it. Yet how can cooperative practitioners simultaneously act within and beyond a capitalist market system?

A distinct string of anthropological scholarship has paid attention to resemblances of this double movement for decades. A shared focus in this scholarship has been the concept of mimesis.[3] A recent contribution to this field draws on a study of the Siberian Yukaghirs (Willerslev 2007). Among the Yukaghirs, social actors who engage in acts of mimicry must "constantly steer a difficult course between analogy and identity" as "mimesis becomes totalizing [if] the imitator loses himself [*sic*] in what he imitates" (Willerslev 2007: 12). As in this case, the notions of analogy and identity have often been key terms in studies of processes of mimesis, as they account for the difference between being *alike* (analogy) or being *the same* (identity). Moreover, they have also been central to examinations of power relations in processes of mimesis. As the above study among the Yukaghirs shows, mimesis can open up a space of potentiality, as social actors can "imitate significant and powerful others not simply to represent them, but also to exercise power over them" (ibid.: 11). Yet, this raises the question: in which ways do "the copy [have] to resemble the original in order for the copy to take power over what it is a copy of?" (ibid.). The purpose of what follows is to explore how the builders attempted to resolve this question as they tried to "act *like* capitalists," and how they, in this process, balanced the challenge of analogy and identity. Like others, I am thus concerned with understanding how mimetic practice can be applied instrumentally in political and economic activism (Jerne 2025).

Ethnographically, the chapter focuses on the socioeconomic spaces and contexts in which the builders explicated and negotiated the values they sought to produce by working on construction projects. I am particularly concerned with examining how builders have perceived these values to differ from those associated with the broader capitalist market system in Danish society. The purpose of exploring these questions is to demonstrate how the builders have worked to carve out a new value system *from within* the capitalist market system by tinkering with the values they produced through craftwork. The chapter, in other words, seeks to unfold how the builders put their ability to tinker to work in the entangled collaborations, complex supply chains, and ever-evolving urban political economy, which they—as urban builders—have, inevitably, become part of.[4]

To make this argument, I shall outline the trajectory of three selected building projects, and the builders' evaluations of these, to explore how they sought to balance the challenge of analogy or identity inherent in processes of mimesis. This balance has been achieved by their practically and symbolically "investing" and "divesting" in various ways and to different degrees in the three distinct projects. Yet the builders' decision to invest or divest in a given project can end up as a perilous endeavor, as we shall see, since their perception of the value of projects sometimes changes during the work process.

PROJECT 1: REMODELING A FACADE AND "FUTURE-PROOFING" THE CITY

I heard about this project for the first time during an assembly where Erik referred to it as "the construction work of the future." To put it briefly, the project was a typical facade remodeling of a larger multistory housing complex in the inner part of Copenhagen. While this was work that most of the builders were familiar with, this particular project was part of a larger urban renewal scheme to turn Copenhagen's residential districts into "climate-resilient neighborhoods." The development program was managed by the Municipality of Copenhagen and involved several stakeholders, ranging from leading architectural firms to construction material manufacturers. By redesigning streets, "greening" urban spaces and courtyards, and renewing residential housing, the Municipality hoped to "future-proof" the city. The facade remodeling was, it turned out, merely a small piece in a larger visionary puzzle.

The aim of the project was to develop novel solutions to improve the energy efficiency of aging multistory housing while preserving the architectural heritage of the neighborhood. The particular remodeling which the builders would be working on was a trial run for a newly developed technical system comprised of prefabricated elements made from wood, aluminum profiles, and insulation. The builders were tasked with installing the prefabricated elements to the extant building facade. As the work was due to begin, a crew was assigned. Birger was selected as crew supervisor, and the crew consisted of a few newly employed builders and a couple of apprentices. After being introduced to the plan and practicalities of the work, the crew started to set up the construction site. A tall scaffold was built and materials were ordered and organized.

First, the builders added a timber framework to the existing brick facade. As part of this process, some windows were changed or converted into balconies to improve the indoor climate and lighting conditions of the housing units. Subsequently, the prefabricated elements were attached to the timber framework and the front of the building was replaced. As part of the reconstruction, ventilation, wiring, and drainage systems were also upgraded to, among other things, enable rainwater reuse.

A couple of months into the project, the Municipality invited stakeholders and the public to a *rejsegilde* (topping out ceremony) to celebrate the completion of the program's first milestones. Topping out is an ancient Scandinavian tradition that involves a sort of blessing ceremony to celebrate the completion of a building.[5] This particular ceremony took place in a courtyard surrounded by a cluster of housing complexes that the builders were in the process of remodeling. As I entered the courtyard, I instantly felt the festive atmosphere. Someone was serving coffee at a table and another was grilling sausages on the barbecue—a typical feature at a Danish topping out ceremony. The size of the crowd was, however, unusually big: close to fifty people had gathered for the event. The official program further stated that one of the mayors of Copenhagen and the minister of housing would arrive later. I had expected to see some of the builders from the crew at the ceremony, but I spotted only Erik. I wondered where the other builders were.

The prefabricated materials used in the project were displayed on a wall along with architectural drawings of the remodeling. I walked over to view the exhibition. Erik approached me and said, almost laughing, "Someone has to comment on the stupidity of this project. Do I really have to do it?" He pointed at the structure showcased on the wall and explained that the leftover materials were not suitable for recycling as wood and insulation can only be recycled separately. Consequently, all of the material leftovers had to be disposed of in a separate depository for mineral wool products. "In a few years, people will laugh at projects like these," he said in a loud voice. Erik's perspective surprised me. "Why are you part of the project?" I asked. He shrugged his shoulders, "It's work," adding that it is also a way of getting involved in urban planning in the city. "Now, we're part of the task force working on sustainable urban renewal in Copenhagen," he said with a sneaky smile.

A few weeks later, I talked to some of the builders who were working on this project. I realized that they were, like Erik, quite skeptical about the direction in which the project was heading. Adam, who had worked on the project for some time, seemed especially disappointed. After an afternoon assembly, he swiped through some pictures on his phone that he had taken during the workday. He showed some of them to Astrid and me and described some of the difficulties of adapting the new system to the existing construction. Adam remarked mournfully that it was tragic to see what they (the Municipality) were planning to do with housing in Copenhagen. Astrid responded that projects like these made her feel blue. Adam emphasized that the new system only resulted in excessive use of materials. Astrid shook her head.

The excessive use of materials in contemporary building construction was a returning concern among the builders at KLAR. According to them, reusability is key to reducing the future impact of construction on climate change. The neglect of this concern in the above project, therefore, sparked criticism among them. As Adam and Erik's comments demonstrate, they started to lose faith in the project, and its large institutional framework drew further skepticism about stakeholder incentives.

Indeed, this was not the only project that in one way or another ended up disappointing the builders at KLAR; projects often, it seemed, fell short of fulfilling the builders' hopeful aspirations. For example, this was the case with the project where the builders installed the many drywalls (the retrofitting of the shelter). Although the drywall project had initially sounded interesting, certain adjustments were made to comply with an updated planning permission order from the Municipality as the work was close to commencing, which ended up changing the direction of the project. According to the builders I spoke to, the architectural company had consequently withdrawn the innovative ideas initially guiding the project, and it had ended up being a repetition of conventional construction methods and materials.

These situations left the builders with a conundrum, because they, despite their growing skepticism about the projects, were contractually obliged to complete them. Hence, they seemingly had little choice other than to finalize the work. Yet, as the builders' missing participation in the topping out ceremony—an event where craftworkers have historically been important guests—demonstrates, they did occasionally find other ways of expressing their dissatisfaction with projects which they considered futile. Yet how should we understand the diverse strategies applied by the builders in their efforts to handle and occasionally showcase their dissatisfaction?

THE OBSCURATION OF PRODUCTION PROCESSES

The builders' refusal to participate in the topping out ceremony calls to mind what has been described as quotidian acts of resistance. An example of such acts of resistance is when subordinate actors refuse to accept definitions of reality imposed from "above."[6] This could be one way to explain the builders' rejection of the topping out ceremony. This rather minor act of opposition, one could argue, reveals their refusal to accept the ideological framework of the project as defined by municipal stakeholders and similar actors. While this could be a valid interpretation, theoretical conceptions of quotidian acts of resistance also have certain weaknesses. More specifically, their basic categorizations and conceptualization of human agency and particularly the use of binaries to categorize subordinate and superior actors have often been critiqued as they are too simplistic to account for potential shifts in positioning that can occur between such categories.[7] Indeed, this binary would probably locate the builders within the social category of subordinate, which seems insufficient to describe agentive subjects like the builders at KLAR. Hence, we need a more complex understanding of agency to understand the diverse strategies applied by the builders in their efforts to handle and occasionally showcase their dissatisfaction. A brief return to one of the conversations Erik and I had regarding the facade project described above will further illuminate this perspective.

During an interview, I asked Erik what the builders usually do in situations when the course of a project, like the facade project, takes an undesirable turn. "I could feel how all of the energy disappeared at that moment. Now, we simply have to finish the project as quickly as possible, make some money, and leave as soon as possible," he explained. Our dialogue continued:

Maia: But how do you navigate the needs of the different clients? Do you think it is important to make compromises?

Erik: I like to challenge all of our clients. But when someone wants business as usual, they'll get business as usual.

Maia: So you're not a hardliner in these situations?

Erik: No, but they might also lose something. Something they could have gained without a cost.

Maia: What's that?

Erik: The energy. They won't receive any love, they won't get any additional work, we won't stick around a bit longer, we won't organize any additional meetings.

What Erik communicates in this brief exchange is that, although one might be caught in contractual obligations, one can always choose to withdraw "energy" from projects. This "energy," it seems, covers different actions and sentiments, ranging from "love," "additional work," and "additional meetings," to simply spending some extra time on a given task. So, rephrasing Erik's argument: if clients or collaborators shifted the direction of a project or decided to use materials or methods that the builders disagreed with, then the builders' work effort might also change.

Here we begin to see not only why a more complex understanding of agency is required to comprehend the builders' actions, but also how the builders differentiate between the various construction projects, not just in terms of the actual time spent working on them, but also in terms of the symbolic importance associated with and invested in them. As Erik's explanation suggests, they do so by imbuing certain projects with more "energy" than others. Yet how are we to understand this category of "energy" and the value that it seemingly might add to construction projects?

One of the central topics of economic anthropology, namely value and its social origins, can help unfold this line of inquiry. These studies have a long legacy in anthropology.[8] In more recent work, scholars have built on insights from this legacy to show how characteristics, such as alienation, normally linked to the category of either the "gift" or the "commodity" can also be associated with the other. Certain objects, such as silver from a Mexican mining co-op, can emerge as "inalienable commodities" (Ferry 2002), or artisanal cheese from the United States can be perceived as an "unfinished commodity" (Paxson 2013). From a more general perspective, craft commodities are generally "imbued with and are the bearers of the social identities of their makers and for this reason retain certain inalienable properties" (Terrio 2000: 71). That is, "possessions that are imbued with the intrinsic and ineffable identities of their owners" (Weiner 1992: 6). Overall, these studies show that for objects to emerge *as* commodities, a certain kind of work is needed. It is precisely this point concerning the indeterminacy of the value and exchange of commodities that can help us understand Erik's description of "energy"; this might be exactly the kind of work that the builders are doing as they differentiate between and reassess the projects they are engaged in. To accomplish this work of differentiation and value creation, the builders are seemingly, if we follow Erik's explanation, imbuing certain projects with "energy" through a form of "symbolic investment," whereas they remove "energy" from others through a kind of "symbolic divestment."[9]

Let me exemplify this by returning to the facade project outlined above. Now, we can consider the builders' refusal to participate in the topping out ceremony as an attempt to dissociate themselves from the project. From a different perspective, the builders' lack of participation could suggest that they were somehow trying to conceal their own participation in the work. By "performing an 'objective' relation" (Højer and Pedersen 2019: 163) to the project, the builders indirectly concealed the labor and social relations constituent of their work. By abandoning the ceremony, the builders thus deliberately embraced and performed a creative form of "commodity fetishism," as they actively obscured the production process from the finished project. By engaging with this creative form of "commodity fetishism" the builders thus managed to establish distinct, and thus also diverse, relations to the projects they worked on. By symbolically investing and divesting in the projects, the builders were, in other words, able to construct different identities tailored to each of the projects they worked on. This is a key strategy in their efforts to balance the dangers of mimicking capitalist logics. To ensure that they do not come too close—that is, develop a relation of identity or sameness—to the production of value in a capitalist market system, the builders deliberately sought to either obscure or, as I shall later demonstrate in more detail, to emphasize their relation to the work they performed in individual construction projects.

Yet seeking to imbue projects with different kinds of "energy" can create confusion, as it assumes that the builders know exactly when and how to either invest or divest their "energy" in each project. Resolving this puzzle could potentially be a challenge. This was, for instance, the case in the refurbished rooftop house project. I recount the completion of this project in the following section to show how Astrid came to view this particular project as an ambiguous endeavor.

PROJECT 2: REPURPOSED MATERIALS AND COLLABORATIVE ENTANGLEMENTS

The final stage of this project comprised the installment of the rooftop houses at their destined location: a newly erected five-story building in a suburban area of Copenhagen. Sune, Astrid, and I drove to the site in one of KLAR's trucks, while a crane truck picked up the small wooden houses at the workshop, transferred them to the site and subsequently lifted them to the top of the building. The relocation was a complex but swift task, Sune explained as we were driving in the truck. He had done it several times, but Astrid and I were new to this. The work would take place in stages, Sune said. When the crane truck arrived, the driver would lift the house to the roof. Our job was to steer them according to the sill plate preinstalled on the roof—and to take the strips and hooks off the house once in place. Subsequently, the truck driver would drive back to the workshop and pick up another house. This would perhaps take an hour, during which we could drink coffee and get some food, Sune said and smiled crookedly.

As we arrived at the site, we climbed up to the roof, each carrying the requisite tools: screwdrivers, impact wrenches, a couple of buckets with screws, some crowbars, and a large hammer. Astrid and I took a walk as we reached the top to see the houses already located on the roof. "The truck is here," Sune shouted from the other side of the roof after a while. The lifting began. I stepped back, awaiting orders from Sune. He hollered at Astrid, who was standing at the front part of the house, "Push more!" Astrid was shoving with her entire body. I rushed to help her. The house was slowly approaching the sill plate, while Astrid and I were standing on our toes pushing. The house was lowered down to only a few inches above the plate. Extreme precision was needed. "Try to push it with a crowbar," Sune commanded and indicated to the driver that he should lift the house slightly. On the second attempt, we succeeded.

Pursuant to the plan, the crane truck left after the first couple of houses had been installed on the rooftop. It was time for the awaited break. Sune took the coffeepot and walked toward a sunny spot at the other end of the rooftop. Astrid and I followed suit. After the exchange of a few everyday concerns, the topic of our conversation changed to the project stakeholders. Sune seemed like he was skeptical of the other companies taking part in the project. I asked whether he or Astrid knew who they were. Astrid shook her head. I had done a bit of research on this specific project, so I casually mentioned the name of the contractor, the investor financing the entire project and a few of the companies that had also taken part. Astrid turned her gaze and looked straight at me. "Who is paying for this?" she asked with a concerned look on her face. I told her that, as far as I knew, the contractor was a large private equity fund. Astrid looked at me with a worried expression, "Are they one of the bad ones? Are they similar to the others?" I answered that they were currently financing a large amount of real estate development in Copenhagen. "You could probably say that they work in real estate speculation," I ended up answering, perhaps to Astrid's disappointment.

The role and responsibility of private equity funds in the current urban development of Copenhagen had been a recurrent topic of discussion between Astrid and me from the outset of my fieldwork. Astrid introduced the subject during one of our first lunches together, where she critically uttered that, "everyone can end up a property shark under these circumstances." I asked her what it might, in her opinion, require to alter or reverse the development of the city. She looked at me, discouraged, and answered "That's a good question. What do you think?" In answering her own question, Astrid resumed her explanation after a brief pause, "I think change emerges in collectives where people develop new principles. You need to raise the low point and make sure that everyone commits to a set of new common rules." Our initial talk left me with several questions, which I posed on later occasions when Astrid and I continued our conversation on this or related topics.

Many of the builders at KLAR were, like Astrid, skeptical of the current urban development of Copenhagen, and especially the growing influence of actors such as private equity funds, real estate developers, and capital investors, who were all, according to the builders, lining up to take part in flipping urban land for profit. During a few assemblies, in the discussion group, and at a couple of public seminars on urban development convened at KLAR, the builders discussed how these actors currently affected the development of the city.

One recurrent question ran through these discussions: How should the builders situate their own work—both political and practical—within these larger economic frameworks? One of the dilemmas mentioned and discussed by Astrid and others was that the builders, with their work retrofitting the existing housing stock of Copenhagen, inevitably contributed to the rising house prices in the city. Their daily craftwork, in other words, contributed to shaping the future material, economic, and political urban landscape of Copenhagen. I heard several of the builders frame this concern by stating that they—with their often beautiful and costly renovations—are building a city that they cannot themselves afford to live in. When making this point, the builders often referred to their efforts to introduce novel and more environmentally friendly materials and methods into building construction. In these projects, costs could not always be a determining factor, which meant that the builders ended up working for clients who could afford and appreciate such innovation. Their line of reasoning thus implied that they, by developing products that primarily served a niche, also built against their own belief of the city as an inclusive space.

As this reveals, Astrid's remark regarding the contractor of the rooftop house project was a manifestation of a complex set of concerns regarding the impact of the builders' work on the current political economy of the urban development of Copenhagen. Yet, as her reaction to my description of the collaborative framework of the project indicates, discerning the potential effects of a given construction project could be a challenging task. Although the builders had initially been supportive of this specific construction project owing to its focus on refurbished construction materials, the revelation of who the contractor of the project was (potentially a private financial actor) might also make the impact of the project more dubious, at least in the eyes of Astrid. Drawing on the discussion on energy and value from the previous section, it could thus seem as if Astrid had unwittingly invested energy in the work of a project, from which she would rather, in fact, divest.

As this case shows, the builders were not always capable of knowing to what extent they were compromising their commitment to the urban space they worked in and (for many) inhabited. Astrid's concerned remarks on this particular project and the builders' wider discussions on the contemporary urban economy of Copenhagen reveal that they considered the value production of, for instance, private financial actors differently from their own. Indeed, as Erik also explained in the conversation that I recounted at the opening of this chapter, these actors are, in Erik's view at least, "draining value" as they "withdraw the value from those who have created it." As Erik further underlined, he considered KLAR as different from actors such as these, since the co-op "benefit[s] the collective."

Yet, as my outline of this specific project shows, the builders occasionally came very close to capitalist actors, such as private financial actors. While this proximity worried Astrid, as we saw above, for Erik, he considered it a possible opportunity to influence these actors. During a meeting in the discussion group, Erik argued that the builders, by collaborating with such actors, could potentially influence the priorities of investment and pension funds, and thus introduce agendas such as environmentally friendly construction materials and methods. Proximity thus offered, in Erik's opinion, a possible opportunity to engender change in building construction.

The divergent perspectives of Astrid and Erik in this discussion take us back to the aforementioned challenges and dangers of analogy and identity in processes of mimesis. That is, the challenges associated with the difference between being *alike* or being *the same*. Because, although the basic movement within acts of mimicry is toward similarity, these movements actually depend on the opposite—that is, difference. Indeed, "without difference, the imitator and imitated would collapse into each other, would become one, making any exercise of power impossible" (Willerslev 2007: 11). To balance the question of identity and analogy, the builders, in other words, have to stay alert to difference.

In some projects such as the one discussed above, in Astrid's opinion at least, the distance—or difference—between the builders and the capitalist market that they sought to tinker with was close (and perhaps too close) to collapsing. For the same reason, it was considered of utmost importance that due care was exercised when selecting collaborators.

Choosing and Sustaining the Right Collaborative Alliances

To understand who the builders at KLAR collaborated with, we must first survey the different stakeholders commonly involved in construction projects. Overall, the builders (and other construction professionals in Denmark) distinguish between being either the "contractor" or the "subcontractor" in a given construction project. In the former case, they were responsible for the turnkey contract, for speaking directly with the client or the advisory company, and hiring companies to act as subcontractors. In the latter, they were simply hired to perform specific tasks. The builders further distinguished between the following actors: "clients"—sometimes represented by construction consultants (who finance projects); "collaborators"; and "subcontractors." Clients were further separated into two categories: "public clients" and "private clients." The prime difference between these appeared to be the level of detail. Projects for public clients were usually planned in great detail, as these had to follow regulations in minute detail, whereas private clients could be more audacious (although private individuals often choose not to be audacious, according to the builders, since they financed projects with their hard-earned savings). Most of the builders seemed to know who the client was when they were building for private individuals, but clients could also be trickier to identify in certain collaborative constellations, as we saw in the previous section. The builders defined collaborators widely as actors with whom they co-designed projects. This could, for instance, be architectural or engineering companies. Last, projects (particularly the larger ones) also included numerous subcontractors. This category comprises a wide range of companies with other specializations, including but not limited to bricklaying services, plumbing and heating services, and scaffolding companies.

While this overview of the different positions and roles in a construction project might seem straightforward, it could occasionally be difficult to unravel which companies and actors the builders—explicitly or implicitly—collaborate with. Like the rooftop house project previously described, most construction projects involved several different actors and stakeholders ranging from other construction companies, architects and engineers, to clients and construction consultants. One has to look behind the scenes, as these connections were rarely obvious, which I sometimes did during my fieldwork to identify who the other stakeholders were on a given project.

During an interview, I asked Erik how they chose their collaborators in a given project. "It's about price, time, loyalty and accuracy," he stated after he had described a few examples of companies they had collaborated with for a long time. He further added that they did not necessarily have to "share the same worldview," but mutual respect was necessary. "We can't work with people who scold other people. It simply does not work," he stressed. "They have to live up to certain standards, they have to behave properly. They have to conform to our values and dogma. They have to deliver on time. We won't accept any trouble," he elaborated. Last, he emphasized that one detail is nonnegotiable: they have to be members of a union, as the builders would not support any contravention of collective agreements.

Although Erik's list of criteria on what determines whether an enterprise constitutes a "good" or "bad" collaborator seems straightforward, these criteria, on closer inspection, are not measurable variables. Rather, Erik seemingly talks about a multitude of principles ranging from "price," "time," "loyalty," "behaving properly," "conforming to [KLAR's] values and dogma" to "accuracy." Ensuring that other enterprises (or representatives from these enterprises) fulfill these criteria must be a strenuous task I thought after our conversation, as the meaning and significance of each of these criteria are evidently open to interpretation.

As I began noticing the other subcontracted craftworkers on construction sites and the logos on their workwear, I recognized that many of the same people or representatives from the same enterprises reappeared. That is, particularly on the projects where the builders at KLAR took on the role of contractors, they seemed to collaborate with the same enterprises. There was, I suppose, a practical reason for this. By simply working with the people and enterprises whom they knew in advance, they did not have to spend any additional time on finding new collaborators.

Yet, I often got the impression that this informality did not always make the collaboration run smoothly. During projects, the builders would often quarrel regarding exactly how or when a piece of work should be done or when a payment was due. For instance, in the rooftop house project, it seemed as if the builders were both taking pleasure in the collaboration with the architectural company, and simultaneously struggling to agree on the details. However, despite a number of disagreements, the builders were keenly invested in continuing the collaboration with the architectural company. In fact, they developed three independent projects with this very same company during my fieldwork, as the architects of this company, like the builders, aspired to work with recycled materials in building construction.

Hence, it seems as if finding the right collaborators was not only a question of avoiding certain actors; it was also about attracting and maintaining relations with other enterprises and professionals within the construction industry and beyond, who apparently shared the builders' "values and dogma," as Erik stated. Indeed, it seemed as if their collaboration with other companies was guided by a form of reciprocity, as the enterprises continued to offer projects to one another.

What might the builders' efforts to choose and sustain the right collaborative alliances tell us about the kinds of values they aspired to produce or circulate through relations and exchanges of construction projects? A third and final example of a project will allow us to explore this question further. Although this specific project was in many ways spectacular, exploring the builders' representation of it illuminates certain features of the value system they were seemingly striving to create.

PROJECT 3: THE TRIUMPHANT YET NONEXISTENT URBAN WIND TURBINES

In contrast to the projects described above, this particular undertaking took place nearly a decade ago. Frode was the one who initially told me about this rather peculiar venture. He had from the outset been one of the leading figures of the project. In the following, I provide a description of the project based primarily on Frode's account.

Apart from their aspirations to reduce the environmental impact of construction, the builders at KLAR were also concerned with wider questions related to the impact of urban living on climate change, particularly in relation to urban energy transitions. Their concern about this issue had, a decade ago, prompted them to invest in a number of urban wind turbines, which they installed on the roofs of buildings in the city, to test whether they could produce sufficient electricity to cover the annual use of a small urban household. Erik termed it, "Building-integrated wind energy."

During one summer in the late 2000s, the builders installed the first turbine on the rooftop of KLAR's main office. The turbine was small, silent, and durable, measuring 2 meters tall, with three blades. In contrast to the turbines located across the Danish countryside, the main rotor shaft was positioned vertically in order to make the turbine more suitable for multidirectional wind. This particular turbine was, therefore, designed specifically for urban settings in which the built environment interferes with wind conditions.

To begin with, the builders spent a considerable amount of time persuading people to take part in the project. For the experiment to proceed as planned, at least some of the turbines had to be sited in the city center to test their performance there. Although many seemed reluctant to get involved to begin with, despite the builders' reassurance that they would remove the turbine if the experiment failed, eventually a few participants came forward.

The challenge of finding suitable locations for the turbines was superseded by the task of obtaining official permissions for their installation. As the project proceeded, the builders struggled to gain the Municipality's approval for the proposed locations, as well as to secure permits from electricity supply companies to connect the turbines to the grid. While the builders had gained the support of the Mayor of Technical and Environmental Affairs, the administration received their requests reluctantly. Accordingly, the builders turned to the media to pressure the Municipality to speed up the review of their application. The Municipality quickly responded, reminding the builders and the public that the installment of wind turbines is a complicated matter, while also promising that they would soon be ready with official permits.

Although they were left with the impression that the Municipality was stalling the project, the builders continued to push forward, and they finally secured the permissions needed. A couple of months later, they installed eight turbines in the capital and other large Danish cities. Some were located on top of industrial constructions on the peri-urban outskirts, others on the roofs of residential buildings in the city centers. Initially, the builders decided to pay for the turbines themselves by using the cooperative's savings and after-work hours. It was further agreed that the owners of the locations would get the electricity produced for free in gratitude for their support. Frode added that they had bought the most expensive materials to ensure that the material setup did not inhibit the experiment. Erik told a local newspaper: "We consider it a rational investment. It shouldn't take more than fifteen to twenty years before the initial investment is returned. However, for me, this is also an ideological project that allows people to put up their own turbines and produce electricity from wind energy in the city." He thus underscored the symbolic significance of the project.

After having secured the permissions needed, the project took off. Soon after, the wind turbine emerged as a KLAR trademark, and the builders received close to two thousand inquiries after appearing at a fair in Copenhagen. The excitement had overwhelmed them, to put it mildly. "People kept calling, asking whether they could get one too," Frode explained, "But we told them to wait. We had to see how they would function first." Institutions and companies were particularly keen on getting a turbine so they could signpost their engagement with sustainable energy production, Frode added.

The turbines initially got off to a great start as the wind connected easily to the attached generator. But soon after, the wind slowed down and disconnected from the generator. From the outset of the project, the builders were further keenly aware that the turbines should neither bother neighbors nor blemish buildings. However, both of these considerations proved challenging. Frode recalled that the neighbors complained that the turbines glinted, the blades turned out to be rather noisy and the changing wind conditions in the city caused the turbine to constantly switch on and off. Moreover, the builders soon realized that even when the wind was in their favor, the turbines were not performing as expected. Consequently, they enlisted a researcher to test the productivity of the turbines a few months into the experiment. The researcher concluded that the turbines were producing less than 70 percent of the energy promised by the manufacturer. The researcher, therefore, suggested that it was "probably better to simply turn off the light or shut down your computer if you want to do something serious about the energy problem." The project continued for some months, before "it was put on ice," in Erik's words. As the builders uninstalled the turbines, most of the temporary owners were quite disappointed. They had seemingly enjoyed taking part in the experiment.

During an interview, Frode elucidated some of the practical challenges that the builders had encountered and further reflected on the project's impact:

> We had so much trouble with the turbines, also with the technical stuff—the lights flashed into people's homes; the blades made loud noises as they turned; and they frequently ran out of control. But, we also brought some things up for discussion in Copenhagen. We were on the front pages of the newspapers on several occasions. There were lots of discussions about the project. So the project not only developed the co-op, as it made us famous in some way, it also fostered a discussion about transcending boundaries. Yeah, it might not be possible to put turbines on rooftops in the city—it was probably also a ridiculous idea—but it started some interesting conversations about all sorts of things. I think the turbines put other things in motion. Although the project was not a success from an economic perspective, I consider it a success in other ways. To test boundaries and push the system—the city dwellers and the Municipality in this case—that some people in fact joined in on the project. It might not be a success, but you have to test new approaches. Otherwise, we'll never develop new solutions.

Despite its relatively short lifespan and the economic costs, Frode considered the turbine project to be one of KLAR's greatest successes over the past twenty years. The technical faults of the turbines did not, according to Frode, exceed the gains incurred from the public debate mobilized by the project. Erik seemed to hint at something similar to Frode, when he stated that this was also "an ideological project." In his view, the aim of the project was to mobilize individuals and collectives to join the debate on urban energy transformations.

As we have seen, the builders clearly considered this a valuable project. Indeed, this was also one of the projects that had made it onto KLAR's wall of fame—a colorful picture of a turbine decorated the main office of the co-op, hanging next to an image of a large hemispherical wooden frame, representing another valuable project undertaken by the builders (see Figure 6.2). The builders had, in other words, somehow turned this costly, yet nonexistent project into an artful installation. A trophy indeed.

Such acts of "showing off" could easily be dismissed as merely cynical and cunning examples of deliberate marketing. Yet, doing so would also imply embracing the "common sense" understanding and ideology of "economic man"; thereby reducing Erik, Frode, and the rest of the builders to strategic, self-optimizing individuals. This would only constitute yet another attempt to put the maximizing individual back into anthropological theory (Graeber 2001). Instead, I suggest we consider the builders' ongoing representations of the turbines, visually and verbally, as attempts to uphold a connection with the project. By continuously spreading the word about the project through newspaper articles and other media accounts, the builders not only

Figure 6.2. The construction of the framing for a recreational space. Photo by Brian Berg.

brought projects such as these into the public debate, they also emphasized the connection between KLAR and the turbines.

Here, I suggest, we see an example of how the builders invested symbolically in a project and thereby sought to inscribe themselves into the project precisely because they could see their own values reflected within it (ibid.). In doing so, they also constructed a particular identity for the turbines as symbols of active engagement with urban energy transformations. By converting such projects into singularized artful installations, and underscoring that they were the proud creators of these constructions, they also turned the turbines into inalienable possessions that are ideally not supposed to be exchanged. Moving further along this analytical track, it can be stressed that such objects carry relational capacities, as their circulation creates associations and alliances between individuals or groups who might not otherwise be connected.

Drawing on this assertion, we can begin to see how this particular project, and Frode's positive evaluation of it, was deeply connected to the kinds of relations that it established. More precisely, the relations produced through this project were seemingly the type of relations that the builders valued and strived to create as a basis for their ideological vision of transforming the construction industry and urban energy production. The builders lost monetary value and the project failed, yet this was not the kind of value the builders aspired to create. Rather, they wanted to build relations and enhance KLAR's reputation.

Indeed, as we learned from Frode's explanation, the value of the project was not to be found in the successful installation and use of the turbines. Rather, value was produced in the public debate mobilized by the project and by the fact that urban citizens and actors wanted to take part in the project.

In my conversations with Frode about the urban turbines, he finalized his description of the project by underlining that, "It's not because I think we can change the entire world. But I do think that we set some things in motion." I asked him if the project had disappointed him in any way. He explained that it probably was not a success from a marketing perspective. The workload had also been shattering. Nonetheless, he repeated his message that such experiments are necessary:

> We spent so much money and time on the project. And it didn't work out, it simply didn't. If we had been reasonable in some way, we could have told ourselves that from the outset of the project. But, on the other hand, you also have to try something out sometimes—we might learn something new. It might be that reason does not really determine everything. There might be something that could have created some kind of opening or a gap that would have only emerged if we had in fact tried it out, right?

In his own calm way, Frode alluded to one of the key elements that the builders sought to create and exchange through the value production of their work: the possibility of experimentation and invention. As he stated, the project with the urban turbines could potentially "create some kind of opening or gap" that they had not been capable of seeing beforehand. Indeed, looking back at the three cases presented in this chapter, the possibility of experimentation and invention has characterized all three projects, although they did not, to the same extent, succeed in fulfilling this possibility. The builders, in other words, seemingly assessed the value of projects through these hopes and promises of possible experimentation and invention. As we saw in the earlier cases, they withdrew from projects when the promise of potential was broken. Consequently, it is this particular promise, I propose, that has become a key value that guides the builders in their work. It is also the collective devotion to experimentation and invention under contingent circumstances that I seek to grasp with the notion of *tinkering together*.

CONCLUDING REMARKS

Since the inception of KLAR in the early 2000s, the builders have engaged with countless construction projects ranging from regular construction work, such as retrofitting windows, to the installment of urban wind turbines. The builders have evidently come to consider some of these projects as more valuable than others. By detailing how the builders related to and (re)assessed three distinct construction projects in different ways, this chapter has shown how the builders were able to construct different identities tailored to each of the projects they worked on. The creation of different identities is one of the strategies applied by the builders as they constantly tried to avoid being absorbed by the capitalist market system that they—as urban builders—engaged with on a daily basis. Through constant assessments and symbolic investments/divestments, the builders sought to tinker with the value productions defined by the entangled collaborations, complex supply chains, and ever-evolving urban political economy defining construction in the city, as they aspired to engender change within the urban landscape they inhabited.

It has repeatedly been highlighted that co-ops and similar associations often become enthralled by capitalism. Yet the relation between the economic practices and ideas pursued by the builders at KLAR and other contemporary cooperative practitioners in Denmark, and dominant economic systems and logics, such as capitalism, might be one of proximity and imbrication rather than pure opposition or accommodation. Throughout the chapter, I have unpacked the builders' attempts to "act like capitalists" to show how they try to embrace the ambiguities, tensions, and uncertainties produced by this proximity. As we saw in the case of the rooftop houses, it can, at times, be a perilous endeavor, as the builders constantly have to balance the question of analogy or identity, which inherently shapes their attempt to mimic the workings of capitalism. They have, in other words, to strike the right balance between too little or too much engagement with capitalist transactions and tendencies. Exploring this double movement is exactly what allows us to move beyond a binary approach to cooperativism that either celebrates or criticizes these organizations, as it enables us to see cooperative practitioners' complicated relation to capitalist practices; practices which they might simultaneously refuse, ridicule, and reproduce.

In making this argument, this last chapter of the book has also returned to some of the questions that I raised in the Introduction to underscore how contemporary forms of cooperativism might also be conceived of as attempts to forge novel modalities of knowing, reasoning, and engaging with a capitalist economy, while in many cases working against it from within. In this final chapter, we have seen how the builders have applied what I have described throughout this book as the ability to tinker together as they sought to build a different value system from within the capitalist market system by somehow turning it against itself. These insights concerning how proximity to the market is negotiated are vital if we are to understand the wider processes of tinkering among the builders at KLAR. Indeed, proximity is a premise for engaging with the work of tinkering. It is, in other words, only by allowing oneself to be close, while simultaneously keeping a distance, that the ability and possibility to tinker can be upheld.

NOTES

This section includes ethnography previously published in: Ebsen, Maia. 2022. The missing builders: craftwork and crafty resistance in the "eco-metropolis" of Copenhagen. *Journal of Organizational Ethnography* 11(1): 79–92.

1. The question of whether it is possible to realize one political vision (e.g., socialism) in isolation from the encompassing society has been a recurrent concern in political theory associated with Marxism and classical Anarchism. However, in this chapter, I focus on how this question has come to shape discussion on cooperativism.
2. In assuming this analytical focus, I draw especially on the approach to capitalism developed by Hirokazu Miyazaki (2013) in his study of a group of derivatives traders in Japan. Key to this approach "is to demonstrate the importance of ethnographic attention to the specific uses to which categories of economic analysis are put in particular ethnographic settings" (Miyazaki 2013:11–12). I draw on this insight as I attend to capitalism as a "category of economic analysis" in this chapter. By tracing the builders' reflections, I, similar to Miyazaki, "seek to take [the builders'] thinking seriously as a window into their practical and theoretical engagement with the market and capitalism more generally" (ibid.: 41).
3. The concept of mimesis can be traced back to James George Frazer's (1920 [2009]) comparative study of magic and religion *The Golden Bough*, and Michael Taussig's (1993) subsequent anthropological reinterpretation presented in *Mimesis and Alterity: A Particular History of the Senses.*
4. Several ethnographers have recently presented accounts of the complex systems in urban construction; see Dharia (2022) for an example of such a study.
5. Historically, a contractor was obliged to invite builders to a topping out to celebrate the completed work. If the contractors omitted this celebration, the builders working on the project would cause trouble, for instance, by making a human-size doll dressed as a bricklayer with affixed bottles, and attaching it to a gallows at the top of the building (see, e.g., Fode, Møller and Hastrup 1984 for a more elaborate historical account).
6. This notion is advanced by James C. Scott (1985) in his seminal work *Weapons of the Weak.*
7. Kondo (1990), among others, presents this critique. She is particularly critical of the use of the terms "rich" and "poor" (ibid.: 220–21).
8. Malinowski's (1922) study of the Kula exchange of necklaces and bracelets across the Trobriand Islands, and Marcel Mauss's (1925) examination of the norms and customs governing gift-giving are seminal works in this field. Drawing on insights from Mauss, anthropologists began to explore how the logics of "gift economies" and "commodity economies" diverged (Gregory 1982). This dichotomy was subsequently challenged by numerous scholars, focusing on "the social life of commodities" (Appadurai 1986) and on "the cultural biography of things" (Kopytoff 1986).
9. I borrow the notions of "symbolic investment" and "symbolic divestment" from Péter Berta (2009). Berta traces how the Gabors, a Transylvanian Roma ethnic subgroup, turn silver beakers and tankards purchased from non-Roma antique dealers, auction houses and museums into prestige items by de-contextualizing the beakers from their Gazo heritage (the Gazo is another "non-Roma" ethnic subgroup living in Transylvanian rural settlements) through engagement with a creative and constitutive "commodity fetishism." This conceals the importance of the labor and social relations that were once necessary for the beakers' production, thus actively obscuring the production process of the beakers.

CONCLUSION

Taking Politics into One's Own Hands

"Denmark will get stupider and poorer without good craftsmanship and strong professional identities," states former bricklayer and unionist-turned-politician Mattias Tesfaye in his 2013 book, *Wise hands:—In defense of craftwork and professionalism* [my translation]. Throughout the book, Tesfaye, who currently serves as the Minister for Education and Children in the Danish Parliament, surveys historical and contemporary societal developments that, in his view, have diminished the status of skilled craftwork in Danish society. Such developments range from the opening of the first Fordist-inspired factory in Copenhagen in 1919 to the recent trajectory of vocational education, as well as contemporary shifts in the Danish labor market. Yet, as he writes, "Letters and words can do much, but not all knowledge is available through language—much knowledge is stored in the body, and can only be conveyed through the hands" (Tesfaye 2013: 23). "Bright heads" and "wise hands," Tesfaye argues, must be reunited.

Tesfaye's concerns mirror those of scholars such as Richard Sennett, who similarly reflects on the devaluation of skilled work in his book *The Craftsman* (2008). "Craftsmanship may suggest a way of life that waned with the advent of industrial society—but this is misleading," writes Sennett on one of the opening pages, and adds that craftwork, in his view, "names an enduring, basic human impulse, the desire to do a job well for its own sake" (Sennett 2008: 11). Sennett's work underscores that it is not only in the Danish context that the manual work of craft practice has seemingly lost its significance.

In this book, I have followed a group of builders working in the Danish craft co-op KLAR who share a commitment to reinvigorating skilled work. Despite the composite nature of the group, nearly everyone is a strong believer in the act of making. In this respect, craftwork is, to many of them, not only a livelihood; it is also envisioned as a vehicle for political activism and social change. Yet, while the builders share with public intellectuals and scholars a keen interest in reviving the value of craftwork, this work is not, to them, about words and books. Rather, it is about taking politics into their own hands.

Across the previous pages, I have explored what this pursuit entails through a detailed analysis of the builders' daily work at construction sites, their discussions at assemblies, their efforts to rethink building practices and projects, and their attempts to disrupt larger social structures, including dominant economic systems such as capitalism. In doing so, I have ethnographically theorized the double meaning of the builders' aspirations to take politics into *their own hands*. First, KLAR's launch was guided by founding members' desire to "do things in [their] own way"; a desire cultivated through their involvement in the social movements surging in Copenhagen in the 1980s. Second, I have argued that the builders' political actions also emerge from their hands as they intentionally hone a skillset through their daily craftwork, which they then extrapolate to other social domains. Through the practicalities of craftwork, the builders at KLAR learn to carefully repair, refine, recalibrate, re-model, or simply renew their craft skills, selves, and larger social structures in Denmark, such as building conventions and economic orders.

Although the builders rarely articulated this skillset in explicit terms, I found the concept of tinkering to be a useful heuristic for understanding the transformative capacity they aim to cultivate through their daily craftwork. Across the book, I have shown variously how the builders bring their aspiration and ability to tinker together: to work on the ongoing adjustments they make of the practical organization of their assemblies in an effort to enhance their participatory foundations; in their efforts to change the Danish building regulations in order to bring questions of diversity to bear on building materials; and last, in their efforts to change the value systems they as urban builders inevitably become part of, as they seek to tinker with capitalism by somehow turning it against itself. To grasp how the builders at KLAR strategically and intentionally tinker with various social orders, this book has ethnographically advanced the concept of *tinkering together*. The transformative action of tinkering together is, as I have shown, guided by an aspiration to continuously experiment with various projects and interventions rather than imagine radically alternative ways of working and living.

By illuminating the relation between the transformative actions of the builders at KLAR and their daily engagement with craftwork, this book contributes to a renewed conversation about shifts in meaning of politics in Denmark and beyond since the turn of the century. This is a period in which the claim that we live in "post-political" times has become a compelling assertion; one that has also gained traction in works on cooperativism (Kasmir 1996). However, scholars have recently begun to question whether this notion has ever been empirically accurate, arguing instead that the capacity for critical politics is always broadly distributed (e.g., Li 2019; Postero and Elinoff 2019). According to these scholars, the question of politics is inherently an ethnographic one (Candea 2011b). In this book, I have followed a similar path by exploring how the domain of the political might itself be a site of contestation. More precisely, I have proposed that by examining people like the builders at KLAR—whose transformative actions may depart from conventional notions of politics, yet who nonetheless describe their actions as political—we can extend our understanding of what constitutes political action today. In the remainder of this conclusion, I want to discuss some implications of this claim by further reflecting upon some of the findings, conclusions, and perspectives of this book.

* * *

In the aftermaths of the diverse socioeconomic and political crises in the first decade of the twenty-first century, primarily the 2008 financial collapse, interest in co-ops and similar associations has resurfaced in Denmark and many other countries, as these organizational forms are positioned as more inclusive, just, and localized modes of business. This book has traced a concrete case of this cooperative resurgence in Denmark by exploring how the founding and subsequent generations of KLAR's builders seek to invigorate this organizational form. As I have shown, the builders' aspiration to ensure a "jointly owned and democratically controlled enterprise" is not easily translated into practice. Yet despite endless quarrels over collective ownership and democratic control, the builders—sometimes to my surprise—rarely seemed to lose faith in their cooperativist aspirations. While their ongoing efforts to muddle through the practical challenges and contradictions of cooperativism continuously tested the limits of their project, it seemingly did not, as we have seen, prompt them to abandon the possibility of its realization altogether. Quite the contrary, I argue that these struggles served not only to reaffirm the fundamental vision of cooperativism, but also to adapt and renew it.

Co-ops are often criticized for failing to live up to their professed ideals. Some scholars assert that the pragmatism often associated with cooperative projects poses a challenge to intellectual endeavors as it "often stops short our thinking and cuts off our imaginations" (Kasmir 1996: 200). Yet rather than assess whether or not co-ops and similar associations fulfill the intended purpose of an ostensibly fixed organizational form, this book has examined what forms of life cooperative organizations enable that are not easily captured in terms of a relationship of negation or submission to existing hegemonic orders. Indeed, only by carefully tracing the details of social life in these organizations—including their tribulations—can we, I argue, grasp that cooperativism is not an all-or-nothing proposition. Rather, as we have seen, it is an elusive project that demands continuous reinvention. In my view, intellectual nourishment is exactly to be found in tracing social actors' readiness to tinker with the elusive nature and messiness of cooperativism and political action more broadly.

Keeping an elusive project like a co-op going requires a considerable amount of hard work. At KLAR, the daily work starts at an unearthly hour and continues, at times, into the evening as the builders convene for assemblies after work. During my fieldwork, I was often struck by many of the builders' persistent efforts to work hard—including their embrace of laborious construction work. Indeed, from the outset of their training, apprentices at KLAR are expected to accept the bodily hardship and endurance of craftwork. Yet, as we have seen, many in fact consider the embodied methods of craftwork as potentialities through which they can transform themselves into certain subjects. This is an independent, ingenious, and agentive subject that never relaxes into the convenience of the status quo, but is always capable and willing to repair, refine, recalibrate, re-model, or simply renew itself and the social contexts it inhabits. Put differently, I argue that the political subject that the builders seek to cultivate is, in brief, a persistent, agile, and above all a hard-working subject.

Putting these insights into perspective, one could argue that the builders at KLAR reproduce a conventional Scandinavian social doctrine: a willingness and commitment to hard work. Indeed, the Scandinavian belief in hard work has not only been underlined by anthropologists; scholars from other disciplines have also taken notice, asserting for instance that "rather than being motivated by economic reasons, work in Scandinavia is more like the fulfillment of a religious calling" (Nelson 2017: 27). Much seems to indicate that the "Protestant work ethic" described by Max Weber (1930) remains a fundamental principle in the Scandinavian countries. With their daily toil and commitment to hard work, it could easily be argued that the builders at KLAR reproduce this cultural norm. However, as with any other political project, the builders cannot fully extricate themselves from the social reality they seek to alter. Oppositional practices and ideas always run the risk of reproducing certain social doctrines and arrangements, while they seek to fracture or disassemble others.

Yet the significance of hard work is not the same for everyone working at KLAR. As I have described, the co-op seeks to provide people who—for various reasons—are excluded from the labor market with an opportunity to earn a livelihood for themselves, and thus to be included in the workforce. As social policy in Denmark has, in accordance with international trends, generally shifted from welfare to "workfare" since the turn of the century, welfare programs are increasingly conditioned by work requirements. To offer a job to people like Yusuf is thus also to offer him legitimate standing within the contemporary Danish state.

While builders like Yusuf may not have much of a choice when it comes to work, several of the builders from the younger generation are inherently skeptical of the maxim of hard work that shapes KLAR. They question whether formalized work arrangements can ever have emancipatory potential, and some of them rather strive to create lives for themselves in which work plays a minor role. Given the social tensions examined in this ethnography, it is perhaps no surprise that several of the builders whom we have encountered no longer work at the co-op today. Some of the people who decided to leave KLAR did so to pursue their aspirations to live a life without formalized work obligations. Others, I have heard, have moved to jobs at conventional construction enterprises; perhaps because they started questioning KLAR's purpose and framework, or perhaps owing to financial or other private reasons. A few, however, left KLAR to launch their own craft co-ops.

In the opening pages of this book, I recounted a conversation I had with Erik in which he said that KLAR, in his view, is a "story of freedom." As we have seen over the course of the chapters, and as the different professional trajectories of ex-builders also underscore, these perceptions of freedom do not always align. Yet, as I have argued, these perceptions are nonetheless shaped by a similar directionality, as the forms of freedom that the builders aspire to are not necessarily a freedom *from* external interferences. Consider how Erik expanded on his characterization of KLAR as "a story of freedom": "If I want to spend my weekends on sorting nails and screws, I can do that without anyone interfering." As this brief remark underlines, the freedom that Erik describes is a liberty to do what he wants. Likewise, Liv's story, detailed in Chapter 2, also underscores this point, as it reveals that freedom for her, an apprentice, is not a question of finding refuge from external forces. Rather, it appears to be a freedom to expose herself to these forces in the service of self-crafting. I argue that such emic concepts of freedom—like "sorting nails and screws" and strenuous construction work—challenge the abstract or absolute conceptions of freedom (Freedom with a capital F) that have generally occupied anthropologists (Sopranzetti 2017). Indeed, it is only by pursuing such localized understandings of freedom—that is, by turning freedom into an ethnographic question—that we can grasp the complexities of social actors' emancipatory politics.

Freedom has been a central concern of this book. Indeed, it was by exploring this very question that I arrived at the concept of a *tinkering together*. More precisely, I came to consider the builders' ongoing work of deliberate and attentive tinkering as a means through which they strategically engage with transformative potentials; that is, in search of a sense of freedom to "do things in [their] own way." Specifically in the Danish context, where there is a nearly invisible boundary between civil society and the state, the builders' efforts to tinker strategically with various social orders, including legal frameworks, can emerge as an efficacious mode of political action. Indeed, tinkering always relies on such proximity.

In contrast to other accounts of politics in anthropology, the transformative actions that I have explored in this book are not necessarily conditioned by privation or constraint. This perhaps raises the question of whether tinkering together is inherently a transformative action or whether it is perhaps better conceptualized as a mode of agency. If tinkering had been an individual endeavor, "agency" may well have been appropriate. But exactly because the builders at KLAR strive to build new forms of commonality by bringing people together across differences in an attempt to act together, their cooperative enterprise, I argue, constitutes a world-building project and thus also a transformative action. While the ability and willingness to tinker may not be evenly distributed among the different people who join KLAR, their collective engagement, their *tinkering together*, is, as we have seen, guided by an aspiration to benefit everyone working at the co-op. Above all, it is guided by a desire to show that building practices and craftwork more broadly can be harnessed to solve challenging social, political, and environmental issues. My hope with this book is that by conveying the desires, dedication, diligence, and dreams that the builders at KLAR put into crafting buildings and better futures, I have unfolded the intricate yet ever-evolving possibilities of taking politics into one's own hands.

REFERENCES

Abram, Simone. 2017. "Contradiction in Contemporary Political Life: Meeting Bureaucracy in Norwegian Municipal Government." *The Journal of the Royal Anthropological Institute* 23: 27–44.

Ajslev, Jeppe Z. N., Henrik L. Lund, Jeppe L. Møller, Roger Persson, and Lars L. Andersen. 2013. "Habituating Pain: Questioning Pain and Physical Strain as Inextricable Conditions in the Construction Industry." *Nordic Journal of Working Life Studies* 3(3): 195–218.

Ajslev, Jeppe Z. N., Jeppe L. Møller, Roger Persson, and Lars L. Andersen. 2017. "Trading Health for Money: Agential Struggles in the (Re) Configuration of Subjectivity, the Body and Pain among Construction Workers." *Work, Employment and Society* 31(6): 887–903.

Alexandrakis, Othon. 2016. *Impulse to Act: A New Anthropology of Resistance and Social Justice.* Bloomington: Indiana University Press.

Als, Jeppe, Jesper Clausen, and Arne Oksen. 1979. *Arbejderkooperationen: En beskrivelse og analyse af den arbejderkooperative virksomhedsform, eksemplificeret ved kooperative virksomheder i Århus* [Worker Cooperation: A Description and Analysis of the Worker-Owned Enterprise Form, Illustrated by Cooperative Enterprises in Aarhus]. København: SOC.

Anderson, Benedict. 1991. *Imagined Communities: Reflections on the Origin and Spread of Nationalism.* London: Verso.

Anderson, Sally. 2008. *Civil Sociality: Children, Sport, and Cultural Policy in Denmark.* Charlotte, NC: Information Age Pub.

Andreassen, Randi. 1998. "Gossip in Henningsvær." *Etnofoor* 11(2): 41–56.

Appadurai, Arjun. 1986. "Introduction: Commodities and the Politics of Value." In *The Social Life of Things: Commodities in Cultural Perspective*, 3–63. Cambridge: Cambridge University Press.

Applebaum, Herbert A. 1999. *Construction Workers, U.S.A.* Westport, CT: Greenwood Publishing Group.

Arnholtz, Jens, Jakob Krause-Jensen, and Ida Juul. 2015. "Introduktion til forandringer i bygge- og anlægsbranchens arbejdsliv" [Introduction to Changes in Working Life in the Construction Industry]. *Tidsskrift for Arbejdsliv* 17(2): 5–10.

Arnholtz, Jens, and Line Eldring. 2015. "Varying Perceptions of Social Dumping in Similar Countries." In *Market Expansion and Social Dumping in Europe*, ed. Magdalena Bernaciak, 80–96. Abingdon: Routledge.

Atkinson, Robert. 1998. *The Life Story Interview*. London: SAGE.
Attwood, D. M., and B. S. Baviskar. 1987. "Why Do Some Co-operatives Work but Not Others? A Comparative Analysis of Sugar Co-operatives in India." *Economic and Political Weekly* 22(26): A38–56.
Attwood, D. W. and B. S. Baviskar. 1988. *Who Shares? Co-operatives and Rural Development*. Delhi: Oxford University Press.
Baarts, Charlotte. 2004. "Viden og kunnen: En antropologisk analyse af sikkerhed på en byggeplads" [Knowledge and Skills: An Anthropological Analysis of Safety on a Construction Site]. PhD thesis. København: University of Copenhagen.
Bear, Laura, Karen Ho, Anna Lowenhaupt Tsing, and Sylvia Yanagisako. 2015. "Gens: A Feminist Manifesto for the Study of Capitalism." Theorizing the Contemporary, *Fieldsights*. Retrieved March 30, 2026 from https://culanth.org/fieldsights/gens-a-feminist-manifesto-for-the-study-of-capitalism.
Beck, Ulrich. 1992. *Risk Society: Towards a New Modernity*. London: SAGE.
Beltrán, Héctor. 2023. *Code Work: Hacking across the US/México Techno-Borderlands*. Princeton, NJ: Princeton University Press.
Berta, Péter. 2009. "Materialising Ethnicity: Commodity Fetishism and Symbolic Re-creation of Objects among the Gabor Roma (Romania)." *Social Anthropology* 17(2): 184–97.
Bertelsen, Sven. 1997. *Bellahøj, Ballerup, Brøndby Strand: 25 år der industrialiserede byggeriet* [Bellahøj, Ballerup, Brøndby Strand: 25 Years of Industrialized Construction]. København: SBI (Statens Byggeforskningsinstitut).
Blim, Michael. 2005. "Review of Producing Culture and Capital: Family Firms in Italy, by Sylvia Yanagisako." *American Anthropologist* 107(2): 317–18.
Bloch, Maurice. 1975. "Introduction." In *Political Language and Oratory in Traditional Society*. London: Academic Press.
Boas, Franz. 1897. "III—The Potlaches." In *The Social Organization and the Secret Societies of the Kwakiutl Indians*, 341–57. Washington, DC: Government Printing Office.
Boni, Stefano. 2015. "Assemblies and the Struggle to Diffuse Power: Ethnographic Examples and Contemporary Practices." *Focaal* 2015(72): 9–22.
Bosk, Charles L., and Raymond G. de Vries. 2004. "Bureaucracies of Mass Deception: Institutional Review Boards and the Ethics of Ethnographic Research." *The Annals of the American Academy of Political and Social Science* 595: 249–63.
Bottomore, Tom. 1991. *A Dictionary of Marxist Thought*. Oxford: Blackwell.
Brown, Hannah, Adam Reed, and Thomas Yarrow. 2017. "Introduction: Towards an Ethnography of Meeting." *Journal of the Royal Anthropological Institute* 23(S1): 10–26.
Bruun, Maja Højer. 2011. "Egalitarianism and Community in Danish Housing Cooperatives: Proper Forms of Sharing and Being Together." *Social Analysis* 55(2): 62–83.
———. 2012. "Social Life and Moral Economies in Danish Cooperative Housing: Community, Property and Value." PhD thesis. København: University of Copenhagen.
———. 2013. "Som én stor familie: husfællesskab og slægtskab i danske andelsboligforeninger" [Like One Big Family: Communal Living and Kinship in Danish Housing Cooperatives]. In *Familie og slægtskab: Antropologiske perspektiver* [Family and Kinship: Anthropological Perspectives], ed. Hanne Overgaard Mogensen and Karen Fog Olwig. Frederiksberg: Samfundslitteratur.
———. 2018. "Social Imaginaries and Egalitarian Practices in the Era of Neoliberalization." In *Egalitarianism in Scandinavia: Historical and Contemporary Perspectives*, ed. Synnøve Bendixsen, Mary Bente Bringslid, and Halvard Vike, 135–55. Cham: Springer International Publishing.

Bruun, Maja Højer, Gry Skrædderdal Jakobsen, and Stine Krøijer. 2011. "Introduction: The Concern for Sociality; Practicing Equality and Hierarchy in Denmark." *Social Analysis* 55(2): 1–19.

Bruun, Maja Højer, Stine Krøjer, and Mikkel Rytter. 2015. "Indledende Perspektiver: Forandringsstaten Og Selvstændighedssamfundet" [Introductory Perspectives: The Transformative State and the Self-Reliant Society]. *Tidsskriftet Antropologi* 72: 63–81.

Bryer, Alice. 2010. "Beyond Bureaucracies?: The Struggle for Social Responsibility in the Argentine Workers' Cooperatives." *Critique of Anthropology* 30(1): 41–61.

Burawoy, Michael. 2010. "From Polanyi to Pollyanna: The False Optimism of Global Labor Studies." *Global Labour Journal* 1(2): 301–13.

Callon, Michel. 1998. "Introduction: The Embeddedness of Economic Markets in Economics." *Sociological Review* 46(1): 1–57.

Candea, Matei. 2011a. "Endo/Exo." *Common Knowledge* 17(1): 146–50.

———. 2011b. " 'Our Division of the Universe': Making a Space for the Non-Political in the Anthropology of Politics." *Current Anthropology* 52(3): 309–34.

Caplan, Pat. 2000. "Introduction." In *Risk Revisited*, 1–28. London: Pluto Press.

Carrier, James G. 2009. "Market and Economy in Environmental Conservation in Jamaica." In *Market and Society*, ed. Chris Hann and Keith Hart, 240–55. Cambridge: Cambridge University Press.

Checker, Melissa. 2007. " 'But I Know It's True': Environmental Risk Assessment, Justice, and Anthropology." *Human Organization* 66(2): 112–24.

Cooper, Eugene. 1980. *The Wood-Carvers of Hong Kong: Craft Production in the World Capitalist Periphery.* Cambridge, New York: Cambridge University Press.

Dale, Gareth. 2010. *Karl Polanyi: The Limits of the Market.* Oxford: Polity Press.

———. 2012. "Double Movements and Pendular Forces: Polanyian Perspectives on the Neoliberal Age." *Current Sociology* 60(1): 3–27.

Dharia, Namita Vijay. 2022. *The Industrial Ephemeral: Labor and Love in Indian Architecture and Construction.* Berkeley: University of California Press.

Douglas, Mary, and Aaron Wildawsky. 1982. "Introduction: Can We Know the Risks We Face?" In *Risk and Culture: An Essay on the Selection of Technological and Environmental Dangers*, 1–15. Berkeley: University of California Press.

Dragojlovic, Ana, and Annemarie Samuels. 2021. "Tracing Silences: Towards an Anthropology of the Unspoken and Unspeakable." *History and Anthropology* 32(4): 1–9.

Dübeck, Inger, and Vagn Dybdahl. 1983. *Håndværkets kulturhistorie* [The Cultural History of Craft]. København: Håndværksrådet.

Düzel, Esin. 2024. "The Afterlife of Sacrifice in the Kurdish Movement." *Cultural Anthropology* 39(4): 507–32.

Ebsen, Maia. 2021. "Køn, Kroppe og Kontroverser i Håndværksfagene" [Gender, Bodies, and Controversies in the Skilled Trades]. *Økonomi & Politik* 94(1): 16–26.

———. 2022. "The missing builders: craftwork and crafty resistance in the 'eco-metropolis' of Copenhagen." *Journal of Organizational Ethnography* 11(1): 79–92.

Elmqvist, Thomas, José Siri, Erik Andersson, Pippin Anderson, Xuemei Bai, Pranab Kishore Das, Tatu Gatere, et al. 2018. "Urban Tinkering." *Sustainability Science* 13(6): 1549–64.

Engelmark, Jesper. 2014. *Dansk byggeskik: etagebyggeriet gennem 150 år* [Danish Building Traditions: Apartment Construction Through 150 Years]. Herlev: Byggeskik.dk.

Eriksen, Thomas Hylland, James Laidlaw, Jonathan Mair, Keir Martin, and Soumhya Venkatesan. 2015. "The Concept of Neoliberalism Has Become an Obstacle to the Anthropological Understanding of the Twenty-First Century." *Journal of the Royal Anthropological Institute* 21(4): 911–23.

Fassin, Didier. 2014. "The Ethical Turn in Anthropology: Promises and Uncertainties." *HAU: Journal of Ethnographic Theory* 4(1): 429–35.

Faubion, James D. 2011. *An Anthropology of Ethics. New Departures in Anthropology.* Cambridge: Cambridge University Press.

Faulk, Karen Ann. 2008. "If They Touch One of Us, They Touch All of Us: Cooperativism as a Counterlogic to Neoliberal Capitalism." *Anthropological Quarterly* 81(3): 579–614.

Federspiel, Søren. 1997. *Nørrebro—træk af en bydels historie* [Nørrebro: Aspects of a District's History]. København: Nørrebro Lokalhistorisk Forening og Arkiv.

Ferry, Elizabeth Emma. 2002. "Inalienable Commodities: The Production and Circulation of Silver and Patrimony in a Mexican Mining Cooperative." *Cultural Anthropology* 17(3): 331–58.

Fode, Henrik, Jonas Møller, and Bjarne Hastrup. 1984. *Håndværkets kulturhistorie: Kapløbet med industrien (1862–1980)* [The Cultural History of Craft: The Race with Industry (1862–1980)]. København: Håndværksrådet.

Frazer, James George. [1920] 2009. *The Golden Bough—Part 1: The Magic Art and the Evolution of Kings Vol. 1.* Toronto: Macmillan & co.

Gershon, Ilana. 2011. "'Neoliberal Agency.'" *Current Anthropology* 52(4): 537–55.

Gibson-Graham, J. K. 2006. *A Postcapitalist Politics.* Minneapolis: University of Minnesota Press.

Gjerding, Helena Reumert, and Jacob Rønnoe Rask. 2021. *Kooperativ håndbog: iværksætteri i* fællesskab [The Cooperative Handbook: Entrepreneurship in Collaboration]. København: Nemo.

Gluckman, Max. 1963. "Papers in Honor of Melville J. Herskovits: Gossip and Scandal." *Current Anthropology* 4(3): 307–16.

Graeber, David. 2001. *Toward an Anthropological Theory of Value: The False Coin of Our Own Dreams.* New York: Palgrave.

———. 2009. *Direct Action: An Ethnography.* Chico, CA: AK press.

Gregory, Christopher A. 1982. *Gifts and Commodities.* London: Academic Press.

Grelle, Henning. 2012. *Det kooperative alternativ: Arbejderkooperationen i Danmark 1852–2012* [The Cooperative Alternative: Worker Cooperatives in Denmark, 1852–2012]. København: Arbejdermuseet.

Grytnes, Regine. 2018. "A Sense of Security: Carpentry Apprentices Handling Uncertain and Dangerous Work Tasks." *Ethnos: Journal of Anthropology* 83(2): 353–70.

Gullestad, Marianne. 1984. *Kitchen-Table Society: A Case Study of the Family Life and Friendships of Young Working-Class Mothers in Urban Norway.* Oslo: Universitetsforlaget.

———. 1990. "Doing Interpretive Analysis in a Modern Large Scale Society: The Meaning of Peace and Quiet in Norway." *Social Analysis* 29: 38–61.

———. 1992. *The Art of Social Relations: Essays on Culture, Social Action, and Everyday Life in Modern Norway. Scandinavian Library.* Oslo: Scandinavian University Press.

Hann, Chris. 2007. "A New Double Movement? Anthropological Perspectives on Property in the Age of Neoliberalism." *Socio-Economic Review* 5(2): 287–318.

———. 2016. "Cucumbers and Courgettes: Rural Workfare and the New Double Movement in Hungary." *Intersections* 2(2): 38–56.

Hann, Chris, and Keith Hart. 2009. "Introduction: Learning from Polanyi 1." In *Market and Society: The Great Transformation Today,* 1–16. Cambridge: Cambridge University Press.

Haugbolle, Sune. 2018. "Anthropology and political ideology." In *Handbook of Political Anthropology*, ed. B. Thomassen and H. Wydra, 191–204. Cheltenham: Edward Elgar Publishing.

Henkel, Heiko. 2012. "The Political Ideology of Scandinavia after July 22, 2011." *American Anthropologist* 114(2): 353–55.

Henriksen, Lars S., Steven R. Smith, and Anette Zimmer. 2012. "At the Eve of Convergence? Transformations of Social Service Provision in Denmark, Germany, and the United States." *Voluntas* 23(2): 458–501.

Hervik, Peter. 2011. *The Annoying Difference: The Emergence of Danish Neonationalism, Neoracism, and Populism in the Post-1989 World.* New York and Oxford: Berghahn Books.

Herzfeld, Michael. 2004. *The Body Impolitic: Artisans and Artifice in the Global Hierarchy of Value.* Chicago, IL: University of Chicago Press.

———. 2013. "Review of Alive in the Writing: Crafting Ethnography in the Company of Chekhov, by Kirin Narayan." *American Anthropologist* 115(3): 528–29.

Hirslund, Dan V. 2019. "Brokering Labour: The Politics of Markets in the Kathmandu Construction Industry." *Ethnography* 22(4): 495–514.

Hirslund, Dan, Karen Lisa Goldschmidt Salamon, Julie Rahbæk Møller, and Karen Lisa Salamon. 2020. *Prekarisering uden grænser* [Precarization Without Borders]. København: U Press.

Ho, Karen Zouwen. 2009. *Liquidated, an Ethnography of Wall Street.* Durham: Duke University Press.

———. 2015. "Finance, Anthropology Of." In *International Encyclopedia of the Social & Behavioral Sciences,* ed. James D. Wright, 171–76. Amsterdam: Elsevier.

Hobsbawm, Eric, and Terence Ranger. 1983. *The Invention of Tradition.* Cambridge: Cambridge University Press.

Holm, Jesper, and Inger Stauning. 2007. "Hvordan skal vi bygge og bo? Miljøomstilling i byggeriet" [How Should We Build and Live? The Environmental Transition in Construction]. In *Planlægning i teori og praksis: Et tværfagligt perspektiv* [Planning in Theory and Practice: An Interdisciplinary Perspective], ed. Anne Jensen, kapitel 16. Frederiksberg: Roskilde Universitetsforlag.

Holmes, Christopher. 2012. "Problems and Opportunities in Polanyian Analysis Today." *Economy and Society* 41(3): 468–84.

Holmstrom, Mark. 1990. *Industrial Democracy in Italy: Workers Co-ops and the Self-Management Debate.* Aldershot: Avebury.

Højer, Lars, and Morten Axel Pedersen. 2019. *Urban Hunters: Dealing and Dreaming in Times of Transition.* New Haven, CT: Yale University Press.

Hubert, Henri, and Marcel Mauss. 1981. *Sacrifice: Its Nature and Function.* Chicago, IL: The University of Chicago Press.

Ingold, Tim. 2000. *The Perception of the Environment, Essays on Livelihood, Dwelling and Skill.* London: Routledge.

———. 2013. *Making: Anthropology, Archaeology, Art and Architecture.* London: Taylor & Francis Group.

Jackson, Anthony. 1987. *Anthropology at Home*. London: Tavistock.

Jacob, François. 1977. "Evolution and Tinkering." *Science* 196(4295): 1161–66.

Jansky, Bianca. 2024. "Digitized Patients: Elaborative Tinkering and Knowledge Practices in the Open-Source Type 1 Diabetes 'Looper Community.'" *Science, Technology, & Human Values* 49(1): 53–77.

Jenkins, Richard. 2012. *Being Danish: Paradoxes of Identity in Everyday Life*. Copenhagen: Museum Tusculanum.

Jensen, Jens Stissing. 2014. "Sektorielle Spor omkring Dansk Byggeri" [Sectoral Pathways in Danish Construction]. In *Bæredygtig omstilling af bolig og byggeri* [The Sustainable Transition of Housing and Construction], ed. Jesper Holm, Bent Søndergård, Inger Stauning, and Jesper Ole Jensen, 139–61. Frederiksberg: Frydenlund Academic.

Jensen, Kristoffer. 2016. *Brugsen—en anderledes forretning?—1866–2016: dansk brugsbevægelse fra pastor Sonne til det moderne Coop* [Brugsen—A Different Kind of Business? (1866–2016): The Danish Cooperative Retail Movement from Pastor Sonne to the Modern Coop]. Albertslund: Samvirke.

Jerne, C. 2025. *Opposition by Imitation: The Economics of Italian Anti-Mafia Activism*. Minneapolis: University of Minnesota Press.

Jiménez, Alberto Corsín, and Adolfo Estalella. 2017. "Political Exhaustion and the Experiment of Street: Boyle Meets Hobbes in Occupy Madrid." *The Journal of the Royal Anthropological Institute* 23: 110–23.

Jones, Graham. 2011. *Trade of the Tricks Inside the Magician's Craft*. Berkeley: University of California Press.

Jöncke, Steffen. 2011. "Integrating Denmark: The Welfare State as a National(ist) Accomplishment." In *The Question of Integration: Immigration, Exclusion and the Danish Welfare State*, ed. Karen Fog Olwig and Karsten Pærregaard, 30–53. Newcastle upon Tyne: Cambridge Scholars Publisher.

Jørgensen, Andreas Pinstrup. 2020. *Medejer: kunsten at overhale konkurrenter gennem demokratisk ejerskab* [Co-Owner: The Art of Surpassing Competitors through Democratic Ownership]. København: Gyldendal.

Jørgensen, Christian Helms. 2018. "The Modernisation of the Apprenticeship System in Denmark 1945–2015." In *Vocational Education in the Nordic Countries*, ed. Svein Michelsen and Marja–Leena Stenström, 171–90. London: Routledge.

Jørgensen, Christian Helms, and Gudmund Bøndergaard. 2018. "Historical Evolution of Vocational Education in Denmark until 1945." In *Vocational Education in the Nordic Countries*, ed. Svein Michelsen and Marja-Leena Stenström, 84–101. London: Routledge.

Jørgensen, Rikke Egaa. 2017. "Vi er altid faldet mellem flere stole: socialøkonomi og social virksomhed betwixt and between" [Always Between Several Chairs: Social Economy and Social Enterprise Betwixt and Between]. PhD thesis. Roskilde: Roskilde University.

Juul, Ida. 2013. "De danske håndværkeruddannelser i krydsfeltet mellem det europæiske og det nationale" [Danish Vocational Craft Educations at the Intersection of the European and the National]. *Uddannelseshistorie* 47: 60–80.

———. 2016. "Historieskrivningen om de erhvervsfaglige uddannelser" [The Historiography of Vocational Education and Training]. *Uddannelseshistorie* 50: 107–25.

Kasmir, Sharryn. 1996. *The Myth of Mondragón, Cooperatives, Politics, and Working-Class Life in a Basque Town*. Albany: State University of New York Press.

Knorr, Karin D. 1979. "Tinkering toward Success: Prelude to a Theory of Scientific Practice." *Theory and Society* 8(3): 347–76.

Knudsen Anne. 1996. *Her går det godt, send flere penge* [Things Are Going Well - Send More Money]. København: Gyldendal.
Køber, Jesper Vestermark. 2022. *Det lille systemskifte* [The Little System Shift]. 100 danmarkshistorier. Aarhus: Aarhus Universitetsforlag.
Kocksch, Laura. 2024. "Tinkering." In *Fragile Computing: How to Live with Insecure Technologies*, ed. Laura Kocksch, 77–113. Singapore: Springer Nature.
Kondo, Dorinne K. 1990. *Crafting Selves: Power, Gender, and Discourses of Identity in a Japanese Workplace*. Chicago, IL: University of Chicago Press.
Kopytoff, Igor. 1986. "The Cultural Biography of Things: Commoditization as Process." In *The Social Life of Things*, 64–92. Cambridge: Cambridge University Press.
Krøijer, Stine. 2015. *Figurations of the Future, Forms and Temporalities of Left Radical Politics in Northern Europe*. Oxford: Berghahn Books.
Krøijer, Stine, and Inger Sjørslev. 2011. "Autonomy and the Spaciousness of the Social in Denmark: the Conflict between Ungdomshuset and Faderhuset." *Social Analysis* 55(2): 84–105.
Kuper, Adam. 1971. "The Kgalagari Lekgota." In *Councils in Action*, ed. Richards Audrey and Adam Kuper, 80–99. Cambridge Papers in Social Anthropology. Cambridge: Cambridge University Press.
Kyed, Morten. 2014. "Ambulancearbejde, sikkerhed og maskuline rekonfigurationer: Etnografiske fortællinger om kulturelle praksisser under forandring" [Ambulance Work, Safety, and Masculine Reconfigurations: Ethnographic Accounts of Cultural Practices in Transition]. *Dansk Sociologi* 25(3): 70–117.
Laidlaw, James. 2002. "For an Anthropology of Ethics and Freedom." *Journal of the Royal Anthropological Institute* 8(2): 311–32.
Lancy, David F. 1980. "Becoming a Blacksmith in Gbarngasuakwelle." *Anthropology & Education Quarterly* 11(4): 266–74.
———. 2012. "'First You Must Master Pain': The Nature and Purpose of Apprenticeship." *Anthropology of Work Review* 33(2): 113–26.
Laszczkowski, Mateusz. 2019. "Rethinking Resistance through and as Affect." *Anthropological Theory* 19(4): 489–509.
Lave, Jean. 2008. "Epilogue: Situated Learning and Changing Practice." In *Community, Economic Creativity, and Organization*, ed. Joanne Roberts and Ash Amin. Oxford: Oxford University Press.
Lave, Jean, and Etienne Wenger. 2003. *Situated Learning: Legitimate Peripheral Participation*. Cambridge: Cambridge University Press.
Laville, Jean-Louis. 2010. "The Solidarity Economy: An International Movement," trans. Karen Bennett. *RCCS Annual Review* 2: 3–41.
Levien, Michael. 2013. "The Politics of Dispossession: Theorizing India's 'Land Wars'." *Politics & Society* 41(3): 351–94.
Levi-Strauss Claude. 2014 [1978]. *Myth and Meaning*. London: Routledge Great Minds.
Li, Tania Murray. 2019. "Politics, Interrupted." *Anthropological Theory* 19(1): 29–53.
Little, Peter C. 2012. "Another Angle on Pollution Experience: Toward an Anthropology of the Emotional Ecology of Risk Mitigation." *Ethos* 40(4): 431–52.
Lykkeberg, Rune. 2008. *Kampen Om Sandhederne: Om Det Kulturelle Borgerskabs Storhed Og Fald* [The Struggle over Truths: The Rise and Fall of the Cultural Bourgeoisie]. København: Gyldendal.
Madsen My. 2018. "Fællesskabets ingeniører: En antropologisk analyse af sociale studiestartsaktiviteter for ingeniørstuderende" [Engineers of Community: An

Anthropological Analysis of Social Activities for First Year Engineering Students]. PhD thesis. København: University of Copenhagen.
Mahmood, Saba. 2005. *Politics of Piety: The Islamic Revival and the Feminist Subject.* Princeton, NJ: Princeton University Press.
Malinowski, Bronisław. 1922. *Argonauts of the Western Pacific: An Account of Native Enterprise and Adventure in the Archipelagoes of Melanesian New Guinea.* London: G. Routledge & Sons.
Mannheim, Karl. [1928] 1972. "The Problem of Generations." In *Essays on the Sociology of Knowledge*, ed. Paul Kecskemeti, 276–320. London: Routledge.
Marchand, Trevor Hugh James. 2009. *The Masons of Djenné. African Expressive Cultures.* Bloomington: Indiana University Press.
———. 2021. *The Pursuit of Pleasurable Work: Craftwork in Twenty-First Century England.* New York: Berghahn Books.
Martinez, Sylvia Libow, and Gary S. Stager. 2016. *Invent to Learn: Making, Tinkering, and Engineering in the Classroom.* Constructing Modern Knowledge Press.
Mattingly, Cheryl. 2014. "Moral Deliberation and the Agentive Self in Laidlaw's Ethics." *HAU: Journal of Ethnographic Theory* 4(1): 473–86.
Mauss, Marcel. 1925. *The Gift: The Form and Reason for Exchange in Archaic Societies.* London: Routledge.
Mayblin, Maya, and Magnus Course. 2014. "The Other Side of Sacrifice: Introduction." *Ethnos* 79(3): 307–19.
McGranahan, Carole. 2020. *Writing Anthropology: Essays on Craft and Commitment.* Durham, NC: Duke University Press.
McNaughton, Patrick R. 1988. *The Mande Blacksmiths: Knowledge, Power, and Art in West Africa.* Bloomington: Indiana University Press.
Mead, Margaret. 1978. *Culture and Commitment: The New Relationships Between the Generations in the 1970s.* New York: Columbia University Press.
Mikkelsen, Flemming. 2002. *Bevægelser i demokrati. Foreninger og kollektive aktioner i Danmark* [Movements in Democracy: Associations and Collective Action in Denmark]. Aarhus: Aarhus Universitetsforlag.
Mikkelsen, Flemming, and Rene Karpantschof. 2001. "Youth as a Political Movement: Development of the Squatters' and Autonomous Movement in Copenhagen." *International Journal of Urban and Regional Research* 25(3): 593–608.
Miyazaki Hirokazu. 2013. *Arbitraging Japan: Dreams of Capitalism at the End of Finance.* Berkeley: University of California Press.
Moeran, Brian. 1984. *Lost Innocence: Folk Craft Potters of Onta, Japan.* Berkeley: University of California Press.
Mogensen, Hanne Overgaard, and Karen Fog Olwig. 2013. *Familie og slægtskab: Antropologiske perspektiver* [Family and Kinship: Anthropological Perspectives]. Frederiksberg: Samfundslitteratur.
Mol, Annemarie, Ingunn Moser, and Jeannette Pols. 2010. "Care: Putting Practice into Theory." In *Care in Practice*, ed. Annemarie Mol, Ingunn Moser, and Jeannette Pols, 7–25. Bielefeld: Transcript Verlag.
Mordhorst, Mads. 2005. "Andelsbevægelsen mellem national identitet og globalisering" [The Cooperative Movement Between National Identity and Globalization]. In *Virksomhedshistorie* [Business History], ed. Kenn Tarbensen, 48–69. Århus: Den jyske Historiker.

Narayan Kirin. 2012. *Alive in the Writing: Crafting Ethnography in the Company of Chekhov*. Chicago, IL: University of Chicago Press.

Narotzky, Susana. 2004. "The Political Economy of Affects: Community, Friendship, and Family in the Organization of a Spanish Economic Region." In *Workers and Narratives of Survival in Europe: The Management of Precariousness at the End of the Twentieth Century*, ed. Angela Procoli, 57–79. Albany: State University of New York Press.

———. 2007. "'A Cargo Del Futuro'—Between History and Memory: An Account of the 'Fratricidal' Conflict during Revolution and War in Spain (1936—39)." *Critique of Anthropology* 27(4): 411–29.

Narotzky, Susana, and Patricia Homs. 2019. "Within and beyond the Market System: A Case of Organic Food Cooperatives in Catalonia." In *Food Values in Europe*, ed. Valeria Siniscalchi and Krista Harper, 133–46. London: Bloomsbury Publishing Plc.

Nash, June, and Nicholas S. Hopkins. 1976. "Anthropological Approaches to the Study of Cooperatives, Collectives, and Self-Management." In *Popular Participation in Social Change: Cooperatives, Collectives, and Nationalized Industry*, ed. Nicholas S. Hopkins, June Nash and Dandler Jorge, 3–34. Berlin: De Gruyter Mouton.

Nelson, Robert H. 2017. "Rethinking the Lutheran Roots of Nordic Social Democracy." In *Lutheranism and the Nordic Spirit of Social Democracy: A Different Protestant Ethic*, 35–52. Aarhus: Aarhus University Press.

Paap, Kris. 2006. *Working Construction: Why White Working-Class Men Put Themselves—and the Labor Movement—in Harm's Way*. Ithaca, NY: Cornell Paperbacks.

Paine, Robert. 1967. "What Is Gossip About? An Alternative Hypothesis." *Man* 2(2): 278–85.

Parkin, D. 1984. "Political Language." *Annual Review of Anthropology* 13(1): 345–65.

Paxson, Heather. 2013. *The Life of Cheese, Crafting Food and Value in America*. Berkeley: University of California Press.

Peletz, Michael. 2001. "Ambivalence in Kinship since the 1940's." In *Relative Values Reconfiguring Kinship Studies*, ed. Sarah Franklin and Susan McKinnon, 413–44. Durham, NC: Duke University Press.

Petersen, Jørn Henrik. 2014. *Pligt og ret—ret og pligt: refleksioner over den socialdemokratiske idéarv* [Duty and Right—Right and Duty: Reflections on the Social Democratic Intellectual Legacy]. Odense: Syddansk Universitetsforlag.

Petersen, Jørn Henrik, Klaus Petersen, and Niels Finn Christiansen. 2014. *Dansk velfærdshistorie—Hvor glider vi hen?* [Danish Welfare History—Where Are We Heading?] Vol. 6. Dansk Velfærdshistorie [Danish Welfare History]. Odense. Syddansk Universitetsforlag.

Pink, Sarah, Dylan Tutt, and Andrew Dainty. 2013. *Ethnographic Research in the Construction Industry*. London: Routledge.

Plender, Celia. 2021. "The 'Awkwardnesses' of Aid and Exchange: Food Cooperative Practices in Austerity Britain." *Focaal* 1: 1–14.

Polanyi, Karl. 1944. *Great Transformation: The Political and Economic Origins of Our Time*. Boston, MA: Beacon Press.

Polletta, F. 2014. "Participatory Democracy's Moment." *Journal of International Affairs*, 68(1), 79–92.

Portisch, Anna Odland. 2011. "The Craft of Skilful Learning: Kazakh Women's Everyday Craft Practices in Western Mongolia." In *Making Knowledge: Explorations of the Indissoluble Relation between Mind, Body and Environment*, ed. Trevor H. J. Marchand, 59–75. Chichester: Wiley–Blackwell.

Postero, Nancy, and Eli Elinoff. 2019. "Introduction: A Return to Politics." *Anthropological Theory* 19(1): 3–28.

Prasse-Freeman, Elliott. 2020. "Resistance/Refusal: Politics of Manoeuvre under Diffuse Regimes of Governmentality." *Anthropological Theory*: 1–26.

Prudham, Scott. 2013. "Men and Things: Karl Polanyi, Primitive Accumulation, and Their Relevance to a Radical Green Political Economy." *Environment and Planning A: Economy and Space* 45(7): 1569–87.

Quimby, Barbara, Claire M. Nichols, Margaret V. Du Bray, Alida Cantor, Julia C. Bausch, Amber Wutich, Clinton Williams, Sarah Porter, Weston M. Eaton, and Kathryn Brasier. 2023. "Changing Flows: Sociotechnical Tinkering for Adaptive Water Management." *Environmental Management* 71(2): 421–31.

Rajković, Ivan. 2018. "For an Anthropology of the Demoralized: State Pay, Mock-Labour, and Unfreedom in a Serbian Firm." *Journal of the Royal Anthropological Institute* 24(1): 47–70.

Rakopoulos, Theodoros. 2015a. "Solidarity Economy in Contemporary Greece 'Movementality': Economic Democracy and Social Reproduction during Crisis." In *Economy For and Against Democracy*, ed. Keith Hart. New York: Berghahn Books.

———. 2015b. "Which Community for Cooperatives? Peasant Mobilizations, the Mafia, and the Problem of Community Participation in Sicilian Co-ops." *Focaal* (71): 57–70.

———. 2018. *From Clans to Co-ops: Confiscated Mafia Land in Sicily*. New York: Berghahn Books.

———. 2020. "Cooperatives." In *Cambridge Encyclopedia of Anthropology*, ed. Felix Stein, Matei Candea, Sian Lazar, Joel Robbins, Andrew Sanchez, and Rupert Stasch. Haar: Open Knowledge Press.

Rasmussen, Stine, Agnete Meldgaard Hansen, and Ida Juul. 2020. "Udviklingslinjer og forandringer i den aktive arbejdsmarkedspolitik" [Developments and Changes in Active Labor Market Policy]. *Tidsskrift for Arbejdsliv* 21(1): 5–10.

Razsa, Maple. 2015. *Bastards of Utopia: Living Radical Politics after Socialism*. Bloomington: Indiana University Press.

Reed-Danahay, Deborah. 1993. "Talking about Resistance: Ethnography and Theory in Rural France." *Anthropological Quarterly* 66(4): 221–29.

Rofel, Lisa, and Sylvia Junko Yanagisako. 2019. *Fabricating Transnational Capitalism: A Collaborative Ethnography of Italian-Chinese Global Fashion*. Durham, NC: Duke University Press.

Rytter, Mikkel. 2010. "'The Family of Denmark' and 'the Aliens': Kinship Images in Danish Integration Politics." *Ethnos: Journal of Anthropology* 75(3): 301–22.

Schulte-Tenckhoff, Isabelle. 2001. "Misrepresenting the Potlatch." In *Expanding the Economic Concept of Exchange: Deception, Self-Deception and Illusions*, ed. Caroline Gerschlager, 167–88. Boston, MA: Springer US.

Scott, James C. 1985. *Weapons of the Weak: Everyday Forms of Peasant Resistance*. New Haven, CT: Yale University Press.

———. 1998. *Seeing Like a State: How Certain Schemes to Improve the Human Condition Have Failed*. New Haven, CT: Yale University Press.

Sennett, Richard. 2008. *The Craftsman*. London: Allen Lane.

Sievers, Silla Marie Mørch. 2016. "Fragile Heterotopias—A Case Study of a Danish Social Enterprise." *Community Development Journal* 51(1): 77–94.

Singleton, John. 1998. *Learning in Likely Places: Varieties of Apprenticeship in Japan*. Cambridge: Cambridge University Press.

Sjørslev, Inger. 2011. "The Paradox of Integration: Excluding While Claiming to Integrate into Danish Society." In *The Question of Integration: Immigration, Exclusion and the Danish Welfare State*, ed. Karen Fog Olwig and Karsten Pærregaard, 77–93. Cambridge: Cambridge Scholars Publishing.

Skidmore-Hess, Daniel. 2003. "The Danish Party System and the Rise of the Right in the 2001 Parliamentary Election." *International Social Science Review* 78(3/4): 89–110.

Skytte, Claus. 2016. *Den nye andelsbevægelse* [The New Cooperative Movement]. København: Skytsengel.

Snikersproge, Ieva. 2021. "The Emancipatory Promise of Cooperatives in a Historical Perspective: Evidence from an Ice-Cream Factory in France." *History and Anthropology* 32(5): 617–36.

Soanes, Catherine and Stevenson, Angus (eds). (2005). *Oxford Dictionary of English* (2nd edn). Oxford: Oxford University Press.

Sopranzetti, Claudio. 2017. "Framed by Freedom: Emancipation and Oppression in Post-Fordist Thailand." *Cultural Anthropology* 32(1): 68–92.

Steiger, Tina. 2018. "Cycles of the Copenhagen Squatter Movement: From Slumstormer to BZ Brigades and the Autonomous Movement." In *The Urban Politics of Squatters' Movements*, ed. Miguel A. Martínez López, 165–86. New York: Palgrave Macmillan.

Stephen, Lynn. 2005. "Women's Weaving Cooperatives in Oaxaca: An Indigenous Response to Neoliberalism." *Critique of Anthropology* 25(3): 253–78.

Strathern, Marilyn. 2017. "Afterword." *The Journal of the Royal Anthropological Institute* 23: 198–203.

Sutton, D. E. (2014). *Secrets from the Greek Kitchen: Cooking, Skill, and Everyday Life on an Aegean Island*. Berkeley: University of California Press.

Swider, Sarah. 2015. "Building China: Precarious Employment among Migrant Construction Workers." *Work, Employment and Society* 29(1): 41–59.

Taussig Michael. 1993. "In Some Way or Another One Can Protect Oneself From Evil Spirits by Portraying Them." In *Mimesis and Alterity: A Particular History of the Senses*, 1–14. London: Routledge.

Terrio, Susan J. 2000. *Crafting the Culture and History of French Chocolate*. Berkeley: University of California Press.

Tesfaye, Mattias. 2013. *Kloge hænder: Et forsvar for håndværk og faglighed*. [Wise Hands: In Defense of Craftwork and Professionalism]. København: Gyldendal.

Thiel, Darren. 2007. "Class in Construction: London Building Workers, Dirty Work and Physical Cultures." *The British Journal of Sociology* 58(2): 227–51.

Thomsen, Steen. 2017. *The Danish Industrial Foundations*. København: Djøf Forlag.

Tjørnhøj-Thomsen, Tine. 2003. "Samværet—Tilblivelse i tid og rum" [Being Together: Emergence in Time and Space]. In *Ind i verden: En grundbog i antropologisk metode* [Into the World: An Introduction to Anthropological Method], ed. Kirsten Hastrup, 93–115. København: Hans Reitzel.

Tsing, Anna Lowenhaupt. 2015. *The Mushroom at the End of the World: On the Possibility of Life in Capitalist Ruins*. Princeton, NJ: Princeton University Press.

Turner Victor Witter. 1969. *The Ritual Process: Structure and Anti-Structure.* London: Routledge.

Ulin, Robert C. 1995. "Invention and Representation as Cultural Capital: Southwest French Winegrowing History." *American Anthropologist*, 97(3): 519–27.

———. 1996. *Vintages and Traditions: An Ethnohistory of Southwest French Wine Cooperatives.* Washington, DC: Smithsonian.

Van Der Kist, Jasper. 2024. "Making Workable Knowledge for Asylum Decisions: On Tinkering with Country of Origin Information." *Journal of Ethnic and Migration Studies* 50(9): 2309–26.

Vargas-Cetina, Gabriela. 2005. "Anthropology and Cooperatives: From the Community Paradigm to the Ephemeral Association in Chiapas, Mexico." *Critique of Anthropology* 25(3): 229–51.

———. 2011. "Corporations, Cooperatives, and the State: Examples from Italy." *Current Anthropology* 52(S3): S127–36.

Venkatesan, Soumhya. 2010. "Learning to Weave; Weaving to Learn ... What?" *Journal of the Royal Anthropological Institute* 16(May): S158–75.

———. 2023. "Freedom." In *Cambridge Handbook of the Anthropology of Ethics and Morality*, ed. James Laidlaw, 251–80. Cambridge: Cambridge University Press.

Weber, Max. 1930. *The Protestant Ethic and the Spirit of Capitalism.* Newburyport: Dover Publications.

Weiner, Annette B. 1992. "Introduction." In *Inalienable Possessions: The Paradox of Keeping-While-Giving*, 1–22. Berkeley: University of California Press.

Weston, Kath. 1998. "Production as Means, Production as Metaphor: Women's Struggle to Enter the Trades." In *Long Slow Burn*. New York: Routledge.

Willerslev Rane. 2007. *Soul Hunters Hunting, Animism, and Personhood among the Siberian Yukaghirs.* Berkeley: University of California Press.

Wulff, Helena. 2016. "Introducing the Anthropologist as Writer: Across and Within Genres." In *The Anthropologist as Writer*. New York: Berghahn Books.

Yanagisako, Sylvia. 2002. *Producing Culture and Capital: Family Firms in Italy.* Princeton, NJ: Princeton University Press.

Yanagisako, Sylvia Junko, and Carol Lowery Delaney. 1995. *Naturalizing Power: Essays in Feminist Cultural Analysis.* New York: Routledge.

REPORTS

Bennedsen, Morten, and Kasper Meisner Nielsen. 2014. *Familievirksomheder i Danmark Kapitel 1: Definition og udbredelse.* Copenhagen Business School.

Bentsen, Kristian Hedeager, Lise Lam Hansen, Bent Jensen, Claus Larsen, and Peer Ebbesen Skov. 2018. *Aktiviteter uden for det formelle arbejdsmarked: sort arbejde, gør det selv-arbejde og deleøkonomi.* University of Southern Denmark Studies in History and Social Sciences, vol. 575. Odense: Syddansk Universitetsforlag.

Birgisdottir, Harpa, Kai Kanafani, Regitze Kjær Zimmermann, Camilla Marlene, Ernst Andersen, Damir Hatic, Malene Elmbæk, Maria Kamper, Mette Falbe-Hansen, and Torsten Sack-Nielsen. 2019. *Dialogværktøj: Cirkulær værdiskabelse i den eksisterende bygningsmasse.* BUILD: Statens Byggeforsknings Institut.

Fogh Rasmussen, Anders. 2002. "Nytårstale." [New Year's Speech]. January 2002. Copenhagen: Prime Minister's Office.

Gram-Hanssen, Kirsten, Susse Georg, Ellen Tove Christiansen, and Per Kvols Heiselberg. 2017. *How Building Regulations Ignore the Use of Buildings, What That Means for Energy Consumption and What to Do about It.* ECEEE Summer Study Proceedings, June, 2095–2104.

Gram-Hanssen, Kirsten, Jesper Ole Jensen, Anders Rhiger Hansen, Gianluca Trotta, and Katinka Johansen. 2020. *Beboernes betydning for den realiserede varmebesparelse ved renovering af boliger.* SBi 2020:05. København: BUILD.

International Energy Agency (IEA) and United Nations Environment Programme (UNEP). 2018. *2018 Global Status Report: Towards a Zero-Emission, Efficient and Resilient Buildings and Construction Sector.* UN Environment Programme.

Jespersen, Knud J. V., Esma Birdi, Lise Egholm, David Gress, Ove Korsgaard, Peter Kurrild-Klitgaard, Kathrine Lilleør, and Ole Thyssen. 2008. *Demokratikanon.* Undervisningsministeriet.

Johansen, Lars Jannick, Anne Kjær Skovgaard, and Morten Hyllegaard. 2010. *Velfærdens iværksættere – en dansk strategi for socialt iværksætteri.* Mandag Morgen.

Larsen, Mona, Helle Holt, and Malene Rode Larsen. 2016. *Et kønsopdelt arbejdsmarked: udviklingstræk, konsekvenser og forklaringer.* SFI—Det Nationale Forskningscenter for Velfærd.

Mariager, R. M., and Schmidt, R. (2009). *PET's overvågning af protestbevægelser 1945–1989: Fra Atomkampagnen til BZ-Brigaden.* Justitsministeriet.

Pedersen, Camilla Damsø, Søren Dyck-Madsen, and Christian Jarby. 2021. *Anvendelse Af Træ i Byggeriet.* CONCITO & Rådet for grøn omstilling.

Pedersen, Magnus Skovrind, and Frederikke Nayberg. 2019. *Danmarks Demokratiske Virksomheder: Første kortlægning af fuldt demokratisk kontrollerede virksomheder.* Tænketanken Demokratisk Erhverv.

Sørensen, Asger. 2012. *Livet er smukt, mulighederne utallige.* Modkraft, 29.

ONLINE REFERENCES

Beskæftigelsesministeriet. 2021. "Bekendtgørelse om arbejde med montering og nedrivning af isoleringsmaterialer med indhold af syntetiske mineralfibre." Vol. BEK nr 1399 af 25/06/2021. Retrieved April 4, 2021 from www.retsinformation.dk/eli/lta/2021/1399.

Claus, Bjørn. 2020. "Andelsbevægelsen—Den Store Danske på lex.dk." Retrieved October 9, 2021 from https://denstoredanske.lex.dk/andelsbev percentC3 percentA6gelse.

Danmarks Statistik. 2019. "Byggebeskæftigelsen." Retrieved May 5, 2021 from www.dst.dk/da/Statistik/emner/arbejde-indkomst-og-formue/beskaeftigelse/byggebesk aeftigelsen.

Erhvervsuddannelser i Danmark. 2019. "Danmarks Statistik." Retrieved September 4, 2021 from www.dst.dk/da/Statistik/Publikationer/VisPub?cid=32526.

International Cooperative Alliance. 1995. "Cooperative Identity, Values & Principles ICA." Retrieved November 10, 2021 from www.ica.coop/en/whats-co-op/co-operative-identity-values-principles.

Praktikpladsafhængigt AUB-bidrag. 2018. Retrieved February 24, 2026 from www.ft.dk/samling/20181/lovforslag/l104/index.htm.

Westh, Asger, and David Rebouh. 2018. "Efter afsløring: Minister trækkes ind i sag om mineraluld." [After Revelation: Minister is Dragged into Mineral Wool Case]. Fagbladet 3F website, December 17, 2018. Retrieved January 21, 2026 from https://fagbladet3f.dk/minister-traekkes-ind-i-sag-om-mineraluld/.

INDEX

www.ingramcontent.com/pod-product-compliance
Ingram Content Group UK Ltd.
Pitfield, Milton Keynes, MK11 3LW, UK
UKHW021836150926
8656IPUK00004B/18

9 781836 956204